The Authoritative Life of General William Booth

George Scott Railton

Contents

Preface 7
Chapter I
  Childhood and Poverty 10
Chapter II
  Salvation In Youth 18
Chapter III
  Lay Ministry 26
Chapter IV
  Early Ministry 36
Chapter V
  Fight Against Formality 52
Chapter VI
  Revivalism 62
Chapter VII
  East London Beginning 70
Chapter VIII
  Army-making 83
Chapter IX
  Army Leading 89
Chapter X
  Desperate Fighting 99
Chapter XI
  Reproducing The Army in America 109
Chapter XII
  In Australasia 124
Chapter XIII
  Women And Scandinavia 136
Chapter XIV
  Children Conquerors in Holland and Elsewhere 145

Chapter XV
India and Devotees 156

Chapter XVI
South Africa and Colonisation 169

Chapter XVII
Japanese Heroism 187

Chapter XVIII
Co-operating With Governments 192

Chapter XIX
Conquering Death 199

Chapter XX
His Social Work 209

Chapter XXI
Motoring Triumphs 221

Chapter XXII
Our Financial System 230

Chapter XXIII
In Germany in Old Age 242

Chapter XXIV
The End 250

Chapter XXV
Tributes 265

Chapter XXVI
Organisation 293

Chapter XXVII
The Spirit of The Army 303

Chapter XXVIII
The General as a Writer 328

Important Events Connected With
The General's Life And Work 342

THE AUTHORITATIVE LIFE
OF
GENERAL WILLIAM BOOTH

BY

George Scott Railton

WILLIAM BOOTH
Born April 10th. 1829. Died August 20th, 1912.

Preface

I have no hesitation in commending this small volume as containing so far as its space permits, a good picture of my beloved Father and a record of much that made his life of interest and importance to the world.

It does not, of course, profess to cover anything like the whole story of his many years of world-wide service. It could not do so. For any such complete history we must wait for that later production which may, I hope, be possible before very long when there has been time to go fully through the masses of diaries, letters and other papers he has left behind him.

It must not be supposed that I can make myself responsible for every phrase Commissioner Railton has used. I know, however, that perhaps no one except myself had anything like his opportunities, during the last forty years, of knowing and studying my Father's life, both in public and private, and of understanding his thoughts and purposes.

Now we wish this book to accomplish something. We cannot think it possible for anyone, especially a Salvationist, to read it without being compelled ever and anon to ask himself such questions as these:—

"Am I living a life that is at all like this life? Am I, at any rate, willing by God's grace to do anything I can in the same direction, in order that God may be more loved and glorified, and that my fellow men may be raised to a more God-like and happy service? After all, is there not something better for me than money-making, or the search after human applause, or indeed the pursuit of earthly good of any kind?

"If, instead of aiming at that which will all fade away, I turn my attention to making the best of my life for God and for others, may I not also accomplish something that will afford me satisfaction at last and bear reflection in the world to come?"

I hope also that to some, at least, the great message of this life will stand revealed in these pages. I believe it to be that, while God can do little or nothing by us until we are completely submitted and given up to Him, He can work wonders of infinite moment to the world when we are. Asked, a few months before his death, if he would put into a sentence the secret as he saw it, of all the blessings which had attended him during his seventy years of service, The General replied: "Well, if I am to put it into one sentence, I would say that I made up my mind that God Almighty should have all there was of William Booth." It was, in the beginning, that entire devotion to God and its continued maintenance which could, alone, account for the story told in these brief records.

The book is, of course, written in the main from the Salvationist point of view; much of it, indeed, is simply a reproduction of my father's own sayings and writings to his own people. This, to all thoughtful readers, must be our defence against any appearance of self-glorification, or any omission to refer to the work in the world that others are doing for Christ. No attempt has been made to tell the story of The General's "life and times," but simply to note some of the things he said and did himself. And I trust the record may be found useful by all the many servants of God who do not think exactly as he thought, but who yet rejoiced in the triumphs of the Cross through his labours.

To continue and to amplify the results of his work must needs be my continual aim. I am full of hope that this book may bring me some help, not only towards his Memorial Scheme, which contemplates the erection and equipment in London and other Capitals of enlarged premises for the Training of Officers in every branch of the work, or where they already have such buildings, the erection of new Headquarters or Halls; but towards the maintenance and extension in every land of the work he began.

It cannot but be a special gratification to me to know that this book will be received with eager affection in almost every part of the world. How could it ever cease to be my greatest joy to strive more and more after my Father's ideal of linking together men and women of every land and race in one grand competition for the extinction of selfishness by the enlistment of all sorts and conditions of men in one Great Holy War for God and for all that is good?

Whether those into whose hands this volume falls, agree or not with the teachings of The Salvation Army, may God grant them Grace to join heartily at least in this, my Father's great purpose, and so help me to attain the victory for which he lived and died.

    W. Bramwell Booth.
    London International Headquarters
     of The Salvation Army.

    November, 1912.

The Authoritative Life of General William Booth
Founder of The Salvation Army

Chapter I
Childhood and Poverty

William Booth was born in Nottingham, England, on April 10, 1829, and was left, at thirteen, the only son of a widowed and impoverished mother. His father had been one of those builders of houses who so rapidly rose in those days to wealth, but who, largely employing borrowed capital, often found themselves in any time of general scarcity reduced to poverty.

I glory in the fact that The General's ancestry has never been traced, so far as I know, beyond his grandfather. I will venture to say, however, that his forefathers fought with desperation against somebody at least a thousand years ago. Fighting is an inveterate habit of ours in England, and another renowned general has just been recommending all young men to learn to shoot. The constant joy and pride with which our General always spoke of his mother is a tribute to her excellence, as well as the best possible record of his own earliest days. Of her he wrote, in 1893:—

> "I had a good mother. So good she has ever appeared to me that I have often said that all I knew of her life seemed a striking contradiction of the doctrine of human depravity. In my youth I fully accepted that doctrine, and I do not deny it now; but my patient, self-sacrificing mother always appeared to be an exception to the rule.

"I loved my mother. From infancy to manhood I lived in her. Home was not home to me without her. I do not remember any single act of wilful disobedience to her wishes. When my father died I was so passionately attached to my mother that I can recollect that, deeply though I felt his loss, my grief was all but forbidden by the thought that it was not my mother who had been taken from me. And yet one of the regrets that has followed me to the present hour is that I did not sufficiently value the treasure while I possessed it, and that I did not with sufficient tenderness and assiduity at the time, attempt the impossible task of repaying the immeasurable debt I owed to that mother's love.

"She was certainly one of the most unselfish beings it has been my lot to come into contact with. 'Never mind me' was descriptive of her whole life at every time, in every place, and under every circumstance. To make others happy was the end of all her thoughts and aims with regard not only to her children but to her domestics, and indeed to all who came within her influence. To remove misery was her delight. No beggar went empty-handed from her door. The sorrows of any poor wretch were certain of her commiseration, and of a helping hand in their removal, so far as she had ability. The children of misfortune were sure of her pity, and the children of misconduct she pitied almost the more, because, for one reason, they were the cause of sorrow to those who had reason to mourn on their account.

"For many years before she died, love, joy, and peace reigned in her heart, beamed from her countenance, and spoke in her words. Her faith was immovably fixed on Him who is able to save to the uttermost. It was a common expression of confidence with her that 'Jesus would go with her all the way through the journey of life—even to the end. He would not leave her. Her feet were on the Rock.'"

To this testimony to his mother's worth The General added:—

"To those whose eyes may fall on these lines, may I not be excused saying, 'See to it that you honour your father and your mother, not only that your days may be long in the land, but that you may not, in after years, be disturbed by useless longings to have back again the precious ones who so ceaselessly and unselfishly toiled with heart and brain for your profoundest well-being.'

"My mother and father were both Derbyshire people. They were born within a few miles of each other, the former at Somercotes, a small village within a mile or two of Alfreton and the latter at Belper. My mother's father was a well-to-do farmer. Her mother died when she was three years of age; and, her father marrying again, she was taken to the heart and home of a kind uncle and aunt, who reared and educated her, giving her at the same time a sound religious training.

"Years passed of which we have but imperfect knowledge during which, by some means, she drifted to the small town of Ashby-de-la-Zouch. Here she met my father, who was availing himself of the waters as a remedy for his chronic enemy, rheumatism. He offered her marriage. She refused. He left the town indignant, but returned to renew his proposal, which she ultimately accepted. Their marriage followed. Up to this date her path through life had been comparatively a smooth one; but from this hour onward through many long and painful years, it was crowded with difficulties and anxieties.

"My father's fortunes appear to have begun to wane soon after his marriage. At that time he would have passed, I suppose, for a rich man, according to the estimate of riches in those days. But bad times came, and very bad times they were, such as we know little about, despite all the grumbling of this modern era. Nottingham, where the family was then located, suffered heavily, a large proportion of its poorer classes being reduced to the verge of starvation. My father, who had invested the entire savings of his lifetime in small house property, was seriously affected by these calamitous circumstances; in fact, he was ruined.

"The brave way in which my mother stood by his side during that dark and sorrowful season is indelibly written on my memory. She shared his every anxiety, advised him in all his business perplexities, and upheld his spirit as crash followed crash, and one piece of property after another went overboard. Years of heavy affliction followed, during which she was his tender, untiring nurse, comforting and upholding his spirit unto death; and then she stood out all alone to fight the battles of his children amidst the wreck of his fortunes.

"Those days were gloomy indeed; and the wonder now in looking back upon them is that she survived them. It would have seemed a perfectly natural thing if she had died of a broken heart, and been borne away to lie in my father's grave.

"But she had reasons for living. Her children bound her to earth, and for our sakes she toiled on with unswerving devotion and unintermitting care. After a time the waters found a smoother channel, so far as this world's troubles were concerned, and her days were ended, in her eighty-fifth year, in comparative peace."

"During one of my Motor Campaigns to Nottingham," The General wrote on another occasion, "my car took me over the Trent, the dear old river along whose banks I used to wander in my boyhood days, sometimes poring over Young's *Night Thoughts*, reading Henry Kirke White's *Poems*, or, as was frequently the case before my conversion, with a fishing-rod in my hand.

"In those days angling was my favourite sport. I have sat down on those banks many a summer morning at five o'clock, although I rarely caught anything. An old uncle ironically used to have a plate with a napkin on it ready for my catch waiting for me on my return.

"And then the motor brought us to the ancient village of Wilford, with its lovely old avenues of elms fringing the river.

"There were the very meadows in which we children used to revel amongst the bluebells and crocuses which, in those days, spread out their beautiful carpet in the spring-time, to the unspeakable delight of the youngsters from the town.

"But how changed the scene! Most of these rural charms had fled, and in their places were collieries and factories, and machine shops, and streets upon streets of houses for the employes of the growing town. We were only 60,000 in my boyhood, whereas the citizens of Nottingham to-day number 250,000.

"A few years ago the city conferred its freedom upon me as a mark of appreciation and esteem. To God be all the glory that He has helped His poor boy to live for Him, and made even his former enemies to honour him."

But we all know what sort of influences exist in a city that is at once the capital of a county and a commercial centre. The homes of the wealthy and comfortable are found at no great distance from the dwellings of the poor, while in the huge market-places are exhibitions weekly of all the contrasts between town and country life, between the extremest want and the most lavish plenty.

Seventy years ago, life in such a city was nearly as different from what it is to-day as the life of to-day in an American state capital is from that of a Chinese town.

Between the small circle of "old families" who still possessed widespread influence and the masses of the people there was a wide gap. The few respectable charities, generally due to the piety of some long-departed citizen, marked out very strikingly a certain number of those who were considered "deserving poor," and helped to make every one less concerned about all the rest. For all the many thousands struggling day and night to keep themselves and those dependent upon them from starvation, there was little or no pity. It was just "their lot," and they were taught to consider it their duty to be content with it. To envy their richer neighbours, to covet anything they possessed, was a sin that would only ensure for the coveter an eternal and aggravated continuance of his present thirst.

In describing those early years, The General said:—

> "Before my father's death I had been apprenticed by his wish. I was very young, only thirteen years of age, but he could not afford to keep me longer at school, and so out into the world I must go. This event was followed by the formation of companionships whose influence was anything but beneficial. I went down hill morally, and the consequences might have been serious if not eternally disastrous, but that the hand of God was laid on me in a very remarkable manner.
>
> "I had scarcely any income as an apprentice, and was so hard up when my father died, that I could do next to nothing to assist my dear mother and sisters, which was the cause of no little humiliation and grief.
>
> "The system of apprenticeship in those days generally bound a lad for six or seven years. During this time he received little or no wages, and was required to slave from early morning to late evening upon the supposition that he was 'being taught' the business, which, if he had a good master, was probably true. It was a severe but useful time of learning. My master was a Unitarian—that is, he did not believe Christ was the son of God and the Saviour of the

world, but only the best of teachers; yet so little had he learnt of Him that his heaven consisted in making money, strutting about with his gay wife, and regaling himself with worldly amusements.

"At nineteen the weary years of my apprenticeship came to an end. I had done my six years' service, and was heartily glad to be free from the humiliating bondage they had proved. I tried hard to find some kind of labour that would give me more liberty to carry out the aggressive ideas which I had by this time come to entertain as to saving the lost; but I failed. For twelve months I waited. Those months were among the most desolate of my life. No one took the slightest interest in me.

"Failing to find employment in Nottingham, I had to move away. I was loath, very loath, to leave my dear widowed mother and my native town, but I was compelled to do so, and to come to London. In the great city I felt myself unutterably alone. I did not know a soul excepting a brother-in-law, with whom I had not a particle of communion.

"In many respects my new master very closely resembled the old one. In one particular, however, he differed from him very materially, and that was he made a great profession of religion. He believed in the Divinity of Jesus Christ, and in the Church of which he was a member, but seemed to be utterly ignorant of either the theory or practice of experimental godliness. To the spiritual interests of the dead world around him he was as indifferent as were the vicious crowds themselves whom he so heartily despised. All he seemed to me to want was to make money, and all he seemed to want me for was to help him in the sordid selfish task.

"So it was work, work, work, morning, noon, and night. I was practically a white slave, being only allowed my liberty on

Sundays, and an hour or two one night in the week, and even then the rule was 'Home by ten o'clock, or the door will be locked against you.' This law was rigidly enforced in my case, although my employer knew that I travelled long distances preaching the Gospel in which he and his wife professed so loudly to believe. To get home in time, many a Sunday night I have had to run long distances, after walking for miles, and preaching twice during the day."

The contrast between those days and ours can hardly be realised by any of us now. We may put down almost in figures some of the differences that steam and electricity have made, linking all mankind together more closely than Nottingham was then connected with London. But what words can convey any picture of the development of intelligence and sympathy that makes an occurrence in a London back street interest the reading inhabitants of Germany, America, and Australia as intense as those of our own country?

What a consolation it would have been to the apprentice lad, could he have known how all his daily drudgery was fitting him to understand, to comfort, and to help the toiling masses of every race and clime?

In the wonderful providence of God all these changes have been allowed to leave England in as dominating a position as she held when William Booth was born, if not to enhance her greatness and power, far as some may consider beyond what she deserved. And yet all the time, with or without our choice, our own activities, and even our faults and neglects, have been helping other peoples, some of them born on our soil, to become our rivals in everything. Happily the multiplication of plans of intercourse is now merging the whole human race so much into one community that one may hope yet to see the dawn of that fraternity of peoples which may end the present prospects of wars unparalleled in the past. How very much William Booth has contributed to bring that universal brotherhood about this book may suffice to hint.

Chapter II
Salvation In Youth

In convincing him that goodness was the only safe passport to peace and prosperity of any lasting kind, William Booth's mother had happily laid in the heart of her boy the best foundation for a happy life, "Be good, William, and then all will be well," she had said to him over and over again.

But how was he to "be good"? The English National Church, eighty years ago, had reached a depth of cold formality and uselessness which can hardly be imagined now. Nowhere was this more manifest than in the "parish" church. The rich had their allotted pew, a sort of reserved seat, into which no stranger dare enter, deserted though it might be by its holders for months together. For the poor, seats were in some churches placed in the broad aisles or at the back of the pulpit, so conspicuously marking out the inferiority of all who sat in them as almost to serve as a notice to every one that the ideas of Jesus Christ had no place there. Even when an earnest clergyman came to any church, he had really a battle against great prejudices on both sides if he wished to make any of "the common people" feel welcome at "common prayer." But the way the appointed services were "gone through" was only too often such as to make every one look upon the whole matter as one which only concerned the clergy. Especially was this the effect on young people. Anything like interest, or pleasure, in those dull and dreary, not to say "vain" repetitions on their part must indeed have been rare.

It is not surprising then that William Booth saw nothing to attract him in the Church of his fathers. John Wesley, that giant reformer of religion in England, had been dead some forty years, and his life-work had not been allowed to affect "the Church" very profoundly. His followers having seceded from it contrary to his orders and entreaties, had already made several sects, and in the chief of these

William Booth presently found for himself at least a temporary home. Here the services were, to some extent, independent of books; earnest preaching of the truth was often heard from the pulpits, and some degree of real concern for the spiritual advancement of the people was manifested by the preachers.

Under this preaching and these influences, and the singing of Wesley's hymns, the lad was deeply moved. To his last days he sang some of those grand old songs as much as, if not more than, any others; that one, for example, containing the verse:—

> And can I yet delay my little all to give?
> To tear my soul from earth away, for Jesus to receive?
> Nay, but I yield, I yield! I can hold out no more,
> I sink, by dying love compelled, and own Thee conqueror.

The mind that has never yet come in contact with teaching of this character can scarcely comprehend the effect of such thoughts on a young and ardent soul. This Jesus, who gave up Heaven and all that was bright and pleasant to devote Himself to the world's Salvation, was presented to him as coming to ask the surrender of his heart and life to His service, and his heart could not long resist the appeal. It was in no large congregation, however, but in one of the smaller Meetings that William Booth made the glorious sacrifice of himself which he had been made to understand was indispensable to real religion. Speaking some time ago, he thus described that great change:—

> "When as a giddy youth of fifteen I was led to attend Wesley Chapel, Nottingham, I cannot recollect that any individual pressed me in the direction of personal surrender to God. I was wrought upon quite independently of human effort by the Holy Ghost, who created within me a great thirst for a new life.
>
> "I felt that I wanted, in place of the life of self-indulgence, to which I was yielding myself, a happy, conscious sense that I was pleasing God, living right, and spending all my powers to get others into such a life. I saw that all this ought to be, and I

decided that it should be. It is wonderful that I should have reached this decision in view of all the influences then around me. My professedly Christian master never uttered a word to indicate that he believed in anything he could not see, and many of my companions were worldly and sensual, some of them even vicious.

"Yet I had that instinctive belief in God which, in common with my fellow-creatures, I had brought into the world with me. I had no disposition to deny my instincts, which told me that if there was a God His laws ought to have my obedience and His interests my service.

"I felt that it was better to live right than to live wrong, and as to caring for the interests of others instead of my own, the condition of the suffering people around me, people with whom I had been so long familiar, and whose agony seemed to reach its climax about this time, undoubtedly affected me very deeply.

"There were children crying for bread to parents whose own distress was little less terrible to witness.

"One feeling specially forced itself upon me, and I can recollect it as distinctly as though it had transpired only yesterday, and that was the sense of the folly of spending my life in doing things for which I knew I must either repent or be punished in the days to come.

"In my anxiety to get into the right way, I joined the Methodist Church, and attended the Class Meetings, to sing and pray and speak with the rest." (A Class Meeting was the weekly muster of all members of the church, who were expected to tell their leader something of their soul's condition in answer to his inquiries.) "But all the time the inward Light revealed to me that I must not only renounce everything I knew to be sinful, but make restitution, so far as I had the ability, for any wrong I had done to others before I could find peace with God.

"The entrance to the Heavenly Kingdom was closed against me by an evil act of the past which required restitution. In a boyish trading affair I had managed to make a profit out of my companions, whilst giving them to suppose that what I did was all in the way of a generous fellowship. As a testimonial of their gratitude they had given me a silver pencil-case. Merely to return their gift would have been comparatively easy, but to confess the deception I had practised upon them was a humiliation to which for some days I could not bring myself.

"I remember, as if it were but yesterday, the spot in the corner of a room under the chapel, the hour, the resolution to end the matter, the rising up and rushing forth, the finding of the young fellow I had chiefly wronged, the acknowledgment of my sin, the return of the pencil-case—the instant rolling away from my heart of the guilty burden, the peace that came in its place, and the going forth to serve my God and my generation from that hour.

"It was in the open street that this great change passed over me, and if I could only have possessed the flagstone on which I stood at that happy moment, the sight of it occasionally might have been as useful to me as the stones carried up long ago from the bed of the Jordan were to the Israelites who had passed over them dry-shod.

"Since that night, for it was near upon eleven o'clock when the happy change was realised, the business of my life has been not only to make a holy character but to live a life of loving activity in the service of God and man. I have ever felt that true religion consists not only in being holy myself, but in assisting my Crucified Lord in His work of saving men and women, making them into His Soldiers, keeping them faithful to death, and so getting them into Heaven.

"I have had to encounter all sorts of difficulties as I have travelled along this road. The world has been against me, sometimes very intensely, and often very stupidly. I have had difficulties similar to those of other men, with my own bodily appetites, with my mental disposition, and with my natural unbelief.

"Many people, both religious and irreligious, are apt to think that they are more unfavourably constituted than their comrades and neighbours, and that their circumstances and surroundings are peculiarly unfriendly to the discharge of the duties they owe to God and man.

"I have been no exception in this matter. Many a time I have been tempted to say to myself, 'There is no one fixed so awkwardly for holy living and faithful fighting as I am.' But I have been encouraged to resist the delusion by remembering the words of the Apostle Paul: 'There hath no temptation taken you but such as is common to man.'

"I am not pretending to say that I have worked harder, or practised more self-denial, or endured more hardships at any particular time of my life than have those around me; but I do want those who feel any interest in me to understand that faithfulness to God in the discharge of duty and the maintenance of a good conscience have cost me as severe a struggle as they can cost any Salvation Soldier in London, Berlin, Paris, New York, or Tokio to-day.

"One reason for the victory I daily gained from the moment of my conversion was, no doubt, my complete and immediate separation from the godless world. I turned my back on it. I gave it up, having made up my mind beforehand that if I did go in for God I would do so with all my might. Rather than yearning for the world's pleasures, books, gains, or recreations, I found my new nature leading me to come away from it all. It had lost all charm for me. What were all the novels, even those of Sir Walter Scott or Fenimore Cooper, compared with the story of my Saviour? What were the choicest orators compared with Paul? What was the hope of money-earning, even with all my desire to help my poor mother and sisters, in comparison with the imperishable wealth of ingathered souls? I soon began to despise everything the world had to offer me.

"In those days I felt, as I believe many Converts do, that I could willingly and joyfully travel to the ends of the earth for Jesus Christ, and suffer anything imaginable to help the souls of other men. Jesus Christ had baptised me, according to His eternal promise, with His Spirit and with Fire.

"Yet the surroundings of my early life were all in opposition to this whole-hearted devotion. No one at first took me by the hand and urged me forward, or gave me any instruction or hint likely to help me in the difficulties I had at once to encounter in my consecration to this service."

This clear experience and teaching of an absolutely new life, that "eternal life" which Jesus Christ promises to all His true followers, is indispensable to the right understanding of everything in connexion with the career we are recording. Without such an experience nothing of what follows could have been possible. With it the continual resistance to every contrary teaching and influence, and the strenuous struggle by all possible means to propagate it are inevitable.

One is amazed at this time of day, to find intelligent men writing as though there were some mysticism, or something quite beyond ordinary understanding, in this theory of conversion, or regeneration.

Precisely the process which The General thus describes in his own case must of necessity follow any thoughtful and prayerful consideration of the mission and Gospel of Christ. Either we must reject the whole Bible story or we must admit that "all we like sheep have gone astray," taking our own course, in contempt of God's wishes. To be convinced of that must plunge any soul into just such a depth of sorrow and anxiety as left this lad no rest until he had found peace in submission to his God. No outside influences or appearances can either produce or be substituted for the deep, inward resolve of the wandering soul, "I will arise, and go to my Father." Whether that decision be come to in some crowded Meeting, or in the loneliness of some midnight hour is quite unimportant. But how can there be true repentance, or the beginning of reconciliation with God, until that point is reached?

And whenever that returning to God takes place, there is the same abundant pardon, the same change of heart, the same new birth, which has here been described. What can be more simple and matter of fact? Take away the need and possibility of such "conversion," and this whole life becomes a delusion, and the proclamation of Jesus Christ as a Saviour of men inexcusable. What has created any mystery around the question amongst Christians, if not the sacramental theory, which more or less contradicts it all? In almost all Christian Churches a theory is set up that a baby by some ceremonial act becomes suddenly regenerated, "made a child of God, and an heir of His Kingdom."

If that were the case, there could, of course, have been no need for the later regeneration of that child; but I do not believe that an ecclesiastic could be found, from the Vatican to the most remote island-parish where children are "christened," who would profess to have seen such a regenerated child alive. There is notoriously no such change accomplished in any one, until the individual himself, convinced of his own godless condition, cries to God for His Salvation, and receives that great gift.

What a foundation for life was the certainty which that lad got as he knelt in that little room in Nottingham! Into that same "full assurance" he was later on to lead many millions—young and old—of many lands. The simple Army verse:—

> I know thy sins are all forgiven,
> Glory to the Bleeding Lamb!
> And I am on my way to Heaven,
> Glory to the Bleeding Lamb!

embalms for ever that grand starting-point of the soul, from which our people have been able, in ignorance of almost everything else of Divine truth, to commence a career of holy living, and of loving effort for the souls of others.

How much more weight those few words carry than the most eloquent address bereft of that certainty of tone could ever have!

That certainty which rests not upon any study of books, even of the Bible itself, but upon the soul's own believing vision of the Lamb of God who has taken its sins away; that certainty which changes in a moment the prison darkness of the sin-chained into the light and joy and power of the liberated slave of Christ; that is the great conquest of the Salvation Soldier everywhere.

And yet, perhaps, in the eyes of an unbelieving world, and a doubting Church, that was General Booth's great offence all through life. To think of having uneducated and formerly godless people "bawling" the "mysteries of the faith" through the streets of "Christian" cities, where it had hitherto been thought inconsistent with Christian humility for any one to dare to say they really knew Him "whom to know is life eternal"! Oh, that was the root objection to all The General's preaching and action.

And it was one of the most valuable features of his whole career that wherever he or his messengers went there came that same certainty which from the days of Bethlehem onwards Jesus Christ came to bring to every man.

"By faith we know!" If every outward manifestation of The General's successes could be swept off the world to-morrow, this positive faith in the one Saviour would be capable of reproducing all its blessed results over again, wherever it was preserved, or renewed. Any so-called faith which gives no certainty must needs be hustled out of the way of an investigating, hurrying, wealth-seeking age. Only those who are certain that they have found the Lord can be capable of inducing others to seek and find Him.

Chapter III
Lay Ministry

Convictions such as we have just been reading of were bound to lead to immediate action. But it is most interesting to find that William Booth's first regular service for Christ was not called forth by any church, but simply by the spontaneous efforts of one or two young Converts like himself. No one could be more inclined towards the use of organisation and system than he always was, and yet he always advocated an organisation so open to all, and a system so elastic, that zeal might never be repressed, but only made the most of. It is, perhaps, fortunate that we have in one of his addresses to his own young Officers the following description of the way he began to work for the Salvation of his fellow-townsmen:—

"Directly after my conversion I had a bad attack of fever, and was brought to the very edge of the grave. But God raised me up, and led me out to work for Him, after a fashion which, considering my youth and inexperience, must be pronounced remarkable. While recovering from this illness, which left me far from strong, I received a note from a companion, Will Sansom, asking me to make haste and get well again, and help him in a Mission he had started in a slum part of the town. No sooner was I able to get about than I gladly joined him.

"The Meetings we held were very remarkable for those days. We used to take out a chair into the street, and one of us mounting it would give out a hymn, which we then sang with the help of, at the most, three or four people. Then I would talk to the people, and invite them to come with us to a Meeting in one of the houses.

"How I worked in those days! Remember that I was only an apprentice lad of fifteen or sixteen. I used to leave business at 7 o'clock, or soon after, and go visiting the sick, then these street Meetings, and afterwards to some Meeting in a cottage, where we would often get some one saved. After the Meeting I would often go to see some dying person, arriving home about midnight to rest all I could before rising next morning in time to reach my place of business at 7 A.M. That was sharp exercise! How I can remember rushing along the streets during my forty minutes' dinner-time, reading the Bible or C. G. Finney's *Lectures on Revivals of Religion* as I went, careful, too, not to be a minute late. And at this time I was far from strong physically; but full of difficulties as those days were, they were nevertheless wonderful seasons of blessing, and left pleasant memories that endure to this hour.

"The leading men of the church to which I belonged were afraid I was going too fast, and gave me plenty of cautions, quaking and fearing at my every new departure; but none gave me a word of encouragement. And yet the Society of which for those six apprentice years I was a faithful member, was literally my heaven on earth. Truly, I thought then there was one God, that John Wesley was His prophet, and that the Methodists were His special people. The church was at the time, I believe, one thousand members strong. Much as I loved them, however, I mingled but little with them, and had time for but few of their great gatherings, having chosen the Meadow Platts as my parish, because my heart then as now went out after the poorest of the poor.

"Thus my conversion made me, in a moment, a preacher of the Gospel. The idea never dawned on me that any line was to be drawn between one who had nothing else to do but preach and a saved apprentice lad who only wanted 'to spread through all the earth abroad,' as we used to sing, the fame of our Saviour. I have lived, thank God, to witness the separation between layman and cleric become more and more obscured, and to see Jesus Christ's idea of changing in a moment ignorant fishermen into fishers of men nearer and nearer realisation.

"But I had to battle for ten of the best years of my youth against the barriers the Churches set up to prevent this natural following of the Lamb wherever He leads. At that time they all but compelled those who wished to minister to the souls of men to speak in unnatural language and tones, and adopt habits of mind and life which so completely separated them from the crowd as to make them into a sort of princely caste, whom the masses of every clime outwardly reverenced and inwardly despised.

"Lad though I was, a group of new Converts and other earnest souls soon gathered around me, and greater things seemed to be ahead when a great trial overtook me. The bosom friend already referred to was taken from my side. We had been like David and Jonathan in the intensity of our union and fellowship in our work for God. He had a fine appearance, was a beautiful singer, and possessed a wonderful gift in prayer. After I had spoken in our Open-Air Meeting he would kneel down and wrestle with God until it seemed as though he would move the very stones on which he knelt, as well as the hearts of the people who heard him. Of how few of those men called ministers or priests can anything like this be said!

"But the unexpected blow came. He fell into consumption. His relations carried him up and down the country for change of air and scene. All was done that could be done to save his life, but in vain. The last change was to the Isle of Wight. In that lovely spot the final hope fled. I remember their bringing him home to die. He bade farewell to earth, and went triumphantly to Heaven singing—

> And when to Jordan's flood I come,
>   Jehovah rules the tide,
>   And the waters He'll divide,
>   And the heavenly host will shout—
>   "Welcome Home!"

"What a trial that loss was to my young heart! It was rendered all the greater from the fact that I had to go forward all alone in face of an opposition which suddenly sprang up from the leading functionaries of the church."

The consecration which William Booth made of himself to this work, with all the zeal and novelty with which it was characterised, was due, no doubt, to the teaching, influence, and example of James Caughey, a remarkable American minister who visited the town. Largely free from European opinions and customs in religious matters, and seeking only to advance the cause of Jesus Christ with all possible speed, this man to a very large extent liberated William Booth for life from any one set of plans, and led him towards that perfect faith in God's guidance which made him capable of new departures to any extent.

The old-fashioned representatives of officialdom grumbled in vain at novelties which have now become accepted necessities of all mission work.

"But just about this time," The General has told us, "another difficulty started across my path in connexion with my business. I have told you how intense had been the action of my conscience before my conversion. But after my conversion it was naturally ever increasingly sensitive to every question of right and wrong, with a great preponderance as to the importance of what was right over what was wrong. Ever since that day it has led me to measure my own actions, and judge my own character by the standard of truth set up in my soul by the Bible and the Holy Ghost; and it has not permitted me to allow myself in the doing of things which I have felt were wrong without great inward torture. I have always had a great horror of hypocrisy—that is, of being unreal or false, however fashionable the cursed thing might be, or whatever worldly temptation might strive to lead me on to the track. In this I was tested again and again in those early days, and at last there came a crisis.

"Our business was a large one and the assistants were none too many. On Saturdays there was always great pressure. Work often continued into the early hours of Sunday. Now I had strong notions in my youth and for long after—indeed, I entertain them now—about the great importance of keeping the Sunday, or Sabbath as we always called it, clear of unnecessary work.

"For instance, I walked in my young days thousands of miles on the Sabbath, when I could for a trifling sum have ridden at ease, rather than use any compulsory labour of man or beast for the promotion of my comfort. I still think we ought to abstain from all unnecessary work ourselves, and, as far as possible, arrange for everybody about us to have one day's rest in seven. But, as I was saying, I objected to working at my business on the Sabbath, which I interpreted to mean after twelve o'clock on Saturday night. My relatives and many of my religious friends laughed at my scruples; but I paid no heed to them, and told my master I would not do it, though he replied that if that were so he would simply discharge me. I told him I was willing to begin on Monday morning as soon as the clock struck twelve, and work until the clock struck twelve on Saturday night, but that not one hour or one minute of Sunday would I work for him or all his money.

"He kept his word, put me into the street, and I was laughed at by everybody as a sort of fool. But I held out, and within seven days he gave in, and, thinking my scrupulous conscience might serve his turn he told me to come back again. I did so, and before another fortnight had passed he went off with his young wife to Paris, leaving the responsibilities of a business involving the income and expenditure of hundreds of pounds weekly on my young shoulders.

"So I did not lose by that transaction in any way. With no little suffering on four separate occasions, contrary to the judgments of all around me, I have thus left every friend I had in the world, and gone straight into what appeared positive ruin, so far as this world was concerned, to meet the demands of conscience. But I have trusted God, and done the right, and in every separate instance I can now see that I have gained both for this world and the next as the result.

"During all the period of my lay preaching, both in Nottingham and London, I had to grapple with other difficulties. What with one thing and another I had a great struggle at times to keep my head above the waters, and my heart alive with peace and love. But I held on to God and His grace, and the never-failing joy that I experienced in leading souls to Christ carried me through."

How can anybody fail to see how much more the masses are likely to be influenced by the preaching, no matter how defective oratorically, of one who has thus lived in the midst of them—living, in fact, their very life of anxiety, suffering, and toil—than by that of men, however excellent, who come to them with the atmosphere of the study, the college, or the seminary?

And yet, after having been trained for a year in the rough-and-ready oratory of the streets, subject to interruptions and interjected sneers, The General was called upon, in order to be recognised as fit for registration as a lay preacher, to mount the pulpit and preach a "trial sermon"! Accustomed as he had become to talk out his heart with such words and illustrations as involuntarily presented themselves to the simple-minded, though often wicked and always ignorant crowds, who gathered around the chair on which he stood; able without difficulty to hold their attention when he had won it, and drive the truth home to their souls, in spite of the counter-attractions of a busy thoroughfare, he took very hardly to the stiff, cold process of sermonising and sermon-making such as was then in vogue, and it was some time before he had much liberty or made much progress in the business.

Still, in due time he was passed, first as a lay "preacher on trial," and later called as fully qualified to preach at any chapel in the district—this latter after a second year's activities and a "second trial sermon."

When he once got on to this sermon-making line he took the best models he could find—men like John Wesley, George Whitefield, and, above all, C. G. Finney, who he could be certain had never sought in their preaching for human applause, but for the glory of God and the good of souls alone.

In the Psalms, as in the Gospels and the Acts of the Apostles, we have the most unmistakable guidance upon this subject, showing it to have been God's purpose so to pour out His Spirit upon all flesh that all His people should be true prophets—not all, of course, of the same calibre or style, but all capable of warning and teaching, in all wisdom, every one whom they could reach.

The work of the ministry is another thing altogether. Let no one suppose that The Salvation Army at all underrates the "separation" unto His work of those whom God has chosen for entire devotion to some task, whatever it be. As to those whom we take away from their secular calling to become our Officers, I will only say here that we judge of their fitness not alone by their ability to speak, but by their having proved themselves to be so devoted to the poor that we can rely upon their readiness to act as servants of the very neediest in any way that lies within their power. Only two persons at each of our Stations, the Officers actually in command, receive any payment whatever from The Army. All the others associated with us, many of them wearing our uniform and holding some particular office, give freely their leisure-time and money to the work, and may be spoken of as "lay preachers."

Our young "local preacher" generally spent his Sundays in some distant village where he had been appointed to preach, just as is the case in these days with thousands of our Soldiers.

"My homeward walk, often alone through the dark, muddy fields and lanes," he tells us, "would be enlivened by snatches of the songs we had been singing in our Meetings, and late into the night people might have heard my solitary prayers and praises. 'Don't sit up singing till twelve o'clock after a hard day's work,' was one of the first needed pieces of practical advice I got from my best adviser of later years."

"But we never felt we could have too much of God's service and praise, and scarcely regarded the grave itself as a terminus for our usefulness; for in the case of a girl who had attended our Cottage Meetings, and who had died of consumption, we lads organised something very like one of our present-day Salvation Army Funerals.

"Having ministered to the poor girl's necessities during her sickness, comforted her in her last hours of pain, sung hymns of triumph round her bed as her spirit took its passage to the skies, we had the right, as her only friends, to order her funeral, and we resolved to make the most of it for the good of her neighbours.

"Although it was in the depth of winter, and snow lay thick on the ground, we brought the coffin out into the street, sang and prayed around it, and urged the few neighbours who stood shivering by, or listening at their doors and windows, to prepare for their dying day. We then processioned to the Cholera Burial Ground, as the cemetery in which the poorest of Nottingham were buried was called, obtaining permission from the Chaplain to hold another little Meeting by the grave-side, after he had read the ordinary Service. I cannot but feel that the hand of God was upon me in those days, teaching me how much lay preachers could do."

How wonderful that the lad who did all that in the teeth of religious convention and opinion should have lived to organise just such battles and just such funerals all round the world, and to train hundreds of thousands of Soldiers of Christ to do likewise! What a termination to his own career he was preparing all the time, when the City of London was to suspend the traffic of many of its busiest thoroughfares for hours to let his coffin pass through with a procession of his uniformed Soldiers a mile long!

With regard to the question of a "Call to the ministry," that bugbear of so many souls, The General constantly expressed himself as follows:—

> "How can anybody with spiritual eyesight talk of having no call, when there are such multitudes around them who never hear a word about God, and never intend to; who can never hear, indeed, without the sort of preacher who will force himself upon them? Can a man keep right in his own soul, who can see all that, and yet stand waiting for a 'call' to preach? Would they wait so for a 'call' to help any one to escape from a burning building, or to snatch a sinking child from a watery grave?
>
> "Does not growth in grace, or even ordinary growth of intelligence, necessarily bring with it that deepened sense of eternal truths which must intensify the conviction of duty to the perishing world?
>
> "Does not an unselfish love, the love that goes out towards the unloving, demand of a truly loving soul immediate action for the Salvation of the unloved?"
>
> "And, are there not persons who know that they possess special gifts, such as robust health, natural eloquence or power of voice, which specially make them responsible for doing something for souls?

"And yet I do not at all forget, that above and beyond all these things, there does come to some a special and direct call, which it is peculiarly fatal to disregard, and peculiarly strengthening to enjoy and act upon.

"I believe that there have been many eminently holy and useful men who never had such a call; but that does not at all prevent any one from asking God for it, or blessing Him for His special kindness when He gives it."

There is, I think, no doubt that God did give to young William Booth such a call, although he never spoke of it, perhaps lest he might discourage any who, without enjoying any such manifestation, acted upon the principles just referred to. At any rate, he battled through any season of doubt he had with regard to it, and came out into a certainty that left him no room for question or fear.

Chapter IV
Early Ministry

We cannot wonder that God Himself rarely seems to find it wise, even if it be possible, to fit men for His most important enterprises in a few years, or by means of one simple process of instruction. Consider the diversity of men's minds and lives, and the varying currents of thought and opinion which are found in the various parts of the world at different periods of even one century, and it will at once be seen how impossible we should all immediately pronounce it to fit one man by means of one pathway of service to be the minister and leader of the followers of Christ in every part of the world.

Christ Himself was kept in an obscurity we cannot penetrate for thirty years before He was made known to the comparatively small people amongst whom all His time on earth was to be spent. Moses was not called till he was eighty years old, having spent forty years amidst the splendours of one of the grandest courts of the ancient world, and forty more amidst the sheep on a desert border!

How was the ardent English lad who came to serve in a London shop during the week, and to do the work of a lay preacher on Sundays, to be fitted to form and lead a great Christian Order of devotees out of every nation, and to instruct and direct them in helping their fellow-men of every race in every necessity that could arise? To prepare a man merely to preach the Gospel a few years of service in that work might suffice; but then we should probably have seen a man merely interested in the numbers of his own audiences and the effect produced upon them by his own preaching.

For William Booth a much more tedious and roundabout journey was needed. He must first of all preach his way up from the counter to the pulpit, and he must then have twenty years of varied experiences in ministerial service amongst widely differing Churches, before he could be fit to take up his appointed place, outside all the Churches, to raise from amongst every class a new force for the exaltation of Christ amongst all men.

For so great a work he must needs have a helpmeet, and he was to find her when she was still physically as weak and unlikely for the great task as he was, and as entirely severed from all existing organisations. Catherine Mumford, like himself, innocent of any unkind feeling towards her Church, had been excluded from it, simply because she would not pledge herself to keep entirely away from the Reform party.

Unable really at the time to do more than teach a class in the Sunday School, and occasionally visit a sick person, she nevertheless, by the fervour of her action, made herself a power that was felt, and threw all her influence on the side of any whole-hearted religious or temperance effort. The anxiety of both these two young people not to allow any thought for their own happiness to interfere with their duty to God and to their fellows delayed their marriage for years; and when they did marry it was with the perfect resolve on both sides to make everything in their own life and home subordinate to the great work to which they had given themselves.

Neither of them at the time dreamed of Mrs. Booth's speaking in public, much less that they were together to become the liberators of woman from the silence imposed on her by almost every organisation of Christ's followers. Having known both of them intimately during the years in which The Salvation Army was being formed, I can positively contradict the absurdly exaggerated statement that The General would have had little or no success in life but for the talents and attractive ministry of Mrs. Booth. She was a helpmeet in the most perfect sense, never, even when herself reduced to illness and helplessness, desiring to absorb either time or attention that he could give to the great War in which she always encouraged him as no other ever could. Remaining to her latest hour a woman of the tenderest and most modest character, she shrank from public duty, and merely submitted so far as she felt "constrained," for Christ's sake, to association with anything that she was convinced ought to be done to gain the ears of men for the Gospel, however contrary it might be to her own tastes and wishes. Perhaps her most valuable contribution to the construction of The General's life was her ability to explain to him opinions and tastes differing widely from his own, and to sustain and defend his general defiance of the usual traditions and customs of "society."

CATHERINE BOOTH
Born January 17th, 1829. Died October 4th, 1890.

His own feelings about it all he has described in these words:—

"The sensations of a new-comer to London from the country, are always somewhat disagreeable, if he comes to work. The immensity of the city must especially strike him as he crosses it for the first time and passes through its different areas. The general turn-out into a few great thoroughfares, on Saturday nights especially, gives a sensation of enormous bulk. The manifest poverty of so many in the most populous streets must appeal to any heart. The language of the drinking crowds must needs give a rather worse than a true impression of all.

"The crowding pressure and activity of so many must almost oppress one not accustomed to it. The number of public-houses, theatres, and music-halls must give a young enthusiast for Christ a sickening impression. The enormous number of hawkers must also have given a rather exaggerated idea of the poverty and cupidity which nevertheless prevailed. The Churches in those days gave the very uttermost idea of spiritual death and blindness to the existing condition of things; at that time very few of them were open more than one evening per week. There were no Young Men's or Young Women's Christian Associations, no P.S.A.'s, no Brotherhoods, no Central Missions, no extra effort to attract the attention of the godless crowds; for miles there was not an announcement of anything special in the religious line to be seen.

"To any one who cared to enter the places of worship, their deathly contrast with the streets was even worse. The absence of week-night services must have made any stranger despair of finding even society or diversion. A Methodist sufficiently in earnest to get inside to the 'class' would find a handful of people reluctant to bear any witness to the power of God.

"Despite the many novelties introduced since those days, the activities of the world being so much greater, the contrast must look even more striking in our own time."

Imagine a young man accustomed to daily labour for the poor, coming into such a world as that!

Thought about what they sang and said in the private gatherings of the Methodist Societies could only deepen and intensify the feeling of monstrosity. They sang frequently:—

> He taught me how to watch and pray,
> And live rejoicing every day.

But where were the rejoicing people? Where was there indeed anybody who, either in or out of a religious service, dared to express his joy in the Lord—or wished to express anything. It was as if religious societies had become wet blankets to suppress any approach to a hearty expression of religious faith. Nevertheless, by God's grace, it all worked in this case not to crush but to infuriate and stir the new-comer to action.

Preaching, under such circumstances, was a relief to such a soul, and necessarily became more and more desperate.

One hearing of William Booth was enough for Mr. Rabbits, a practical, go-ahead man, who had raised up out of the old-fashioned little business of his forefathers one of the great "stores" of London, and who longed to see the same sort of development take place in connexion with the old-fashioned, perfectly correct, and yet all but lifeless institutions that professed to represent Jesus Christ the Saviour of the world. His sense of the contrast between this preacher and others whom he knew was proportionately rapid and acute. The effects produced on hearers were the same at every turn.

This living preaching was and is a perfect fit with all the rush of the world outside, and the helplessness of the poor souls around.

William Booth was, as we have seen, only seventeen when he was fully recognised as a preacher of the Gospel according to the custom of the Methodist Churches, and at nineteen his minister urged him to give up his life to the ministry. At that time, however, he felt himself too weak physically for a ministerial career, and in this view his doctor concurred. So determined was he to accomplish his purpose, however, that he begged the doctor not to express his opinion to the minister, but to allow the matter to stand over for a year. Unless a man with a nervous system like his was "framed like a bullock," and had "a chest like a prize-fighter," he would break down, said the physician, and seeing that he was not so built, he would be "done for" in twelve months. The doctor went to the grave very soon afterwards, whereas The General continued preaching for over sixty years after that pronouncement.

At this period, some of the Wesleyans who were discontented with their leaders in London broke into revolt, and there was so much bitter feeling on both sides, that the main object of John Wesley—the exaltation of Christ for the Salvation of men—was for the moment almost lost sight of.

Mr. Booth joined with the most earnest people he could find; but though they gave him opportunity to hold Meetings, he wrote to one of his old associates:—

> "How are you going on? I wish I knew you were happy, living to God and working for Jesus.
>
> "I preached on Sabbath last to a respectable but dull and lifeless congregation. Notwithstanding this I had liberty in both prayer and preaching. I had not any one to say 'Amen' or 'Praise the Lord' during the whole of the service. I want some of you here with me in the Prayer Meetings, and then we should carry all before us."

Thus we see emerging from the obscurity of a poor home a conqueror, fired with one ambition, out of harmony with every then existing Christian organisation, because of that strange old feeling, so often expressed in the Psalms of David, that the praises of God ought to be heard from all men's lips alike, and that everything else ought to give way to His will and His pleasure.

In speaking to his Officers later on he said:—

> "When the great separation from the Wesleyan Church took place, Mr. Rabbits said to me one day: 'You must leave business, and wholly devote yourself to preaching the Gospel.'

"'Impossible,' I answered. 'There is no way for me. Nobody wants me.' 'Yes,' said he, 'the people with whom you have allied yourself want an evangelist.'

"'They cannot support me,' I replied; 'and I cannot live on air.'

"'That is true, no doubt,' was his answer. 'How much can you live on?'

"I reckoned up carefully. I knew I should have to provide my own quarters and to pay for my cooking; and as to the living itself, I did not understand in those days how this could be managed in as cheap a fashion as I do now. After a careful calculation, I told him that I did not see how I could get along with less than twelve shillings a week.

"'Nonsense,' he said; 'you cannot do with less than twenty shillings a week, I am sure.'

"'All right,' I said, 'have it your own way, if you will; but where is the twenty shillings to come from?'

"'I will supply it,' he said, 'for the first three months at least.'

"'Very good,' I answered. And the bargain was struck there and then.

"I at once gave notice to my master, who was very angry, and said, 'If it is money you want, that need not part us.' I told him that money had nothing to do with the question, that all I wanted was the opportunity to spend my life and powers in publishing the

Saviour to a lost world. And so I packed my portmanteau, and went out to begin a new life.

"My first need was some place to lay my head. After a little time spent in the search, I found quarters in the Walworth district, where I expected to work, and took two rooms in the house of a widow at five shillings a week, with attendance. This I reckoned at the time was a pretty good bargain. I then went to a furniture shop, and bought some chairs and a bed, and a few other necessaries. I felt quite set up. It was my birthday, a Good Friday, and on the same day I fell in love with my future wife.

"But the people would have nothing to do with me. They 'did not want a parson.' They reckoned they were all parsons, so that at the end of the three months' engagement the weekly income came to an end; and, indeed, I would not have renewed the engagement on any terms. There was nothing for me to do but to sell my furniture and live on the proceeds, which did not supply me for a very long time. I declare to you that at that time I was so fixed as not to know which way to turn.

"In my emergency a remarkable way opened for me to enter college and become a Congregational minister. But after long waiting, several examinations, trial sermons and the like, I was informed that on the completion of my training I should be expected to believe and preach what is known as Calvinism. After reading a book which fully explained the doctrine, I threw it at the wall opposite me, and said I would sooner starve than preach such doctrine, one special feature of which was that only a select few could be saved.[1]

---

1 The general tendency towards indifference quite as much as the better impulses of our age have produced such a toning down of the teachings of Calvin, both in and out of Switzerland, that it may be startling to some to be reminded that, except the Lutheran and Methodist, every Church still has in its list of Doctrines those of Election and Predestination. If it were true that every human being

"My little stock of money was exhausted. I remember that I gave the last sixpence I had in the world to a poor woman whose daughter lay dying; but within a week I received a letter inviting me to the charge of a Methodist Circuit in Lincolnshire, and from that moment my difficulties of that kind became much less serious.

"The Spalding people welcomed me as though I had been an angel from Heaven, providing me with every earthly blessing within their ability, and proposing that I should stay with them for ever. They wanted me to marry right away, offered to furnish me a house, provide me with a horse to enable me more readily to get about the country, and proposed other things that they thought would please me.

"With them I spent perhaps the happiest eighteen months of my life. Of course my horizon was much more limited in those days than it is now, and consequently required less to fill it.

"Although I was only twenty-three years of age and Lincolnshire was one of the counties that had been most privileged with able Methodist preaching for half a century before, and I had to immediately follow in Spalding a somewhat renowned minister, God helped me very wonderfully to make myself at home, and become a power amongst the people.

"I felt some nervousness when on my first November Sunday I was confronted by such a large congregation as greeted me. In the morning I had very little liberty; but good was done, as I

---

was predestined, before birth, either to a good or a bad life, there would, of course, be no meaning in a Saviour or a Gospel; and we can understand the indignation of this honest lad, when he was asked to undertake to teach such things. He never learned how to reconcile the profession of a set of doctrines one does not believe with any religion. The recollection of this incident helped him in limiting to the utmost possible extent, the Doctrinal Declarations of The Army. But whatever he asked any one to subscribe to he expected them truly to believe and earnestly to teach.

afterwards learned. In the afternoon we had a Prayer, or After-Meeting, at which one young woman wept bitterly. I urged her to come to the communion rail at night. She did so, and the Lord saved her. She afterwards sent me a letter thanking me for urging her to come out. In the evening I had great liberty, and fourteen men and women came to the communion rail; many, if not all, finding the Saviour.

"On the Monday I preached there again. Four came forward, three of whom professed to find Salvation. I exerted myself very much, felt very deeply, and prayed very earnestly over an old man who had been a backslider for seven years. He wept bitterly, and prayed to the Lord to save him, if He could wash a heart as black as Hell. By exerting myself so much I made myself very ill, and was confined to the house during the rest of the week. My host and hostess were very kind to me.

"The next Sunday I started from home rather unwell. I had to go to Donnington, some miles away, in the morning and evening, and to Swineshead Bridge in the afternoon.

"But at night God helped me to preach in such a way that many came out, and fourteen names were taken of those who really seemed satisfactory. It was, indeed, a melting, moving time.

"I was kneeling, talking to a Penitent, when somebody touched me on the shoulder, and said, 'Here is a lady who has come to seek Salvation. Her son came to hear you at Spalding, and was induced to seek the Saviour, and now she has come to hear you, and she wants Salvation, too." The Lord had mercy upon her, and she went away rejoicing.

"At Swineshead Bridge—the very name gives some idea of the utterly rural character of the population—I was to preach on three successive evenings, in the hope of promoting a Revival there. Many things seemed to be against the project; but the Lord was for us. Two people came out on the Monday evening, and God saved them both. This raised our faith and cheered our spirits, especially as we knew that several more souls were in distress.

"On the Tuesday the congregation was better. The news had spread that the Lord was saving, and that seldom fails to bring a crowd wherever it may be. That evening the word was with power, and six souls cried for mercy. At the earnest solicitations of the people, I decided to stay the remainder of the week, and urged them to pray earnestly, with the result that many more sought and found Salvation, and the little Society was nearly doubled.

"On the Saturday, just before I started home on the omnibus, a plain, unsophisticated Christian came and said, 'O sir, let me have hold of your hand.' When he had seized it between both his, with tears streaming down his face, he said, 'Glory be to God that ever you came here. My wife before her conversion was a cruel persecutor, and a sharp thorn in my side. She would go home from the Prayer Meeting before me, and as full of the Devil as possible; she would oppose and revile me; but now, sir, she is just the contrary, and my house, instead of being a little Hell has become a little Paradise.' This was only one of a number of cases in which husbands rejoiced over wives, and wives over husbands, for whom they had long prayed, being saved.

"I shall always remember with pleasure the week I spent at Swineshead Bridge, because I prayed more and preached with more of the spirit of expectation and faith, and then saw more success than in any previous week of my life. I dwell upon it as, perhaps, the week which most effectually settled my conviction for ever that it was God's purpose by my using the simplest means to bring souls into liberty, and to break into the cold and formal state of things to which His people only too readily settle down."

For the sake of readers who have never seen Meetings such as The General for so many years conducted, it seems at once necessary to explain what is meant by the terms "seeking mercy" or "Salvation," the "cries for mercy," and, above all, the "Mercy-Seat," or "Penitent-Form," which appear so constantly in all reports of his work.

From the first beginnings of his Cottage Meetings as a lad in Nottingham, he always aimed at leading every sinner to repentance, and he always required that repentance should be openly manifested by the Penitent coming out in the presence of others, to kneel before God, to confess to Him, and to seek His pardon.

This is merely in accordance with the ancient customs practised by the Jews in their Temple, to which practice Jesus Christ so strikingly calls attention in His Parable of the Publican, who cried, "God be merciful to me a sinner." The Psalms of David abound with just such cries for deliverance, and with declarations that God heard and answered all those who so cried to Him in the anguish of their guilt.

The General was never blind to the fact that open acts of contrition like this may be feigned, or produced by a mere passing excitement; but having seen so much of the indifference with which men generally continue in sin, even when they admit their consciousness of guilt and danger, he always thought the risk of undue excitement, or too hasty action, comparatively small.

The "Penitent-Form" of The Salvation Army is simply a form or a row of seats, immediately in front of the platform, at which all who wish to seek Salvation are invited to kneel, as a public demonstration of their resolution to abandon their sins, and to live henceforth to please God. Those who kneel there are urged to pray for God's forgiveness, and when they believe that He does forgive them to thank Him for doing so. Whilst kneeling there they are spoken to by persons who, having passed through the same experience, can point out to them the evils and dangers they must henceforth avoid, and the first duties which a true repentance must demand of them.

There are many cases, for example, in which the Penitent is urged to give up at once some worldly habit or companionship, or to make confession of, and restitution for, some wrong done to others. An Officer or Soldier accompanies the Penitent to his home or to his employer, should such a course appear likely to help him to effect any reconciliation, or take any other step to which his conscience calls him. The names and addresses of all Penitents are recorded, so that they may be afterwards visited and helped to carry out the promises they have made to God.

For convenience' sake, in very large Meetings, such as those The General himself held, where hundreds at a time come to the Penitent-Form, a room called the Registration Room is used for the making of the necessary inquiries and records. In this room those who decide to join The Army have a small piece of ribbon of The Army's colours at once attached to their coats. But this Registration Room must in no way be confused with an "Inquiry Room," where seeking souls can go aside unseen. The General was always extremely opposed to the use of any plan other than that of the Penitent-Form, lest there should be any distinction made between one class and another, or an easier path contrived for those who wish to avoid a bold avowal of Christ.

And he always refused to allow any such use of the Bible in connexion with Penitents as has been usual in Inquiry Rooms, where the people have been taught that if they only believed the words of some text, all would be well with them. The faith to which The General desired all who came to the Penitent-Form to be led is not the mere belief of some statement, but that confidence in God's faithfulness to all His promises, which brings peace to the soul.

Nothing could be more unjust than the representation that by the use of the Penitent-Form an attempt is made to work up excitement, or emotion. Experience has proved, everywhere, that nothing tends so rapidly to allay the painful anxiety of a soul, hesitating before the great decision, as the opportunity to take at once, and publicly, a decisive step. We often sing:—

> Only a step, only a step,
> Why not take it now?
> Come, and thy sins confessing,
> Thou shalt receive a blessing;
> Do not reject the mercy
> So freely offered thee.

But the Penitent-Form is no modern invention, nor can it be claimed as the speciality of any set of religionists. Even heathen people in past ages have provided similar opportunities for those who felt a special need either to thank their God for blessings received, or to seek His help in any specific case, to come forward in an open way, and confess their wants, their confidence, or their gratitude, at some altar or shrine.

Shame upon us all that objection should ever be made to equally public avowals of penitence, of submission, of faith, or of devotion to the Saviour of the world. The General, at any rate, never wavered in demanding the most speedy and decisive action of this kind, and he probably led more souls to the Penitent-Form than any man who has ever lived.

In Germany especially it has frequently been objected that the soul which is "compelled" to take a certain course has in that very fact manifested a debased and partly-destroyed condition, and that nothing can excuse the organisation of methods of compulsion. With any such theory one could not but have considerable sympathy, were it not for the undeniable fact that almost all "civilised" people are perpetually under the extreme pressure of society around them, which is opposed to prayer, or to any movement of the soul in that direction.

To check and overcome that very palpable compulsion on the wrong side, the most desperate action of God's servants in all ages has never been found strong enough. Hence there has come about another sort of compulsion, within the souls of all God's messengers. It could not but be more agreeable to flesh and blood if the minds of men could more easily be induced to turn from the things that are seen to those which are invisible. But this has never yet been the case. Hence all who really hear God's voice cannot but become alarmed as to the manifest danger that His warnings may remain entirely unheeded. When once any soul is truly enlightened, it cannot but put forth every devisable effort to compel the attention of others.

The Army is only the complete organisation of such efforts for permanent efficiency. We may have had to use more extreme methods than many before us, because, unlike those who are the publicly recognised advocates of Christ, we have, in the first instance, no regular hearers at all, and have generally only the ear of the people so long as we can retain it, against a hundred competitions. And yet, to those who live near enough to notice it, the exercise of force by means of church steeples and bells is far more violent, all the year round, than the utmost attack of the average Corps upon some few occasions.

Who complains of the compulsion of railway servants, who by bell, flag, and whistle, glaring announcements, or in any other way, urge desiring passengers to get into their train, before it is too late? Wherever a true faith in the Gospel exists, The General's organisation of compulsory plans for the Salvation of souls will not only be approved, but regarded as one of the great glories of his life.

The "Will you go?" of The Army, wherever its songs are heard, has ever been more than a kindly invitation. It has been an urging to which millions of undecided souls will for ever owe their deliverance from the dilatory and hindering influences around them, into an earnest start towards a heavenly life.

That is why The General taught so many millions to sing, in their varied languages, his own song:—

> O boundless Salvation! deep ocean of love,
> O fulness of mercy Christ brought from above!
> The whole world redeeming, so rich and so free,
> Now flowing for all men—come, roll over me!
>
> My sins they are many, their stains are so deep,
> And bitter the tears of remorse that I weep;
> But useless is weeping, thou great crimson sea,
> Thy waters can cleanse me, come, roll over me!
>
> My tempers are fitful, my passions are strong.
> They bind my poor soul, and they force me to wrong;
> Beneath thy blest billows deliverance I see,
> Oh, come, mighty ocean, and roll over me!
>
> Now tossed with temptation, then haunted with fears,
> My life has been joyless and useless for years;
> I feel something better most surely would be,
> If once thy pure waters would roll over me.

O ocean of mercy, oft longing I've stood
On the brink of thy wonderful, life-giving flood!
Once more I have reached this soul-cleansing sea,
I will not go back till it rolls over me.

The tide is now flowing, I'm touching the wave,
I hear the loud call of "The Mighty to Save";
My faith's growing bolder—delivered I'll be—
I plunge 'neath the waters, they roll over me.

And now, Hallelujah! the rest of my days
Shall gladly be spent in promoting His praise
Who opened His bosom to pour out this sea
Of boundless Salvation for you and for me.

Chapter V
Fight Against Formality

The Army's invariable principle of avoiding even the appearance of attacking any other association of religionists, or their ideas or practices, renders it difficult to explain fully either why William Booth became the regular minister of a church, or why he gave up that position; and yet he has himself told us sufficient to demonstrate at one stroke not only the entire absence of hostility in his mind, but the absolute separateness of his way of thinking from that which so generally prevails.

The enthusiastic welcome given to The General wherever he went, by the clergy of almost every Church indicates that he had generally convinced them that he had no thought of attacking them or their Churches, even when he most heartily expressed his thankfulness to God for having been able to escape from all those trammels of tradition and form which would have made his great life-work, for all nations, impossible. And I think there are few who would nowadays question that his life, teaching, and example all tended greatly to modify many of the Church formalities of the past.

> "Just before leaving Lincolnshire," he says, "I had been lifted up to a higher plane of the daily round of my beloved work than I had experienced before. Oh, the stagnation into which I had settled down, the contentment of my mind with the love offered me at every turn by the people! I still aimed at the Salvation of the unconverted and the spiritual advance of my people, and still fought for these results. Indeed, I never fell below that. And yet if the After-Meeting was well attended, and if one or two Penitents

responded, I was content, and satisfied myself with that hackneyed excuse for so much unfruitful work, that I had 'sown the seed.' Having cast my bread on the waters, I persuaded myself that I must hope for its being found by and by.

"But I heard of a Rev. Richard Poole who was moving about the country, and the stories told me of the results attending his services had aroused in me memories of the years gone by, when I thought little and cared less about the acceptability of my own performances, so long as I could drag the people from the jaws of Hell.

"I resolved to go and hear him. I found him at the house of a friend before the Meeting, comparatively quiet. How I watched him! But when I had heard him preach from the text, 'Said I not unto thee, that if thou wouldst believe, thou shouldst see the salvation of God,' and had observed the blessed results, I went to my own chamber—I remember that it was over a baker's shop—and resolved that, regardless of man's opinions, and my own gain or position, I would ever seek the one thing.

"Whilst kneeling in that room, there came into my soul a fresh realisation of the greatness of the opportunity before me of leading men and women out of their miseries and their sin, and of my responsibility to go in for that with all my might. In obedience to the heavenly vision, I made a consecration of the present and future, of all I had, and hoped to have, to the fulfilment of this mission, and I believe God accepted the offering.

"I continued my public efforts in line with my new experience."

Happily and freely as William Booth had been allowed to lead his people, however, he and his intended wife both saw that there could be no permanent prospect of victory amongst these "Reformers." The very popularity of a preacher was sure to lead to contention about the sphere of his labours.

> "The people," he writes, "with whom I had come into union were sorely unorganised, and I could not approve of the ultra-radicalism that prevailed. Consequently, I looked about for a Church nearer my notions of system and order, and in the one I chose, the Methodist New Connexion, I found a people who were, in those days, all I could desire, and who received me with as much heartiness as my Lincolnshire friends had done.
>
> "Ignorance has different effects on different people. Some it puffs up with self-satisfaction. To others it is a source of mortifying regret. I belonged to the latter class. I was continually crying out, 'O God, how little I am, and how little I know! Give me a chance of acquiring information, and of learning how more successfully to conduct this all-important business of saving men to which Thou hast called me, and which lies so near my heart.'
>
> "To gratify this yearning for improvement, the Church with which I had come into union gave me, at my request, an opportunity of studying under a then rather celebrated theologian. But instead of better qualifying me for the work of saving men, by imparting to me the knowledge necessary for the task, and showing me in every-day practice how to put it to practical use, I was set to study Latin, Greek, various Sciences, and other subjects, which, as I saw at a glance, could little help me in the all-important work that lay before me. However, I set to work, and, with all the powers I had, commenced to wrestle with my studies.
>
> "My Professor was a man of beautiful disposition, and had an imposing presence. The books he wrote on abstract and difficult theological problems were highly prized in those days. Moreover, he

belonged to a class of preachers, not altogether unknown to-day, who have a real love for that order of preaching which convicts and converts the soul, although unable to practise it themselves. **He knew a good thing when he saw it**.

"The first time he heard me preach was on a Sunday evening. I saw him seated before me, at the end of the church. I knew he was going to judge me, and I realised that my future standing in his estimation, as well as my position in the Society I had now made my home, would probably very much depend on the judgment he formed of me on that occasion.

"I am not ashamed to say that I wanted to stand well with him. I knew also that my simple, practical style was altogether different from his own, and from that of the overwhelming majority of the preachers he was accustomed to approve. But my mind was made up. I had no idea of altering my aim or style to please him, the world, or the Devil.

"I saw dying souls before me, the gates of Heaven wide open on the one hand, and the gates of Hell open on the other, while I saw Jesus Christ with His arms open between the two, crying out to all to come and be saved. My whole soul was in favour of doing what it could to second the invitation of my Lord, and doing it that very night.

"I cannot now remember much about the service, except the sight of my Professor, with his family around him, a proud, worldly daughter sitting at his side. I can remember, however, that in my desire to impress the people with the fact that they could have Salvation there and then, if they would seek it, and, to illustrate their condition, I described a wreck on the ocean, with the affrighted people clinging to the masts between life and death, waving a flag of distress to those on shore, and, in response, the life-boat going off to the rescue. And then I can remember how I reminded my hearers that they had suffered shipwreck on the ocean of time through their sins and rebellion; that they were sinking down to destruction, but that if they would only hoist the signal of distress Jesus Christ would send off the life-boat to their rescue. Then, jumping on the seat at the back of the pulpit, I waved my pocket-handkerchief round and round my head to represent the signal of distress I wanted them to hoist, and closed with an appeal to those who wanted to be rescued to come at once, and in the presence of the audience, to the front of the auditorium. That night twenty-four knelt at the Saviour's feet, and one of them was the proud daughter of my Professor.

"The next morning was the time for examination and criticism of the previous day's work, and I had to appear before this Doctor of Divinity. I entered the room with a fellow-student. He was put through first. After listening to the Doctor's judgment on his performance my turn came. I was not a little curious as to what his opinion would be.

"'Well, Doctor,' I said, 'what have you to say to me? You heard me last night. What is your judgment on my poor performance?'

"'My dear Sir,' he answered, 'I have only one thing to say to you, and that is, go on in the way you have begun, and God will bless you.'

"But other difficulties were not far away, for I had hardly settled down to my studies before I got into a red-hot Revival in a small London church where a remarkable work was done. In an account of this effort my name appeared in the church's Magazine, and I was invited to conduct special efforts in other parts of the country.

This, I must confess, completely upset my plans once more, and I have not been able to find heart or time for either Greek or Latin from that day to this."

How sincerely this curious student longed for improvement is manifested in the following entry in his Journal, written, I presume, on a Monday morning when it was thought that some relaxation of his studies following a Sunday's services would be advantageous:—

"Monday.—Visited the British Museum. Walked up and down there praying that God would enable me to acquire knowledge to increase my power of usefulness."

Who will doubt that that Museum prayer was heard and answered?

The Church he had joined was governed by an annual assembly, called the Conference, at which candidates for the ministry were accepted into it, and were appointed to some sphere of labour called a Circuit. Just before the Conference met he was astonished to hear that it was proposed to appoint him as Superintendent of a London Circuit. He was able to persuade the authorities concerned to alter this intention on the ground of his comparative lack of experience, although he expressed his willingness to take the post of assistant minister under whomsoever the Conference might appoint as Superintendent.

In due course, the appointment was made, and he found himself assistant to a Superintendent who, he tells us, was "stiff, hard, and cold, making up, in part, for the want of heart and thought in his public performances by what sounded like a sanctimonious wail."

This gentleman strongly objected when, as a result of the reports of Mr. Booth's services appearing in the Press, he was urgently invited to visit other places, as he had visited Guernsey. The Conference authorities, however, prevailed, and insisted, in the general interest, upon his place in London being taken by another preacher, and his services being utilised wherever called for.

It was thus by no choice of his own, but by the arrangement of his Church, that Mr. Booth, instead of remaining tied down to the ordinary routine of pastoral life, was sent for some time from place to place to conduct such evangelising Campaigns as his soul delighted in. Who can doubt that God's hand was in this disposal of his time? He was allowed to marry, though his young wife had to content herself with but occasional brief spells of association with him.

His Campaigns were really wonderful in their success. He would go for a fortnight, or even less, to some city where the congregation had dwindled almost to nothing, and where one or two services a week, conducted in a very quiet and formal way, were maintained with difficulty, owing to the indifference or hopelessness of both minister and people. For the period of his stay all the usual programme would be laid aside, however, and he would be left free to carry out his own plans of daily service.

How remarkable to find him so completely carrying with him all who had been accustomed to the old forms, and introducing, with the evident sanction of the president and authorities of his Church, such re-arrangements, records, and reorganisation as he desired.

But the strange, the almost inexplicable thing is that, without his even remarking upon it, all should go back to the old forms the moment his Campaign ended!

What is not at all strange is that there should have grown up within the Church a strong opposition to him, so that, at the end of two and a half years, a majority of the Conference voted against his continuing these Campaigns, and required him to resume the ordinary routine of the ministry. Surely, any one might have foreseen that unless the old forms could be altered in favour of the new regime, the leader of this warfare must submit to the old routine. True, he might try to carry out in his Circuit, to the utmost of his power, his ideas of free and daily warfare; but, unless all who were under him in the various places which constituted a Methodist Circuit would constantly agree and co-operate, no one man could prevent the old forms from prevailing.

But William Booth was no revolutionist, and his willingness and submission to carry on the old routine, with little alteration, for four successive years surely proved that no desire for personal exaltation or mastery, but only the conquest of souls, was his guiding influence.

In those four years, spent in Brighouse and Gateshead, he tried to introduce into the churches as much as he could of the life of warfare which he considered necessary. In one year he so far won over the officialdom of Brighouse that they desired his reappointment; whilst in Gateshead he so transformed the Circuit that before many weeks had passed the Central Chapel, which had hitherto borne the dignified but cool-sounding name of "Bethesda," was dubbed by the mechanics, who formed the bulk of the surrounding population, "The Converting Shop."

To those iron workers, accustomed daily to see masses of metal suddenly changed, whilst in a red-hot state, into any desired form by the action of powerful machinery, set up for the purpose, such a name was both intelligible and expressive.

It, moreover, accorded with the new pastor's idea of the proper utilisation of any building devoted to the worship of Jesus Christ. There ought to be felt there, he thought, that marvellous heat of Divine Love which was implied in Christ's engagement to "baptise" all His followers "with fire," and the services should above all else, be such as would ensure the immediate conversion to God of all who came under their influence.

But in Gateshead The General was to discover the most potent force that could be brought to bear upon all these questions, in the liberation of Mrs. Booth from the customary silence which Church system has almost universally imposed upon woman. It might almost be said that the whole problem of cold formality, as against loving warmth, can be solved by woman's liberation. True, in the ordinary state of things, the most excellent ladies of any church become its most conservative bulwarks; and, fortified, as they imagine, by a few words in one of St. Paul's Epistles, such ladies can oppose every new spiritual force as powerfully as some of them opposed him in Antioch, nineteen hundred years ago. But "daughters" of God who have been liberated by His Spirit generally make short work of any continued opposition.

Mrs. Booth, herself trained and hitherto fettered by this old school of silence, to the astonishment of every one prayed in the church on the first Sunday evening in Gateshead. The opposition of an influential pastor, in a neighbouring city, to the public ministrations of a Mrs. Palmer, a visitor from the United States, very soon afterwards led Mrs. Booth to defend her sister's action in the Press, and thus to see more clearly than before what God could do through her, if she was willing.

The General had not yet seen the importance of this advance, and, in view of his wife's delicate health, had not pressed her into any sort of activity, much as he had valued her perfect fellowship with him in private. But he rejoiced, of course, in her every forward step, and when she not only visited a street of the most godless and drunken people in the neighbourhood, but began to speak in the services, he gave her all the weight of his official as well as his personal sanction, little imagining at the time what a mighty force for the spread of the truth he was thus enlisting.

After faithfully serving the Church in Gateshead for three years, he found the Conference no more willing than before to release him for the evangelistic work which now both he and his wife more and more longed for.

The final scene, when, in a Conference at Liverpool, Mrs. Booth confirmed The General's resolution to refuse to continue even for one more year his submission to form, by calling out "Never!" marked a stage in his career which was decisive in a startling way as to the whole of his future.

> "It is true that I had a wonderful sphere of usefulness and happiness," says The General; "but I was not contented. I had many reasons for dissatisfaction. I was cribbed, cabined, and confined by a body of cold, hard usages, and still colder and harder people. I desired freedom! I felt I was called to a different sphere of labour. I wanted liberty to move forward in it. So when the Conference definitely declined my request to set me free for evangelistic work I bade them farewell.
>
> "It was a heart-breaking business. Here was a great crowd of people all over the land who loved me and my dear wife. I felt a deep regard for them, and to leave them was a sorrow beyond description. But I felt I must follow what appeared to be the beckoning finger of my Lord. So, with my wife and four little children, I left my quarters and went out into the world once more, trusting in God, literally not knowing who would give me a shilling, or what to do or where to go.
>
> "All my earthly friends thought I was mistaken in this action; some of them deemed me mad. I confess that it was one of the most perplexing steps of my life. When I took it every avenue seemed closed against me. There was one thing I could do, however, and that was to trust in God, and wait for His Salvation."

The difficulty of the Church was really insurmountable at that time. Since those days most of the Protestant Churches have learnt that evangelistic work is just as essential as the ordinary pastoral ministrations.

The fact is, that neither the Booths nor the Church were then aware that God, behind all their perplexities, was working out a plan of His own. Who laments that separation to-day? As the evangelists of any Church they could not possibly have become to so large an extent the evangelists of all.

Chapter VI
Revivalism

Not many days passed after William Booth's retirement from the ministry of the Methodist New Connexion before his faith was rewarded by a warm invitation to a small place at the other end of the country. One of his former Converts was a minister in the little seaport Hayle, in Cornwall, and he sent the call, "Come over and help us."

The Church had got into the stagnant condition which is so commonly experienced wherever contentment with routine long holds sway. Mr. and Mrs. Booth were not only welcomed, but given a free hand to take any course they pleased to fill the building with hearers, and to secure their Salvation.

Fighting now together, as they had learnt to do at Gateshead, they saw results more rapid and striking than they had ever known before, although they found themselves face to face with a population more disinclined for novelty, and especially for the novelties they introduced, than any they had before had to deal with. The General thus described at the time for the Connexional Magazine some of his first battles in Cornwall:—

"Hayle, Cornwall.

"When in London, you requested me to send now and then a report of the Lord's working in connexion with my ministry, and thinking that the following account of the Revival now in progress here will be interesting to you, I forward it. We arrived here on the 10th inst., and commenced labour on the following Sabbath. The chapel was crowded. Gracious influences accompanied the word. Many appeared to be deeply convicted of sin, but no decided cases of conversion took place that day. On Monday afternoon we had a service for Christians, and spoke on the hindrances to Christian labour and Christian joy. Evening, chapel crowded. Very solemn season. Nearly all the congregation stayed to the Prayer Meeting that followed, and many appeared deeply affected, but refused to seek the mercy of God. A strong prejudice prevails here against the custom of inviting anxious inquirers to any particular part of the building. The friends told me that this plan never had succeeded in Cornwall; but I thought it the best, considering the crowded state of the chapel, and therefore determined to try it. I gave a short address, and again invited those who wished to decide for Christ to come forward. After waiting a minute or two, the solemn silence was broken by the cries of a woman who at once left her pew, and fell down at the Mercy-Seat, and became the first-fruits of what I trust will be a glorious harvest of immortal souls. She was quickly followed by others, when a scene ensued beyond description. The cries and groans were piercing in the extreme; and when the stricken spirits apprehended Jesus as their Saviour, the shouts of praise and thanksgiving were in proportion to the previous sorrow.

"Tuesday Evening.—Congregation again large. Prayer Meeting similar to Monday night, and some very blessed cases of conversion.

"Wednesday.—Chapel full. Mrs. Booth spoke with much influence and power. Glorious Prayer Meeting. An old woman who found the Saviour jumped on her feet, and shouted, with her face beaming with heavenly radiance, 'He's saved me! Glory to God! He's saved me, an old sinner, sixty-three. Glory to God!' Other cases of great interest transpired, and the people, with swimming eyes, and glowing hearts, sang—

"'Praise God, from whom all blessings flow.'

"Thursday.—Preached from 'Him that cometh to Me I will in nowise cast out.' Had a blessed Meeting. A woman who had herself found Jesus during the week, pointed me to her husband. Found him fully enlightened and deeply convicted. I urged him to immediate decision and the full surrender of himself to God. He came out, and fell down among the Penitents. He remained there about an hour. The Meeting could not be concluded until near eleven o'clock, and many were very reluctant to retire even then.

"Friday.—The first thing this morning my host informed me that he had just heard of a mason who had been at the services every night, and who had resolved to stop work until he found the Lord. Soon after a young lady came in to tell us of a woman who had found peace during the night. At the family altar this morning, a woman in the employ of the gentleman with whom we are staying commenced to bemoan her sinful condition and to cry for mercy. I asked her to remain, and pointed her to Jesus, and she soon found rest through believing. In the afternoon, met several anxious persons for prayer and conversation. In the evening we had announced a public Prayer Meeting. Before we reached the chapel we could hear the cries and prayers of those already assembled. On entering, we found a strong man praising God at the top of his voice for hearing his prayer and pardoning his sins. It was the mason. He had been under deep concern for three days; had not slept at all the night before, but after a day's agony, he had found Jesus; and such tumultuous, rapturous joy I think I never witnessed. Again and again, during the evening, he broke out with a voice that drowned all others, and rose above our songs of praise ascribing glory to Jesus for what He had done for his soul. There were many other cases of almost equal interest. The Meeting was not closed until eleven.

"About midnight, the Rev. J. Shone, the minister in charge of the church, was called out to visit a woman who was in great distress. He afterwards described her agony in seeking, and her joy in finding, the Lord, together with the sympathy and exultation of her friends with her, as one of the most thrilling scenes he ever witnessed."

In a later report The General wrote:—

"Hayle, Cornwall.

"The work of the Lord here goes on gloriously. The services have progressed with increasing power and success, and now the whole neighbourhood is moved. Conversion is the topic of conversation in all sorts of society. Every night, crowds are unable to gain admission to the sanctuary. The oldest man in the church cannot remember any religious movement of equal power. During the second week, the Wesleyans opened a large room for united Prayer Meetings at noon; since then, by their invitation, we have on several occasions spoken in their chapels to densely crowded audiences; services being simultaneously conducted in the chapel where the movement originally commenced. One remarkable and gratifying feature of the work is the large number of men who are found every night amongst those who are anxious. Never have I seen so many men at the same time smiting their breasts, and crying, 'God be merciful to me a sinner,' Strong men, old men, young men, weeping like children, broken-hearted on account of their sins. A number of these are sailors, and scarcely a ship has gone out of this port the last few days without taking among its crew one or more souls newly-born for Heaven."

Can it be believed that just such victories as these led to the closing of almost all the Churches against him?

"In these days," The General has more recently written, "it has become almost the fashion for the Churches to hold yearly 'revival' or 'special' services, but forty years ago they were as unanimously opposed to anything of the kind, and compelled me to gain outside every Church organisation the one liberty I desired—to seek and save the lost ones, who never enter any place of worship whatever.

"Let nobody suppose that I cherish any resentment against any of the Churches on account of their former treatment of me, or that I have a desire to throw a stone at any of them. From any such feelings I believe that God has most mercifully preserved me all my life, and I rejoice in the kindness on this account with which they load me now in every land, as testimonies to that fact.

"But I want to make it clear to readers in lands far away from Christendom why I was driven into the formation of an Organisation entirely outside every Christian Church in order to accomplish my object, and why my people everywhere, whilst having no more desire than myself to come into dispute, or even discussion, with any Church near them, must needs act as independently of them all as I have done, no matter how friendly they may now be to us.

"Nothing could be more charming than the present attitude towards us of every religious community in the United States, from the Roman Catholics, whose Archbishop has publicly commended us, to the Mormons, who are generally regarded as enemies of all Christianity, and the Friends (commonly called Quakers) whose ideas of worship seem to be at the uttermost extreme from ours. All are satisfied that I and my people are not wishful to find fault with any religious body whatever, but to spend all our time and energy in combating the great evils of godlessness and selfishness which threaten to sweep away all the people everywhere from any thought above material things.

"Yet we have had to forbid our people to accept too often the pressing invitations that pour upon them from all sides to hold Meetings in Church buildings, lest they should lose touch with the masses outside, and begin to be content with audiences of admirers.

"The thirty-six years of my life whilst I was groping about in vain for a home and fellowship amongst Churches gave me to understand, as only experience can, what are the thoughts and feelings of the millions in Christian lands, who not only never enter a church, but who feel it to be inconceivable that they ever should do so.

"If this experience has been invaluable to us in Christian lands, how much more so is it in the far vaster countries of Asia and Africa, where our work is only as yet in its beginnings. When I went to Japan, the entire missionary community everywhere united to uphold me as the exemplar of true Christlike action for the good of all men. But the leaders of all the five sects of Buddhism were no less unanimous in their welcome to me, or in their expressions of prayerful desire for the success of my work.

"In India and Africa I have repeatedly seen supporting me in my indoor and outdoor demonstrations the leaders of the Hindu, Parsee, Sikh, Buddhist, Jewish, and Mohammedan communities, who had never met with the Christians in so friendly a way before. I cannot think this would have been the case had I ever become settled amongst any Christian body in this country.

"Can any one wonder then that I see in all the unpleasant experiences of my early days the hand of God Himself, leading me by a way that I knew not—that I could scarcely believe indeed at the time to be His way. Why should it have been so difficult for a man, who only wished to lead the lost ones to the great Shepherd who seeks them all to get or to remain within any existing fold, if it was not that there lay before me and my Soldiers conquests infinitely greater and more important than had ever yet been made?

"Oh, with what impatience I turn from the very thought of any of the squabbles of Christian sects when I see all around me the millions who want to avoid any thought of their great Friend and Father, and of the coming Judge before whom we must all, perhaps this very day, appear."

How easily excuses, which sound most plausible, are found for every sort of negligence in the service of God—indeed, for not serving Him at all!

"It is not my way, you see," says some one, who does not like to make any open profession of interest in Jesus Christ, as though our own preferences or opinions were to be the governing consideration in all that affects the interests of "our Lord"!

The General has proved that the old ideas connected with "the Master" can not only be revived but acted up to in our day, and the sense of shame for idle excuses drive out all the paltry pleas set up for indifference to the general ruin.

"At this season, nothing can be done" is as coolly pleaded to-day as if "in season, out of season" had never been written in our Divine Order-Book.

How often our forces in the midst of fairs, and race-days, and "slack times," have demonstrated that real soldiers of Christ can snatch victory, just when all around seems to ensure their defeat!

When The General began to form his Army, it was ordinarily assumed as a settled principle that Open-Air Work could only be done in fine weather, and the theory is still existent in many quarters. As if the comfort and convenience of "the workers," and not the danger and misery of the people, were to fix the times of such effort!

"But the people will not come," is even now pleaded as an excuse for the omission or abandonment of any imaginable attempt to do good. As if the people's general disinclination for anything that has to do with God were not the precise reason for His wish to "send out" His servants!

"Such a plan would never succeed here," is an almost invariable excuse made for not undertaking anything new. The General was never blind to differences between this and that locality and population. But he insisted that no plan that could be devised by those on any given spot, and especially no plan that has manifestly been blessed and used by God elsewhere should be dismissed without proper, earnest trial.

"But that has never been done, or has never done well here," seemed to him rather a reason for trying it with, perhaps, some little modification than for leaving a plan untried. The inexorable law to which he insisted that everything should bend was that nothing can excuse inactivity and want of enterprise where souls are perishing. And he was spared to see even Governments beginning to recognise that it is inexcusable to let sin triumph in "a Christian country." He proved that it was possible to raise up "Christian Soldiers," who would not only sing, or hear singing, in beautiful melody about "Marching, onward as to War"; but who would really do it, even when, it led to real battle.

Chapter VII
East London Beginning

What were Mr. and Mrs. Booth to do? They were excluded from most of the Churches in which during the last twenty years they had led so many souls to Christ. They found themselves out of harmony with most of the undenominational evangelists of the day, and, moreover, they had experienced throughout even the brightest of their past years a gnawing dissatisfaction with much of their work, which The General thus described in the preface to his book, ***In Darkest England, and the Way Out***:—

> "All the way through my career I have keenly felt the remedial measures usually enumerated in Christian programmes, and ordinarily employed by Christian philanthropy, to be lamentably inadequate for any effectual dealing with the despairing miseries of the outcast classes. The rescued are appallingly few, a ghastly minority compared with the multitudes who struggle and sink in the open-mouthed abyss. Alike, therefore, my humanity and my Christianity, if I may speak of them as in any way separate from each other, have cried out for some comprehensive method of reaching and saving the perishing crowds."

The Booths had settled in a London home, finding that they must needs have some fixed resting-place for their children, and that abundant opportunities of one kind or another could be found for them both in the metropolis. But The General, who was "waiting upon God, and wondering what would happen" to open his way to the unchurched masses, received an invitation to undertake some services in a tent which had been erected in an old burial-ground in Whitechapel, the expected missioner having fallen ill! He consented, and he thus describes his experiences:—

> "When I saw those masses of poor people, so many of them evidently without God or hope in the world, and found that they so readily and eagerly listened to me, following from Open-Air Meeting to tent, and accepting, in many instances, my invitation to kneel at the Saviour's feet there and then, my whole heart went out to them. I walked back to our West-End home and said to my wife:—
>
> "'O Kate, I have found my destiny! These are the people for whose Salvation I have been longing all these years. As I passed by the doors of the flaming gin-palaces to-night I seemed to hear a voice sounding in my ears, "Where can you go and find such heathen as these, and where is there so great a need for your labours?" And there and then in my soul I offered myself and you and the children up to this great work. Those people shall be our people, and they shall have our God for their God.'"

Mrs. Booth herself wrote:—

> "I remember the emotion that this produced in my soul. I sat gazing into the fire, and the Devil whispered to me, 'This means another departure, another start in life!' The question of our support constituted a serious difficulty. Hitherto we had been able to meet our expenses out of the collections which we had made from our more respectable audiences. But it was impossible to suppose that we could do so among the poverty-stricken East-Enders—we were afraid even to ask for a collection in such a locality.
>
> "Nevertheless, I did not answer discouragingly. After a momentary pause for thought and prayer, I replied, 'Well, if you feel you ought to stay, stay. We have trusted the Lord ***once*** for our support, and we can trust Him ***again***!'"

"That night," says The General, "The Salvation Army was born."

Before long God moved the heart of one of the most benevolent men in England, Mr. Samuel Morley, to promise them his influence and support without any condition but the continuance of the work thus begun. But no amount of monetary help could have placed The General in a position to establish anything like the permanent work he desired. He writes:—

> "I had hardly got successfully started on this new path before my old experience of difficulty met me once more. On the third Sunday morning, I think it was, we found the old tent which formed our cathedral, blown down, and so damaged by the fall, as well as so rotten, that it could not be put up again. Another tent was impossible, as we had no money to buy one; so, as no suitable building could be obtained, there was nothing for it but for us to do our best out of doors.
>
> "After a time we secured an old dancing-room for Sunday Meetings. But, there being no seats in it, our Converts had to come at 4 o'clock on Sunday morning to bring the benches in, and work till midnight, or later still, when the day's Meetings were over, to move them out again. For our week-night Meetings we had hired an old shed, formerly used to store rags in, and there we fought for months."

What a testimony to the character of the work already accomplished, and the readiness of the little force already raised to toil like pioneer soldiers for the love of Christ!

Most of the Converts of those days "had been forgiven much." The following letter from one of them may give some idea both of the nature of the work done, and the surrounding circumstances:—

"Dear Sir,—I have reason to bless the hour that God put the thought into your head to open the Mission at the East-End of London, for it has been the means of making me and my family happy in the love of Christ; it has turned me from a drunkard, blasphemer, and liar, to a true believing Christian. At the age of thirteen, I went as a waiter-boy in a public-house, where I remained until I was sixteen. Here I learned to love the flavour of drink, and I never lost it until I was converted to God, through the blessed words spoken in the open air. When I look back, and think how I have beaten my poor wife—it was through the drink—it makes me ashamed of myself. It was the word and the blow, but sometimes the blow first. After I got sober, sometimes it would make me ashamed to look at her black eyes; but I do thank God there is no fear of black eyes now; for we are very happy together.

"I am a stoker and engine-driver, and I wonder I have never had an explosion, for I have been drunk for a week at a time. On one occasion, I had been drunk overnight, and was not very sober in the morning. I went to work at half-past five, instead of five, and, without looking to see if there was any water in the boiler, I began stoking the fire up. The fright sobered me. It cost above L100 before it was fit for work again. But that did not alter me, only for the worse. I broke up my home. I got worse, after that, and cared for nothing. Half my wages went in drink, my wife was afraid to speak to me, and the poor children would get anywhere out of my way. Afterwards I was discharged; but although I soon got another job, I could not leave off the drink. I was reckoned a regular drunkard. I lost place after place, and was out of work several weeks at a time; for they did not care to employ a drunkard. Still, I would have beer somehow, I did not care how. I have given one and sixpence for the loan of a shilling, and though there was not a bit of bread at home, the shilling went in beer.

"I have often had the police called in for ill-using my wife. On one occasion she ran down to her mother's, with her face bleeding; but I went to bed. When I woke, I saw she was not there, so I went out and got drunk. I came home and got a large carving-knife, put it up my sleeve, and went down to her mother's, with the intention of killing her; but they saw the knife. The police were called in, and I was taken to Spitalfields Station. But no one coming to press the charge, I got off.

"Eight years ago God thought fit to lay me on a bed of sickness for thirteen weeks, and I was given up by all the doctors. When I got better, people thought I would alter my life, and become a steady man; but no, I was as bad as ever. While I was at work, another time, drunk, I lost one of my eyes by an accident; but even that did not make me a sober man, nor make me leave off swearing and cursing. I was generally drunk two or three times on Sundays. The Sunday that I was convinced I was a sinner I had been drunk twice.

"I did not think there was so much happiness for me; but I do thank God for what He has done for me. He has changed my heart, He has filled me full of the love of Christ; and my greatest desire is to tell sinners what a dear Saviour I have found."

Best of all was the demonstration that, out of such material, God was able and ready to raise up a fighting force.

One great difficulty of those days was the obtaining of suitable buildings. For a time a theatre was hired for Sunday Meetings (the law in England then not allowing theatres to give performances on Sundays).

The great buildings to which the people have been accustomed to go for amusement have always proved admirably suited for the gathering of congregations of that sort. A gentleman who had had long experience in mission work thus describes what he saw when he went to spend a "Sunday afternoon with William Booth":—

"On the afternoon of Sunday, January 31st, I was able to see some of the results of William Booth's work in the East of London, by attending his Experience Meeting, held in the East London Theatre. About 2 o'clock some of his helpers and Converts went out from the Mission Hall, where they had been praying together, and held an Open-Air Meeting in front of a large brewery opposite the Hall. The ground was damp and the wind high, but they secured an audience, and then sang hymns along the road, till they came to the theatre, taking in any who chose to follow them. Probably about five hundred were present, though many came in late.

"The Meeting commenced at three, and lasted one hour and a half. During this period fifty-three persons gave their experience, parts of eight hymns were sung, and prayer was offered by four persons. After singing Philip Philips' beautiful hymn, 'I will sing for Jesus,' prayer was offered up by Mr. Booth and two others.

"A young man rose and told of his conversion a year ago, thanking God that he had been kept through the year.

"A negro, of the name of Burton, interested the Meeting much by telling of his first Open-Air Service, which he had held during the past week in Ratcliff Highway, one of the worst places in London. He said, when the people saw him kneel in the gutter, engaged in prayer for them, they thought he was mad. The verse—

> Christ now sits on Zion's hill,
> He receives poor sinners still,

Was then sung.

"A young man under the right-hand gallery, having briefly spoken, one of Mr. Booth's helpers, a Yorkshireman, with a strong voice and hearty manner, told of the Open-Air Meetings, the opposition they encountered, and his determination to go on, in spite of all opposition from men and Devils.

"A middle-aged man on the right, a sailor, told how he was brought to Christ during his passage home from Colombo. One of the Dublin tracts, entitled, 'John's Difficulty,' was the means of his conversion.

"A young man to the right, having told how, as a backslider, he had recently been restored, a cabman said he used to be in the public-houses constantly; but he thanked God he ever heard William Booth, for it led to his conversion.

"Three young men on the right then spoke. The first, who comes five miles to these Meetings, told how he was lost through the drink, and restored by the Gospel; the second said he was unspeakably happy; the third said he would go to the stake for Christ.

"A middle-aged man in the centre spoke of his many trials. His sight was failing him, but the light of Christ shone brilliantly in his soul.

"The chorus—

  Let us walk in the light,

was then sung.

"A young man described his feelings as he had recently passed the place where he was born; and a sister spoke of her husband's conversion, and how they were both now rejoicing in God.

"After a young man on the left had told how his soul had recently revived, another on the right testified to the Lord having pardoned his sins in the theatre on the previous Sunday.

"Two sailors followed. The first spoke of his conversion through reading a tract while on his way to the Indies four months ago. The other said he was going to sea next week, and was going to take some Bibles, hymns, and tracts with him, to see what could be done for Christ on board.

"The verse—

> I believe I shall be there,
> And walk with Him in white,

was then sung.

"A young man of the name of John, sometimes called 'Young Hallelujah,' told of his trials while selling fish in the streets; but he comforted himself by saying, ''Tis better on before.' He had been drawn out in prayer at midnight on the previous night, and had dreamed all night that he was in a Prayer Meeting. He was followed by a converted thief, who told how he was 'picked up,' and of his persecutions daily while working with twenty unconverted men.

"A man in the centre, who had been a great drunkard, said, 'What a miserable wretch I was till the Lord met with me! I used to think I could not do without my pint a day, but the Lord pulled me right bang out of a public-house into a place of worship.'

"He was followed by a young man who was converted at one of the Breakfast Meetings last year, and who said he was exceedingly happy. Another young man on the left said his desire was to speak more and work more for Jesus.

"Two sisters then spoke. The first uttered a brief, inaudible sentence, and the second told of being so happy every day, and wanting to be more faithful.

"The verse—

> Shall we meet beyond the River,
> Where the surges cease to roll?

was then sung.

"A young woman said: 'I well remember the night I first heard Mr. Booth preach here. I had a heavy load of sin upon my shoulders. But I was invited to come on the stage. I did so, and was pointed to Jesus, and I obtained peace.'

"Another told of his conversion by a tract, four years ago, on his passage to Sydney. 'To my sorrow,' he said, 'I became a backslider. But I thank God He ever brought me here. That blessed man, Mr. Booth, preached, and I gave my heart to God afresh. I now take tracts to sea regularly. I have only eighteen shillings a week, but I save my tobacco and beer money to buy tracts.'

"The verse—

> I never shall forget the day
> When Jesus took my sins away,

was then sung.

"A stout man, a navvy, who said he had been one of the biggest drunkards in London, having briefly spoken, was followed by one known as 'Jemmy the butcher,' who keeps a stall in the Whitechapel Road. Some one had cruelly robbed him, but he found consolation by attending the Mission Hall Prayer Meeting.

"Two young lads, recently converted, having given their experience, a dock labourer, converted seventeen months ago, asked the prayers of the Meeting for his wife, yet unconverted. Some of his comrades during the last week said, 'What a difference there is in you now to what there used to be!'

"Three young women followed. The first spoke but a sentence or two. The desire of the second was to live more to Christ. The third had a singularly clear voice, and gave her experience very intelligently. It was a year and a half since she gave her heart to the Saviour; but her husband does not yet see with her. Her desire was to possess holiness of heart, and to know more of the language of Canaan.

"The experience of an old man, who next spoke, was striking. Mr. Booth had announced his intention, some time back, of preaching a sermon on 'The Derby,' at the time of the race that goes by that name. This man was attracted by curiosity, and when listening compared himself to a broken-down horse. This sermon was the means of his conversion.

"The verse then sung was:—

Can you tell me what ship is going to sail?
Oh, the old ship of Zion, Hallelujah!

"Two sisters then spoke. The first had been very much cast down for seven or eight weeks; but she comforted herself by saying, ''Tis better on before.' The second said it was two years since she found peace, and she was very happy.

"A young man told how his sins were taken away. He worked in the city, and some one took him to hear the Rev. E. P. Hammond. He did not find peace then, but afterwards, as a young man was talking to him in the street, he was able to see the way of Salvation, and rejoice in it. He used to fall asleep generally under the preaching. 'But here,' he said, 'under Mr. Booth, I can't sleep.'

"A little boy, one of Mr. Booth's sons (the present General), gave a simple and good testimony. He was followed by a young man, and then an interesting blind girl, whom I had noticed singing heartily in the street, told of her conversion.

"A girl told how she found peace seventeen months ago; and then Mr. Booth offered a few concluding observations and prayed. The Meeting closed by singing:—

> I will not be discouraged,
> For Jesus is my Friend.

"Such is a brief outline of this most interesting Meeting, held Sunday after Sunday. Mr. Booth led the singing by commencing the hymns without even giving them out. But the moment he began, the bulk of the people joined heartily in them. Only one or two verses of each hymn were sung as a rule. Most of them are found in his own admirably compiled Song-Book.

"I could not but wonder at the change which had come over the people. The majority of those present, probably nearly five hundred, owed their conversion to the preaching of Mr. Booth and his helpers. How would they have been spending Sunday afternoon, if this blessed agency had not been set on foot?

"In the evening I preached in the Oriental Music Hall, High Street, Poplar, where five or six hundred persons were assembled. This is one of the more recent branches of Mr. Booth's work, and appears to be in a very prosperous condition. I found two groups of the helpers singing and preaching in the streets, who were only driven in by the rain just before the Meeting commenced inside. This is how the people are laid hold of.

"Shall this good work be hindered for the want of a few hundred pounds?"

The supply of "pounds," alas! though called for in such religious periodicals as at that time were willing to report the work, did not come, and The General says: "After six years' hard work, we had nothing better for our Sunday Night Meetings than a small covered alley attached to a drinking-saloon, together with some old discarded chapels, and a tumble-down penny theatre for week-nights."

At last a drinking-saloon, "The Eastern Star," having been burnt out, was acquired, and rebuilt and fitted as a centre for the Work, to be succeeded ere long by the large covered People's Market in Whitechapel Road, which was for ten years to be The Army's Headquarters, and which is now the Headquarters of its English Men's Social Work.

Throughout all these years of struggle, however, the Converts were being drilled and fitted for the further extension of the Work.

The idea of forming them into a really permanent Organisation only came to their Leader gradually. He says:—

"My first thought was to constitute an evangelistic agency, the Converts going to the Churches. But to this there were three main obstacles:—

i. They would not go where they were sent.
   ii. They were not wanted when they did go.
   iii. I soon found that I wanted them myself."

And the more time he spent amongst them the more the sense of responsibility with regard to them grew upon him. He had discovered what mines of unimagined power for good were to be found amidst the very classes who seemed entirely severed from religious life. There they were, and if only proper machinery could be provided and kept going they could be raised from their present useless, if not pernicious, life to that career of usefulness to others like themselves for which they were so well qualified. They could thus become a treasure of priceless value to their country and to the world.

On the other hand, neglected, or left with no other sort of worship than as yet existed to appeal to them, they must needs become worse and worse, more and more hostile to religion of any kind, more and more unlikely ever to take an interest in anything eternal.

The General could not, therefore, but feel more and more satisfied that he had begun a work that ought to be permanently maintained and enlarged, as opportunity might arise, until it could cope with this state of things wherever it was to be found.

And now that he had at length a centre to which he could invite all his helpers from time to time, there was no hindrance to the carrying out of such a purpose.

With the establishment of a Headquarters that cost L3,500, in one of the main thoroughfares of Eastern London, we may look upon The General as having at last got a footing in the world.

Chapter VIII
Army-making

What a place for a Christian Mission centre was Whitechapel Road! "Just look here," said The General to his eldest son, then a boy of thirteen, as he led him late one Sunday evening through the great swing-doors of a public-house into the crowded bar. "These are the people I want you to live and labour for."

The mere appearance of many a thousand in the neighbourhood, whether inside or outside such houses, was enough to give some idea of the misery of their lives. The language and the laughter with which those ragged, dirty, unkempt men and women accompanied their drinking were such as to leave no doubt that they were wallowing in the mire. At that time, and, indeed, until the Children Act of 1909 came into force, it was the custom of thousands of mothers to take their babies and little children into the public-houses with them, so that the scenes of family misery and ruin were complete.

In many of the side streets and back lanes, where there was little wheel traffic, groups of men and women might have been seen bargaining; for the most dilapidated and greasy articles of old clothing that could still be worn, whilst lads and even children gambled with half-pence, or even with marbles, as if they could not early enough learn how fully to follow the evil courses of their elders. There were, and are still, streets within ten minutes' walk of the Whitechapel Road where dogs and birds were traded in, or betted on, competitions in running and singing being often indispensable to the satisfaction of the buyers and sellers.

By the side of the road along which there was, and is, a continuous stream of waggon and omnibus, as well as foot traffic, was a broad strip of unpaved ground, part of it opposite that Sidney Street which a few years ago became world-renowned as the scene of the battle of the London Police with armed burglars. This was called the Mile End Waste, and was utilised for all the ordinary purposes of a fair ground. The merry-go-rounds, and shows of every description, which competed with the unfailing Punch and Judy, and wooden swings, kept up a continuous din, especially on Saturday nights and Sundays.

Amidst all this the vendors of the vilest songs and books, and of the most astounding medicines, raised their voices so as to attract their own little rings of interested listeners. There, too, men spoke upon almost every imaginable evil theme, denouncing both God and Government in words which one would have thought no decent workman would care to hear. But all who have seen a fair will have some idea of the scene, if they can only imagine all the deepest horrors of appearance and demeanour that drunkenness and poverty, illness and rags, can crowd together within a few hundred yards of space.

Once you can place all that fairly before your imagination you can form some conception of the mind that could look upon it all and hunger to find just there a battlefield for life, as well as of the faith that could reckon upon the victory of the Gospel in such a place. We have all read accounts of missionaries approaching some far-away island shore and seeing the heathen dance round some cannibal feast. But such feasts could not have been very frequent, amidst such limited populations, whereas the ever-changing millions of London have furnished all these years tragedies daily and nightly numerous enough to crowd our memories with scenes no less appalling to the moral sense than anything witnessed on those distant pagan shores. To those who take time to think it out, the marvel of both the eagerness and the reluctance of Mr. and Mrs. Booth to plunge into this human Niagara will appear ever greater. As we look nowadays at the world-wide result of their resolve so to do, despite all their consciousness of ignorance and unfitness for the task, we cannot but see in the whole matter the hand of God Himself, fulfilling His great promise: "Even the captives of the mighty shall be taken away, the prey of the terrible shall be delivered, for I will contend with them that contend with thee, and I will save thy children. And all flesh shall know that I the Lord am thy Saviour, and thy Redeemer, the Mighty One of Jacob."

As long as the God of that solitary, selfish tramp remains determined to redeem and save even the most depraved and abandoned of mankind, its Whitechapels and

Spitalfields, and other moral jungles, can be turned into gardens, blooming with every flower of moral innocence and beauty—if only gardeners, capable of enough trust in God and toil for man, can be found.

The Meetings held at noon daily in front of the new Headquarters set an example of patient, persevering combat which was followed in the Meetings, outdoors or in, held by what was then known as "The Christian Mission." The first name used by "The General Superintendent," as our Founder was then called, was "The East London Christian Revival Society." This was changed to "The East London Christian Mission," and the "East London" being dropped, when the work extended outside London, "The Christian Mission" remained, much as the name was always disliked, from its appearance of implying a slight on all other missions.

The steadily increasing success of the Whitechapel work was such that when I first saw it, after it had only had that centre for two years, the Hall, seating more than 1,200 persons, would be crowded on Sundays, and, although the people had been got together from streets full of drunkenness and hostility, the audiences would be kept under perfect control, once the outer gates were closed, and would listen with the intensest interest to all that was said and sung.

On Sunday nights I have known ten different bands of speakers take their stand at various points along the Whitechapel Road, and when they all marched to the Hall, they could usually make their songs heard above all the din of traffic, and in spite of any attempts at interruption made by the opposition.

The enemy constantly displayed his hostility at the Meetings held in the street, whether in Whitechapel or any of the other poor parishes to which the work had spread, and was not often content with mere cries of derision either. Dirt and garbage would be thrown at us, blows and kicks would come, especially on dark evenings, and the sight of a policeman approaching, so far from being a comfort, was a still worse trial, as he would very rarely show any inclination to protect us, but more generally a wish to make us "move on" just when we had got a good crowd together, on the plea that we were either "obstructing the thoroughfare" or "creating a disturbance."

But what a blessed training for War it all was! The Converts learnt not merely to raise their voices for God, and to persist in their efforts, in spite of every possible discouragement, but to bridle their tongues when abused, to "endure hardness," and manifest a prayerful, loving spirit towards those who despite fully used them. The very fighting made bold and happy Soldiers out of many of the tenderest and most timid Converts.

And yet I am not sure whether a still more important part of The Army-making was not accomplished in the Prayer Meetings, and Holiness Meetings, which came to be more and more popular, until under the name of "Days with God" and "Nights of Prayer" they attracted, in many of the great cities of England, crowds, even of those who did not belong to us, but who wished to find out the secret of our strength, for it was by the light and help got in such Meetings that Converts became "steadfast, unmovable, always abounding in the work of the Lord," so that instead of merely carrying on a "Mission" for so many weeks, months, or years, many of them became reliable warriors for life.

How few of The General's critics, who sneered at his Meetings as though they were mere scenes of "passing excitement" had any idea of the profound teaching he gave his people! The then editor of "The Christian," who took the trouble to visit them, as well as to converse with The General at length, with remarkable prescience wrote, as early as 1871, in his preface to The General's first important publication, "How to Reach the Masses with the Gospel":—

> "The following pages tell a fragment of the story of as wonderful a work, of its kind, as this generation has seen. No doubt it is open to the same kind of criticism as the sculptor's chisel might award to the excavator's pick; but I do not hesitate to believe that for every essential Christian virtue—faith, zeal, self-denial, love, prayer, and the like—numbers of the Converts of this Mission will bear not unfavourable comparison with the choicest members of the most cultivated Churches.
>
> "There is not in this kingdom an agency which more demands the hearty and liberal support of the Church of Christ. In the East of London are crowded and condensed a large proportion of the poorer labouring population of London. The ruined, the unfortunate, the depraved, the feeble ones, outrun in the race of life, gravitate

thither and jostle one another in the daily struggle for bread; thousands remain on the edge of starvation from day to day, and the bulk of these teeming multitudes are as careless of eternity as the heathen, and far more uncared for by the great majority of the professed people of God. Mr. Booth's operations are unparalleled in extent, unsectarian in character, a standing rebuke to the apathy of Christians, and a witness of the willingness of God to show His work unto His servants and to establish the work of their hands upon them."

From the beginning, The General had taught his people to come together for an hour's prayer early each Sunday morning, and to delight in prayer at all times, looking ever to God to deliver them personally from "all evil" and to "make and keep them pure within." These phrases were familiar to all English people; but that their real meaning might not only be taken in but kept ever before his people The General had established two weekly Holiness Meetings in the Mission Halls, one on Sunday morning and the other on Friday evening. These practices, kept up wherever The Army has gone all these forty-five years, have resulted in the cultivation of ideals far above those usual even in the most refined Christian circles.

Nothing has more astonished me, amongst all the torrents of eulogy passed upon The General and his Army since his death, than the almost invariable silence amongst Christian as well as secular papers about these Holiness Meetings, and that teaching of Holiness which were the root and secret of all the success of The Army.

Any capable schoolmaster might compile volumes of rules; but how to get them obeyed is the question. How could it be possible to settle every question of who shall be the greatest in an Army formed largely of the most independent and unruly elements, if there were no superhuman power that could destroy the foundations of envy and ill-feeling, and fill hearts, once wide apart, with the humble love that can prefer others' honour before one's own?

The organisation of The Army has been, and is, in all countries a steady, careful development. But it has only been made possible by the continual maintenance of a complete confidence in God for the needed supplies of wisdom and grace to enable each to submit to others for Christ's sake, to bear and forbear for the good of the whole Army, seeking ever to learn to do better, and yet being willing to be forgotten, and even to be undervalued, misunderstood, and ill-treated by a hasty or unjust superior, for Christ's sake.

General Booth, himself, did not always appear the most patient and kindly of leaders. He would have been the first to admit how he wounded tender hearts, and, perhaps, even repulsed some who could have been of greater helpfulness to him had he been able to endure more patiently their slowness and timidity.

But, conscious as he was of his own defects, he especially rejoiced when his son and successor began to shine as a Holiness teacher, whose weekly Meetings at Whitechapel became a power that was felt all over the world.

The teaching and enjoyment of this great blessing, with all the deliverance from self-seeking and pride which it brings, has made it possible to go on imposing more and more of regulation and discipline on all sorts of men and women without either souring their spirit or transforming The Army's system into mere machinery. The Army will go on to carry out its Founder's purpose better and better the more it learns how to sit constantly at the feet of the one great Master.

Chapter IX
Army Leading

We have seen Mr. Booth beginning on the spot, now marked with a stone, near the site of "The Vine" public-house (since happily pulled down, the site being turned into a public garden) on July 5, 1865, scrambling through the first six years' difficulties until he marched the beginnings of an Army of saved drunkards, infidels, and sinners into a People's Market, transformed into a public Hall and Headquarters.

He called all that "The Christian Mission," with only a slowly dawning consciousness that it was an Army, for six years more.

But he was leading it on, in humble dependence upon God, with increasing speed and force. He was really hindered by many things, amongst them his own ministerial habits of thought and plan. That nothing lasting could be achieved without system and organisation he had always seen. But he had never yet known a formation equal to that of some of the Churches around him which depended upon more or less skilled preachers, and a complete network of elected assemblies. For all purposes of conquest he had got preachers enough out of the public-houses; but he could not imagine their holding regular congregations, or developing the work, without having years for study and just such plans as the Churches had established. Hence, when he wanted leaders for the enlargement of the work he advertised for them in Methodist or other publications. He secured some excellent, well-meaning men, too; but, in almost every instance, they proved to be slower than the troops they were supposed to lead, and a kind of ecclesiastical organisation wrapped them all around with a sort of Saul's armour, in which fighting the heathen was unthinkable. He had got—by the testimony, as we have seen, of impartial observers—such a force as was "unparalleled in extent, unsectarian in character, and a standing rebuke to the apathy of Christians."

But how was he to go further afield with it? He had not a leader ready for its extension outside London. In 1873, Mrs. Booth, however, could not be content without doing something, at least for a season, in England's great naval base, Portsmouth, and, after that, in the sister arsenal city of Chatham. The force of new Converts she gathered in each town must needs be led by somebody, and in each case The General sent men of proved ability to manufacture preachers of their own *fighting* type. After having led Missions in those towns, they went and did likewise in two of the great manufacturing cities of the north. But their first achievements had led The General to venture upon sending out others, of much less ability, to smaller communities, where they were not less successful than the first two.

Already another great difficulty had been solved, for it had been found that congregations of workmen gathered in the provincial towns would give collections generally large enough to defray the local expenses. Thus were cleared away not only two of the main blocks in the path of progress, but all need or desire for the officialdom that had already begun to grow threateningly stiff.

> "After awhile," writes The General, "the work began to spread and show wonderful promise, and then, when everything was looking like progress a new trouble arose. It came about in this wise. Some of the evangelists whom I had engaged to assist me rose up and wanted to convert our Mission into a regular Church, with a Committee of Management and all that sort of thing. They wanted to settle down in quietness. I wanted to go forward at all costs. But I was not to be defeated or turned from the object on which my heart was set in this fashion, so I called them together, and addressing them said, 'My comrades, the formation of another Church is not my aim. There are plenty of Churches. I want to make an Army. Those among you who are willing to help me to realise my purpose can stay with me. Those who do not must separate from me, and I will help them to find situations elsewhere.'"

They one and all chose to stand by The General, for those who were really set upon the formation of deliberative assemblies had already left us.

This was in February, 1877, and in the following July the last Christian Mission Conference met to celebrate the abandonment of the entire system that Conference represented, and to assure The General that he had got a real fighting Army to lead.

It was only at the end of 1878, during which year the "Stations," which we now call Corps, had increased from thirty to eighty, that in a brief description of the work we called the Mission a "Salvation Army." But the very name helped us to increase the speed of our advance.

The rapidity with which The General selected and sent out his Officers reminds one constantly of the stories of the Gospel. One who became one of his foremost helpers, had formerly been a notorious sinner, and had indeed only been converted a fortnight, when because he already showed such splendid qualities he was sent by a girl Officer to The General with the strongest recommendation for acceptance.

It was arranged for him to speak with The General on the platform, after a Meeting. The General, who had, no doubt, observed him during the evening, looked at him for a moment and then said, "You ought to do something for God with those eyes! Good-night!"

"I had never had such a shock," says the Commissioner, as he now is. "If that's being accepted for the Work, I said to myself—what next, I wonder."

But, sure enough, in another three weeks' time he was called out from his place of employment by a Staff Officer, who asked him, "Can you be ready to go to M—— next Monday?" And he went.

This young man had been a devotee of billiards; but had become interested in The Army by seeing two of our "Special" speakers—one a very short Officer, the other a giant doctor from Whitechapel, who weighed some 334 lbs., wheeled up a steep hill in a pig cart, to a great Open-Air Meeting. After listening many times without yielding, he was startled out of his coolness by a large Hall in which he attended a Night of Prayer being burned to the ground the next day. The next evening, with one of his companions, he went to the Penitent-Form and found the mercy of God.

When The General was at all in doubt about a Candidate for Officership, he would often draw such a one out by means of the most discouraging remarks. To one who had gone expecting a hearty welcome, he said, "Well, what good do you think you'll be?" The General's eldest son being present, desiring to help her, remarked upon the high commendation her Officers gave her. He wished to send her off directly to a Corps; but The General, still uncertain, said, "No, send her to Emma," which opened the way for her immediately to leave her business and go to the newly-opened Training Home for women under his daughter's direction.

A similar Home for young men, under the present Chief of the Staff, Commissioner Howard, provided means to take those about whose fitness for the Work there was any doubt, and give them a training prior to sending them on to the Field.

In 1880, The General addressed the Wesleyan Methodist Conference of the United Kingdom. That Conference is one of the most powerful Church assemblies in the world, directing as it does the entire forces of its Church within the British Empire, and consequently influencing very largely all Methodists in the world. It was a remarkable testimony to The General's work that, so early as 1880, its most influential leaders should have been able to arrange, despite considerable opposition, for him to address the Conference which that year sat in London. The President, in welcoming him, warned him that they could only give him a limited time in which to speak.

What an expression of his sense of liberty and power "from on high," that The General should at once have begun by saying, "Mr. President, in our Meetings we are accustomed to bring any speech that seems likely to go on too long to a close by beginning to sing. I shall not take it amiss if you do so in my case." The general laughter with which this suggestion was greeted banished at once any appearance of stiffness from the solemn and exclusive assembly, whose members alone were present. He then proceeded to explain the origin and work of The Army, as follows:—

> "I was told that ninety-five in every hundred of the population of our larger towns and cities never crossed the threshold of any place of worship, and I thought, 'Cannot something be done to reach these people with the Gospel?' Fifteen years ago I thus fell in love with the great crowds of people who seemed to be out of the pale of all Christian Churches. It seemed to me that if we could get them to think about Hell they would be certain to want to turn from it. If we could get them to think about Heaven they would want to go there. If we could get them to think about Christ they would want to rush to His open arms.

"I resolved to try, and 'The Salvation Army' is the outcome of that resolution. In August, 1877, we had 26 Stations. We have now, in 1880, 162. In 1877, we had 35 Evangelists. We have now 285 Evangelists, or, as we now call them, Officers, and in many instances they have the largest audiences in the towns where they are at work.

"We have got all those Officers without any promise or guarantee of salary, and without any assurance that when they reach the railway station to which they book they will find anybody in the town to sympathise with them. The bulk would cheerfully and gladly go anywhere.

"We have got, I think, an improvement upon John Wesley's penny a week and shilling a quarter, by way of financial support from our Converts. We say to them, 'You used to give three or four shillings a week for beer and tobacco before you were converted, and we shall not be content with a penny a week and a shilling a quarter. Give as the Lord has prospered you, and down with the money.'" (Loud laughter.) "When I asked one of my Officers the other day at a Meeting held after a tea, for which the people had paid a shilling each, to announce the collection, the woman-Captain, to my astonishment, simply said, 'Now, friends, go into the collection. Whack it into the baskets.' The whole audience was evidently fond of her, and they very heartily responded.

"If asked to explain our methods, I would say: Firstly, we do not fish in other people's waters, or try to set up a rival sect. Out of the gutters we pick up our Converts, and if there be one man worse than another our Officers rejoice the most over the case of that man.

"When a man gets saved, no matter how low he is, he rises immediately. His wife gets his coat from the pawn-shop, and if she cannot get him a shirt she buys him a paper front, and he gets his head up, and is soon unable to see the hole of the pit from which he has been digged, and would like to convert our rough concern into a chapel, and make things respectable. That is not our plan. We are moral scavengers, netting the very sewers. We want all we can get, but we want the lowest of the low.

"My heart has gone out much after Ireland of late, and ten weeks ago I sent out there a little woman who had been much blessed, and four of her Converts. They landed at Belfast at two o'clock in the morning. They did not know a soul. Our pioneer (contrary to our usual customs) had taken them a lodging. We had said to her, 'Rest yourselves till Sunday morning'; but she was not content with this. After a wash, a cup of tea, and a little sleep, they turned out, found a Christian gentleman who lent them a little hall, had it crowded at once, and now, though only ten weeks have passed away, we have Stations in four other towns, two in Belfast, and two others are getting ready for opening. Blessed results have followed. The people, we are told, come in crowds—they are very poor—they sit and listen and weep, rush out to the Penitent-Form, and many are saved.

"Now, Mr. President, I think I may say that it is a matter for great thankfulness to God that there is a way—a simple, ready way—a cheap way, to get at the masses of the people.

"*Secondly. We get at these people by adapting our measures.* There is a most bitter prejudice, amongst the lower classes, against churches and chapels. I am sorry for this; I did not create it, but it is the fact. They will not go into a church or chapel; but they will go into a theatre or warehouse, and therefore we use these places. In one of our villages we use the pawnshop, and they gave it the name of 'The Salvation Pawnshop,' and many souls were saved there. Let me say that I am not the inventor of all the strange terms that are used in The Army. I did not invent the term 'Hallelujah Lassies.' When I first heard of it I was somewhat shocked; but telegram after telegram brought me word that no buildings would contain the people who came to hear the Hallelujah Lassies. Rough, uncouth fellows liked the term. One had a lassie at home, another went to hear them because he used to call his wife 'Lassie' before he was married. My end was gained, and I was satisfied.

"*Thirdly. We set the Converts to work.*" (Hear, hear.) "As soon as a man gets saved we put him up to say so, and in this testimony lies much of the power of our work. One of our lassies was holding a Meeting in a large town the other day when a conceited fellow came up to her saying, 'What does an ignorant girl like you know about religion? I know more than you do. I can say the Lord's Prayer in Latin.' 'Oh, but,' she replied, 'I can say more than that. I can say the Lord has saved my soul in English.' (Laughter and cheers.)

"*Lastly. We succeed by dint of hard work.* I tell my people that hard work and Holiness will succeed anywhere."

Of course, every day's march forward brought with it lessons that were learned and utilised. Not long could The General continue to interview Candidates himself, and then forms of application were evolved. The Candidate must have every opportunity to understand what would be required of him, and to express his agreement or otherwise with the teachings and principles of The Army. It was made clear to him or her that, whilst called upon to offer up a life-long service to this work for Christ's sake, he must expect no guarantee of salary whatever, and no engagement even to continue to employ him, should he at any time cease to act up to his promises, or show himself to be inefficient in the work.

As for the Soldiers, it was soon required of them that they should sign "Articles of War" before they could be enrolled. These Articles formed so simple and clear an expression of The Army's teachings and system, that the most illiterate in every land could at once take in their practical effect.

The Articles simply required every one to give up the use of intoxicants; to keep from any resorts, habits, company, or language that would be harmful; and to devote all the leisure time, spare energy and money to the War.

As time went on The General published ***Orders and Regulations for Soldiers***, a booklet of 164 pages, and perhaps as complete a handbook for the direction of every department of life, public and private, as was ever written; ***Orders and Regulations for Field Officers***, containing 626 pages of the minutest directions for every branch of the Work; and ***Orders and Regulation's for Staff Officers,*** the most extraordinary directory for the management of missionaries and missionary affairs that could well be packed in 357 pages. At later dates he issued ***Orders and Regulations for Territorial Commissioners and Chief Secretaries***, containing 176 pages, and ***Orders and Regulation's for Social Officers***, the latter a complete explanation of his thoughts and wishes for the conduct of every form of effort for the elevation of the homeless and workless and fallen; and ***Orders and Regulations for Local Officers***, containing precise details as to the duties of all the various non-commissioned or lay Officers, whether engaged in work for old or young. Smaller handbooks of ***Orders and Regulations for Bands and Songster Brigades***, and for almost every other class of agents were also issued from time to time.

Thus, step by step, The General not merely led those who gave themselves up to follow him in the ever-extending War; but furnished them with such simple and clear directions in print as would enable them at any distance from him to study his thoughts, principles, and practices, and sock God's help to do for the people around them all that had been shown to be possible elsewhere.

With such a complete code of instructions there naturally arose a system of reporting and inspection which enabled The General to ascertain, with remarkable accuracy, how far his wishes were being carried out, or neglected, by any of his followers. He sometimes said, "I would like, if I could, to get a return from every man and every woman in The Army as to what they do for God and their fellow-men every day." It soon became impossible, of course, for any one person to examine the returns which were furnished by the Corps; but records were kept, and, as the work increased, Divisional and Provincial Officers were appointed, with particular responsibility for the Work in their areas; so that in even the most distant corners of the world, wherever there is a registered Salvationist, there is some Staff Officer to whom he must report what he is doing, and who is expected periodically to visit each Corps, see that the reports made are accurate, and that the work is not merely being done "somehow," but done as it ought to be, in the Master's Spirit of Love and Hope for the vilest. And all this without the absolute promise of a penny reward to any one! In fact, from the first, The General taught his Officers that they must try to raise all expenses of the work in their Commands within the borders of the districts in which they were operating. He has always regarded it as a proper test of the value of work done that those who see it are willing to pay as much as they can towards its continuance. And, to this day, The Army's resources consist not so much in large gifts from outsiders as of the pence of those who take part in or attend its services.

Regulations are made, from time to time, as to the amount any Officer may draw for himself, according to the cost of living where he is at work, though a considerable number do not regularly receive the full amount. So utterly, indeed, above any such consideration have our Officers, everywhere, proved themselves to be that, to guard against needless sacrifice of health and life, it has been necessary to fix, also, in each country, a minimum allowance, which the Staff Officers must see that the Field Officers receive. Knowing, as I do, that many devoted Officers have, for months together, been down at the minimum level of six shillings per week, in little places where we have no wealthy friends to help a Corps into greater prosperity, I feel it safe to say that never was there a religious society raised and led to victory with so much reliance upon Divine Grace to keep its workers in a perfectly unselfish and happy condition.

Space forbids any description of the heroic labours by which The General and Mrs. Booth, travelling, holding Meetings, and corresponding, managed to extend The Army's work throughout Great Britain; so that before its name had been adopted ten years, it had made itself loved or dreaded in many parts.

At the earliest possible date in The Army's history, The General took steps to get its constitution and rights so legally established that it should be impossible for any one, after his death, to wrest from it or turn to other purposes any of the property which had been acquired for its use by a Deed Poll enrolled in the High Court of Chancery of England, August 7, 1878. The construction, aims and practices of The Army are so defined that its identity can never be disputed. Another Deed Poll, enrolled January 30, 1891, similarly safeguarded The Army's Social Work, so that persons or corporations desiring to contribute only to the Social funds could make sure that they were doing so. Similar Deeds or other provisions are made in every other country where we are at work, containing such references to the British Deeds, that the absolute unity of The Army, and the entire subjection of every part of it to its one General is, in conformity with the laws of each country, secured for all time.

And again a deed dated July 26th, 1904, has provided for the case of a General's death without having first named his successor, or for any other circumstance which might arise rendering a special appointment necessary.

Subsequent chapters will show how wondrously God helped The General to carry on this work in other countries as well as in his own, and we cannot believe that any one will read this book through without being constrained to admit that there has not merely been the accomplishment, under The General's own eye, of an enormous amount of good; but the formation and maintenance of a force for the continual multiplication of it all, in every clime, such as no other leader ever before attempted, or even planned. And then most will be constrained surely to say with us: "It is the Lord's doing, and it is marvellous in our eyes."

Chapter X
Desperate Fighting

One might have supposed that a man who thus raised a force of working people to do good to others, would in a Christian country have been honoured and encouraged by all the better elements, and defended with vigour by the press, the pulpit, and the police against any of the lower sort who might oppose him or his followers.

To the shame of his fellow-countrymen, alas! it must be told that, so far from this being the case, The General was generally treated for the first few years of The Army's work as being unworthy to be received in any decent society, and his followers, as "blasphemers of religion" and "disturbers of the peace," who ought by all possible means to be suppressed.

Those who fattened on the vices of the poor and the opponents of religion generally were undoubtedly the leaders of opposition to his work. There were only too many ignorant ruffians ready to delight in any excuse for disturbance, and very many truly religious people who put down every disturbance so created to The Army's account, and who, without taking the trouble to make any inquiry, denounced it mercilessly.

Condemned almost whenever mentioned, either by press or pulpit, The General and The Army were naturally treated by many authorities and largely by respectable citizens, not only as unworthy of any defence, but as deserving of punishment and imprisonment. In one year alone, 1882, no fewer than 699 of our Officers and Soldiers, 251 of them women and 23 children under fifteen, were brutally assaulted generally whilst marching through the streets singing hymns, though often when attending Meetings in our own hired buildings, and 86, of whom 15 were women, were imprisoned. True, these persecutions almost always gained for us sympathy and friends, as many as 30,000 people coming out in one case to the railway station to welcome an Officer upon his release from prison. Yet, year after year, such attacks were repeated, and, even during the last year, imprisonment was suffered by several Officers for leading Meetings where they had regularly been tolerated for some thirty years; but where some newly-appointed dignitary would rather not see them.

When we ask in wonder how so bitter an opposition to such a leader, or his work, could arise, we always find the sort of explanation which that famous man John Bright once wrote to Mrs. Booth:—

> "The people who mob you would doubtless have mobbed the Apostles. Your faith and patience will prevail. The 'craftsmen' who find 'their craft in danger,' 'the high priests and elders of the people,' whose old-fashioned counsels are disregarded by newly-arrived stirrers-up of men, always complain, and then the governors and magistrates, who may 'care for none of these things,' but who always act 'in the interests of the public peace,' think it best to 'straightly charge these men to speak no more' of Christ."

The General's attitude in face of all these storms was ever the same; "Go straight on" was the pith of all his replies to inquiries, and his own conduct and bearing amidst the most trying hours were always in accord with that counsel. As in the case of many popular leaders of thought in England, the custom was established of meeting him at railway stations, and escorting him with bands and banners, music and song from train to theatre, Town Hall, or whatever the meeting-place might be for the day. When he was received, however, not as in later years with universal acclamations, but with derisive shouts and groans and sometimes with showers of stones and mud, he smiled to see the commotion, and took every opportunity to show his enemies how much he loved them. Already more than fifty years old, and looking decidedly older, when the worst of these storms burst upon him, this bearing often subdued crowds, the moment they really caught sight of his grey beard.

"At Ipswich," says one of our Commissioners, "I remember how he won over the booing crowd by laughingly imitating them, and saying, 'I can boo as well as you.' Riding with Mrs. Booth through one of the worst riots that he experienced, and in full sight of all the violence which nearly cost one of our Officers his life, The General was seen, even when his carriage was all splattered with mud and stones, standing as usual to encourage his Soldiers and to salute the people. Arrived at the great hall he was fitter than most of his people to conduct the Meeting there."

How much his own calm and loving spirit was communicated to many of his followers may best be represented by the remarks of a wounded Lieutenant on that occasion to a local newspaper whilst he was in hospital.

The fact that this Lieutenant had been the champion wrestler of his county, and would never, before his conversion, have allowed any one to take any liberty with him, will explain the way in which from time to time The General acquired Officers capable of overcoming such crowds.

The Lieutenant, riding in the very dress he had once worn as an athlete, but with our Salvation Army band around his helmet, was a perfect target for the enemy.

"When I came to S——, I never thought for one moment that I should have to suffer and to be taken to a hospital for my blessed Master; but I have had a happy time there. I can truly say that the Spirit of God has revealed wondrous things to me since I have been in. Though I have suffered terrible pains, the Great Physician has been close by my side."

(Whilst being removed into the hospital he was heard to whisper "I hope they'll all get saved.") But he goes on, "When I became conscious I found myself in the hospital with a painful head and body; but it was well with my soul. The grace of God constituted my soul's happiness, so much so, that when I thought about Paul and Silas being taken to prison, and how they praised God and sung His praises, my heart sang within me. I could not sing aloud for the pain I was suffering. Could I have done so, I would have made the place ring for the victory the Lord had given me in the battle. Glory to His Name! I remember I had no sleep until twelve o'clock the second night I was in. The first night was an all-night of pain. At the same time it was an all-night with Jesus. He was indeed very precious to my soul. I thought of the sufferings of Christ for me—even then—the chief of all sinners until saved by His grace. Hallelujah for His love to me. My suffering was nothing (though I suffered thirteen weeks) compared to Christ's. Should my blessed Saviour want me to do the work over again, I should do it to-morrow."

"The General," says one of his chosen associates of those times, "always reminded me so of the captain of a vessel in a stormy sea. Perfectly calm himself in a way, yet going resolutely ahead with unerring aim, quickly deciding whenever a decision was needed, and always ready to take all the risks; he trained his folks how to go through everything that came, to victory."

One of the weakest of the many women whom in those days he taught how to rise up out of their ease and go to battle and victory, says of her first sight of him, more than forty years ago, "He gave me the impression in that Meeting of a man of God, whose only aim was the Salvation of souls. I got saved at one of Mrs. Booth's Meetings, when I was still a girl only twelve years old. They used to call me 'Praying Polly.' But, never having had a day's schooling, when he wanted me to become an Officer, I feared my own incompetence. Mrs. Booth said 'You will see God will punish you.' She had seen something of my work in Meetings where I had to take up collections and turn out roughs, and so had no doubt told The General what she thought I could do.

"Sure enough I was laid up completely, lost the use of one limb, and had to use crutches. But just as I came weak out of hospital and penniless, I saw a shilling lying on the ground, picked it up, and with it paid my way across London to The General's house. I thought, 'Oh, if I can only see Mrs. Booth, I'll get her to pray for me, and get help from God.' When I arrived at the door, she was just coming out to go off to the North of England; but she sent her cab away and stayed for a later train, to attend to me. She helped me up the steps and said:—

"'Now then, are you willing to follow God?'

"I didn't feel fit for anything; but I said, 'Yes, if God will only help me, I'll go to the uttermost parts of the earth for Him.'

"Accordingly, after having some care and nursing I recovered strength, and, soon after returning to my Corps, I, in a Meeting when my name was called, forgot my crutches and hobbled to the front without them. How the Soldiers all shouted! The Captain carried them after me on his shoulder home that night.

"After I had been in the War for some months I was ordered to bid farewell to Lancaster, and, whilst resting at a little place near, I received order to go to Scotland. When I was at the station, however, on the Saturday, I got a wire from The General, 'Orders cancelled. Go King's Lynn.' Nobody at the station knew, at first, where it was, and even the stationmaster said, 'You cannot get there to-day.' 'But I must,' I said, 'I have to commence my work there to-morrow.' And he found out there was just a chance, by taking an express part of the way. When I got there, at a quarter to ten at night, I knew of no friend, and found there had been no announcement made in the town. But, on going to a Temperance Hotel to put up, I learned that a gentleman near had the letting of a large hall. I at once went to him.

"'But,' said he, 'we don't let like that, out of business hours. And we are accustomed to get payment in advance of the L2 10 *s.* it costs.'

"As I had only sixpence left, I could pay nothing; but I said to him, 'The Rev. William Booth is responsible. You draw up an agreement. I'll sign, and you shall have the money Monday morning.' Somehow he felt he could not refuse me, and so I had got my hall for Sunday afternoon and evening.

"After a good night's rest, I went out on the Sunday morning and spoke during the forenoon in twelve streets, making, of course, my announcement of the afternoon and evening Meetings. A poor woman who thought I was out singing to get bread came and gave me 11/2 *d.* saying, 'That's all I have; but you shall have it.' I had to do everything myself in the afternoon Meeting, for I could not get anybody who came even to pray. But they gave me twelve shillings. I wanted them to help me hold a Meeting outdoors at 4:30. At 5:30 we had to open the doors, as so many were waiting to get in, and at six the building was packed. We kept up the Meeting till after ten o'clock, by which time seventeen people had come out to seek Salvation.

"The police sent me a message one Sunday evening, during the Meeting, that they wanted me at the police station. I replied that I was engaged that evening; but that I was at their service any time after six the next morning. So they had me up the Monday morning, and sentenced me to a month's imprisonment. But they never enforced it, till I left the town.

"In another place we had no Hall, and I have seen my Soldiers in the early morning trample snow down till it was hard enough for us to kneel upon for our Prayer Meeting.

"In Tipton one of the Converts was called the 'Tipton Devil.' He once sold his dead child's coffin for drink. When we got him, a week later, to the Penitent-Form, and I said to him, 'Now you must pray,' he said, 'I can't pray.' 'But you must,' I said. After waiting a moment, he just clapped his great rough hands together and said,

'O God, jump down my throat and squeeze the Devil out.' And then he said the old child's prayer:—

> Gentle Jesus, meek and mild,
> Look upon a little child;
> Pity my simplicity,
> Suffer me to come to Thee.

If ever a big rough fellow came 'like a little child' to Jesus he did, for his life from that day was absolutely new.

"Another of those men's wives sent for me, and said she feared he was going mad, for he had hung up his old ragged clothes on the wall. But we soon heard him come singing up the street, and he said, 'I've hung them up to remind us all what I was like when Jesus set me free. A lot of our blokes have turned respectable, and gone and joined the chapel, and I thought if ever the Devil comes to tempt me that way I'll show him those clothes, and say, "The hand that was good enough to pick me up will be good enough to lead me on to the finish."'

"So I said to his wife, 'He might do a worse thing: let them hang there, if it helps him any.'"

How The Army won so many of its worst opponents to be its Soldiers comes out beautifully in a more recent story.

"When I was a drunkard," says a poor woman, "I used just to hate The Army. But one day, as I was drinking in the 'King George' public-house, I heard them singing to an old tune of my childhood, and that brought me out. I stood and listened, and the Sergeant of the Cadets, who was leading, came over to me and said:—

"'Isn't it very cold? Hadn't you better go home? Don't go back to them,' she said, nodding towards the public-house. And she started to walk with me, and put her jacket round my shoulders. In that moment I felt that The Salvation Army was something for me."

Not only did this woman get saved, but her husband and children, too, as a result of that loving act.

There came times in many cities, both in England and elsewhere, when our opposers were formally organised against us, under such names as "Opposition and Skeleton Armies," etc. These were organisations, in some instances so formidable, especially on Sunday afternoons, that at one time, in 1882, there would be 1,500 police on extra duty to protect us from their attack. This, of course, we much disliked, and we gave up our marches entirely for a few weeks, so that when we began again the police might get proper control. They never allowed the formation of these bands again, for they had learned their lesson by that time. But how marvellously God helped The General by means of those very oppositions! They brought us into close touch with bodies of young fellows, many of whom have since become leaders amongst us.

Strange and sad that throughout all the years of our most desperate fighting we scarcely ever found men from the "better classes" daring to march with us. One noble exception, Colonel Pepper, of Salisbury, with his wife, never hesitated, in the roughest times, to take their stand with their humblest comrades, glad to go through whatever came. To Mrs. Pepper The General wrote in 1880:—

> "The Colonel will have sent you some information of our Meetings. But any real description is impossible. Manchester has, in many respects, surpassed everything. The Colonel, himself, has pleased me immensely--so humble and willing. When I look at him in the processions, evidently enjoying them, I cannot help wondering at what God hath wrought, and praising Him. London seems your place, and it has been borne in on my mind that the time has come for us to make an attack on the West End, and to raise a Corps there, principally out of the proper and decent people. I don't mean out of the Plymouth Brethren, or the 'evangelical party,' so-called; but out of the wicked and wretched class who have money and position and education, and who are floating to Hell with it all.
>
> "I shrink from suggesting further sacrifices to you. God give you wisdom. We have much success and much trial, and much bitter opposition. We must have more and more success and more trial, and more bitter opposition. We must have more intelligent Officers, and you must help us get them."

That West-End attempt, made later by Mrs. Booth, produced for us, indeed, some Officers who have done much for The Army's advancement; although, perhaps, not another Colonel Pepper. The very attacks made upon us, however, helped to attract the attention of thoughtful people, and to lead to our Meetings persons possessing all the gifts needed for The Army's world-wide extension.

Amongst these were Colonel Mildred Duff, Editress of our papers for the young, and authoress of a number of books; Commissioner W. Elwin Oliphant, then an Anglican Clergyman; Miss Reid, daughter of a former Governor of Madras and now the wife of Commissioner Booth-Tucker, of India; Lieut.-Colonel Mary Bennett, as well as Mrs. de Noe Walker, Dr. and Mrs. Heywood-Smith, and a number of other friends in England and many other lands who, though never becoming Officers, have in various ways been our steadfast and useful friends and supporters.

Surely it can only be a question of time! It is true what our great Master said: "Not many wise men after the flesh, not many mighty, not many noble are called."

But, if in the days of our weakness and contempt, it was given us to win such a force of honourable women and a man now and then, are we to despair, now that all the world is awakened to the value of our work, of winning for it more of the excellent of the earth?

The prosecutions of our people by the police also helped us not only to attain notoriety locally, but to gain a much higher standing generally. As soon as The General could find legal ground for appealing against the magistrates' decisions he did so, and this not only obtained for us judgments that made our pathway clear in the future, but caused the then Lord Chancellor, the late Earl Cairns, Lord Chief Justice Cockburn, Archbishop Tait of Canterbury, Bishop Lightfoot of Durham, and other men of wide influence to speak out in the House of Lords or elsewhere for us.

And yet, throughout his entire career, right down to his last days, The General was at times personally assailed with a malevolence and bitterness that could hardly have been exceeded. It has constantly been suggested, if not openly stated, that he was simply "making a pile" of money for himself; and yet, as will be seen in our chapter on Finance he made the most comprehensive arrangements to render suspicion on this score inexcusable.

But try, if you can, at every turn throughout all this life, whenever you hear of General Booth, to realise what it means for such a man, struggling to carry on and extend such a work, to know every minute, day and night, that he is being accused and suspected of seeking only his own, all the time. Remember that his nature was perhaps abnormally sensitive about any mistrust or suspicion, and about the confidence of those nearest to him. And then you may have some conception of the cross he had always to bear, and of the wounded heart that went about, for years, inside that bold and smiling figure.

And yet there is, thank God! much of the humorous to relieve our tensions in The Army. A brother Commissioner of mine remembers seeing The General sail for the United States for the first time. As the steamer swung off, a bystander remarked, "So he's off?" "Yes." "And when do you go?" "Go? What do you mean?" "Well, you will never see him again now, will you?" And then my comrade fairly took in that the man was alluding to the continual prophecy of those days that The General, once he had got enough, would disappear with all the money he had raised. So that man went down to his house laughing, and has been laughing over it now for twenty-six years!

Perhaps The General gained more than can ever be calculated from having to begin and to carry on his warfare, for a long time, in the very teeth of public opinion.

> We're marching on to war, we are, we are, we are!
> We care not what the people think, nor what they say we are,

was one of the favourite choruses which, in his greatest public demonstrations in this country, as well as in his ordinary Meetings, he taught us to sing.

Only in this spirit of utter disregard for public opinion have God's prophets, in all ages, been able to do their work, and only whilst they remain indifferent to men's scorn and opposition, can the Soldiers of The Salvation Army properly discharge their task of "warning and teaching every man," in all wisdom.

How indispensable this state of mind is to the individual Convert only those who have lived for Christ amongst the hostile surroundings of a great city can really know. That we have now so many resolute comrades, even amongst the young people, who meet with no encouragement, but rather with every sort of contempt and rebuff in their homes, their workshops, and the neighbourhoods in which they live, is alike a remarkable demonstration of the extent to which this great victory has been won, and, at the same time, of the far wider and grander conquests that are yet to come.

The gigantic enterprises that lie before us, if Christ is really to become the First and Last with the millions of Africa, India, Japan, and China, as with those of America and Europe, would be hopeless were we not prepared to raise up Soldiers to this great military height of contempt for civilian opinion.

But it may be that our very attitude in this respect has whetted the enemy's resolution to do all that could be done to prejudice public opinion against us. The very large measure of popularity or, at any rate, respect, so far as The Army generally is concerned, in which we rejoice to-day, must be attributed to the impression created by the calm persistence of The General, and those who have truly followed him, in doing what they believed to be right, and turning from all they believed to be doubtful and wrong, in spite of the general condemnation and opposition of those around them.

The very people who to-day applaud our efforts to assist the poorest and worst to a self-supporting and honourable career, are often blind to the fact that we have only succeeded by doing the very things which they once said we ought not to do, and by turning away from all the old customs to which they would fain have chained us.

Chapter XI
Reproducing The Army in America

So far we have traced the beginnings of The Army in the United Kingdom. But would The General desire or be able to extend it to other countries? With regard to the need for it there is now, at any rate, no dispute in any "Christian country," for almost all intelligent persons, whatever may be their own creed, or want of creed, admit the presence in their great cities, if not elsewhere, of only too many of the sort of persons to whom The Army has proved useful.

But there has been no country in which the need for, or possible value of, The Army has not been at first hotly disputed. We have seen how desperately it was at first opposed in the country of its birth. And that could not have been possible had not so many really religious people looked upon it as an "un-English" sort of thing, "American" in its ideas and in its style of action. When it was beginning in Scotland, many said that it might be tolerated amidst the godless masses across the border, but that its free style of worship especially "on the Lord's Day" could not but be "a scandal" in the land of Sabbath stillness; whilst as to Ireland, we were assured that our outdoor proceedings must needs lead to bloodshed.

When, however, The General resolved to send Officers to America, there was hardly a voice in either Church or Press which did not ridicule the idea of our being of use there. And in the case of almost every other country the same prejudice against English people having "the presumption to think" that they can give lessons in true religion to any other nation has made itself more or less felt, even to this day.

But, happily, The General never took counsel with flesh and blood upon such questions. He knew that, whatever differences might exist between one race and another, there was everywhere the one sad similarity when it came to neglect of God and the soul. That The Army must adapt itself to each new population he had always taught; but that it would ultimately succeed wherever there were masses of godless people, he never doubted.

Really the first extension to the United States came about, however, by no planning of his. A family belonging to one of the home Corps emigrated, in 1879, to Philadelphia, where they commenced to hold Meetings there, meeting with such rapid success that two Corps were raised before the Officers for whom they pleaded could be sent to them.

When The General paid his first visit to America, in 1886, we had already 238 Corps in the Union, under the leadership of 569 Officers, mostly Americans. Ten years later there came that terrible blow to him and to the Work, when his second son, who had been entrusted with its direction for a term, left The Army, and founded a separate organisation. Notwithstanding the misunderstanding which followed, and the check to our progress that was necessarily involved, The Army went steadily forward, and The General visited the country from time to time, receiving on each occasion a very remarkable welcome.

The appreciation of his leadership was always of the more value in the United States, because the disinclination of the American people to accept anything like direction, let alone command, from this side the Atlantic was always so marked. It is this fact which gives such special value to the sort of experiences we are about to record from one of the later tours of The General, that of 1902-3.

Summing up the journey and its general impressions to an old friend, he writes:—

> "Well, I have been busy and no mistake. Day after day, hour after hour, you might say minute after minute, I have had duties calling for immediate attention. Oh, it has been a whirl! But what a wonderful rush of success the nine weeks have been since I landed at New York.

> "The people, the Press, the dignitaries of all classes have combined in the heartiest of welcomes ever given in this country, I suppose, to 'a foreigner' of any nationality. It has been remarkable, and, indeed, surprising, for it was so largely ***unexpected***.

"I have just come into this city of Kansas. The two largest hotels have competed to have the privilege of giving me their best rooms, with free entertainment. A monster brewery that illumines the whole city every night with a search-light has been running alternate slides, one saying, 'Buy our Lager Beer,' and the other, 'General Booth at the Convention Hall Monday night.' The building for my Meeting to-night will hold 8,000 people, and on Saturday 4,000 tickets were already sold.

"You will be a little interested in this because you will know something of the difficulties that seemed to lie ahead of me when I started. God has been very good, and I hope my Campaign will do something towards the forwarding of His wishes in the country."

The reception at New York was one of the most enthusiastic The General ever had. At four o'clock on the Saturday morning, enough of his followers and friends to fill fifteen small steamers had assembled, so as to be sure to be in time to meet his liner. By way of salute, when the great steamer appeared, they discharged seventy-three bombs—one for each year of his life, as yet completed.

The *New York Herald* said of his Sunday there:—

"Eight thousand people heard General William Booth speaking yesterday at the Academy of Music. The rain had no effect in keeping either Salvation Army people or the general public from the Meetings. About one-third of those present wore Salvation Regalia.

"General Booth displayed wonderful energy throughout his fatiguing day's work. His voice has great carrying power, and the speaker was distinctly heard throughout the auditorium. Despite the fact that they could not gain admission to the building, at the evening service, people remained standing in the drenching rain from 7:30 till after 9 o'clock to see The General leave."

"At the close of his last address," says *The Times*, "167 men and women had been persuaded to his point of view, and went to the Mercy-Seat."

How generally the whole country, and not merely the central areas, was stirred by the mere arrival of The General, may be guessed from the following words taken from the ***Omaha Daily News*** article of the Monday for its readers through far-away Nebraska:—

"One of the arrivals on the steamship Philadelphia is General William Booth of The Salvation Army. That vessel never carried before so great a man as this tall, white-haired, white-bearded organiser, enthusiast, and man-lover.

"Wherever men and women suffer and sorrow and despair, wherever little children moan and hunger, there are disciples of William Booth. The man's heart is big enough to take in the world. He has made the strongest distinct impact upon human hearts of any man living. This is a man of the Lincoln type. Like Lincoln he has the saving grace of humour, and sense of proportion. There is something of the mother-heart in these brooding lovers of their kind. There is the constraining love that yearns over darkness and cold and empty hearts. Big hearts are scarce.

"In an age of materialism and greed William Booth has stirred the world with a passion for the welfare of men. His trumpet-call has been like the silvery voice of bugles. His spirit will live, not only in lives made better by his presence, but in the temper of all the laws of the future."

We shall see from the welcomes given to him by great official personages, that these remarks do not in the least exaggerate the feeling created all over the country by the activities of The Army.

GENERAL BRAMWELL BOOTH

Had The General merely made great proposals he would only have been looked upon in the generally favourable way in which men naturally regard every prospector of benevolent schemes. But the country recognised in him the man who, in spite of the extreme poverty of most of his followers, had raised up, and was then leading on, a force of obedient and efficient servants of all men.

The journey was arranged, for economy of time, so as to include a visit to Canada, and its general course was as follows: From New York he travelled to St. John's, New Brunswick, where the Premier, in welcoming him, said the work of The Salvation Army had "placed General Booth in a position perhaps filled by no other religious reformer." From New Brunswick he passed on to Halifax, Nova Scotia, to Montreal (where he was the guest of Earl Grey, the Governor-General), Ottawla, Kingston, Hamilton, London, and Toronto. Thence he returned to the States, and held Meetings in Buffalo, Chicago, Minneapolis, and St. Paul, Des Moines, Kansas City, Denver, Los Angeles, San Francisco, and Oakland, Omaha, St. Joseph, St. Louis, Birmingham, Cincinnati, Cleveland, Pittsburg, Washington, Baltimore, Philadelphia, Worcester, in three of which cities he conducted Councils of Officers, in addition to public Meetings.

The impression invariably made wherever he went, was thus ably summed up by the ***Chicago Interocean***:—

> "No other man *is* General of an Army of people that circles the globe. No emperor commands soldiers serving openly under him in almost every nation of the earth. No other man is called 'commander' by men and women of a hundred nationalities.

> "Aside from his power over the great Organisation of which he is the head, General Booth is one of the world's most remarkable figures. His eloquence stirs and stings, soothes and wins; and this eloquence alone would make him famous, even if he had never undertaken the great work he has done with The Salvation Army.

> "As he speaks, his face is radiant with the fervour that carries conviction. His tall figure and long arms, used energetically in gestures that add force to what is said, his white hair and beard,

and his speaking eyes, make him an orator whose speeches remain
long in the minds of those who hear them. The feeling of the
members of The Army towards their Commander has in it both the love
and reverence of a large flock of their pastor, and, added to this,
the enthusiasm, loyalty, and energetic spirit of an Army."

Where so wonderful a journey is so filled up with Meetings so described, and where, from the very highest to the lowest all speak so warmly of him, it is really difficult within the limited space at our disposal to give, without danger of monotony, or repetition, any adequate idea of what took place. Americans are such habitual organisers of huge demonstrations, and are so generally accustomed to say, publicly, without reserve, what they think, that the expression of what to them may appear perfectly natural runs the risk of creating elsewhere an air of exaggeration and unreality. But if we consider that great American States like Minnesota, Ohio, and Michigan contain more inhabitants than some of the kingdoms of Europe, and that their Governors are men likely to occupy the very highest positions in the government of America, we can realise how effective amongst the masses of the people The General's work must have been before such Governors could be expected to preside at his Meetings, and to speak of him, as they did.

Said Governor Nash, of Ohio:—

"I never had the privilege of meeting you in person, until I
grasped your hand upon this platform. You have not been unknown,
however, to me or to the people of Ohio. You recognise the fact
that you could not perform this work well without the help of God.
That your work has been well performed is well known to us all from
the fact that the Organisation you have made known as The Salvation
Army has spread throughout the world, turning the feet of
multitudes into the paths of righteousness and peace. It has done
good. It has done a great work wherever it has gone. It is for
these reasons that the people of Ohio welcome you most cordially
to-night, and they and I wish you an abundant harvest in your
life's work, and that at the end you may have the peace and rest
and the joy that God gives to all His own good people."

Similar specially religious references to those used by Governor Nash came constantly into the speeches of other leaders who expressed their people's welcomes to The General, showing how faithfully every opportunity was being utilised to exalt Christ, amongst even the most unusual crowds assembled on these occasions.

Governor Cummins, of Iowa, said:—

> "I have long wanted an opportunity to express publicly my appreciation of the grand, noble, and untiring work that every day is being performed by those noble and unselfish men and women, who have gathered under the Flag of The Salvation Army, loved and esteemed throughout the whole world.
>
> "In every army there is a leader. The Salvation Army has a Leader whose commanding figure towers above the Salvationists of the world, and has drawn to himself more love, more respect, and more confidence than at this moment centres in any other human being. Of him it will be said, after he has passed to the beautiful shores of the hereafter, the best that can be said of any man, that the world is better because he lived in it."

Lest The General should have been too much puffed up by all his successes and the praises showered upon him, God almost at the end of the tour allowed an accident which might easily have ended his career; but which only gave him an opportunity to show more conspicuously than ever his resolution to persevere in his ceaseless labours.

It was whilst passing along a dark passage in New York that The General stumbled, and, but for God's great goodness, would have fallen into a cellar. As it was, one leg was very much bruised and hurt. He thus described, in writing, to a friend what followed:—

> "March 13, 1903.--The accident came at a very unfortunate moment, and at the onset it looked like spoiling the closing chapters of the Campaign.

"But God is good. I was favoured with the services of one of the most skilful and experienced surgeons in New York. He put my leg into starch, and then into a plaster of Paris jacket. And by dint of resolution, and the supporting Spirit of my Heavenly Father, I went through the last Meeting with apparent satisfaction to everybody about me, and some little comfort to myself.

"It was a great effort. The Hall is one of the finest and most imposing I ever spoke in. Three tiers of boxes all round full with the swell class of people in whom you are so much interested, with two galleries beyond.

"It called for some little courage to rise up with my walking-stick to steady me; but God helped me through. I hung my stick on the rail, and balanced myself on my feet, and talked the straightest truth I could command for an hour and twenty minutes.

"A little spectacular function followed in the shape of trooping the Colours of the different nationalities amongst whom we are at work in the States, and a midnight torchlight procession, with a massed farewell from the balcony of the Headquarters, closed the Campaign.

"I am doing the voyage fairly well. Of course, it is very wearisome, this lying all the time. The ship is rolling and tossing and pitching considerably, and it looks like doing so, until we get under shelter of the land."

The probable after-effect of these distant Campaigns of The General could not be better described than in the words of one of our American Officers, himself known throughout The Army as one of our most spiritually-minded and intelligent observers:—

"Seventeen years ago," he says, "the writer first heard The General, and it has been his privilege to hear him many times since. Each succeeding effort and series of Meetings seems to eclipse all the rest. It was so in Pittsburg, which, being one of the greatest business centres and home of some of the most virile men of the world, deeply appreciates him.

"He was very weary from his heavy Campaign in Cleveland, but, in spite of this, to me he seemed at his best. He spent no time in angling to get into sympathetic touch with them, but with the precision of a bullet he made direct for the conscience of every man and woman there. Talk about 'naked truth,' 'judgment,' 'daylight,' 'straight preaching.' We had it that night, as I never heard it before. There was no escape. Every honest person there had to pass judgment on himself.

"It was difficult to close that Meeting. The truth was setting men free. Many wept and prayed and submitted to God, and some fairly howled at the revelation God gave them of their character and conduct. It has been my privilege to hear such preachers as Beecher, Matthew, Simpson, and Phillips Brooks, and such orators as Wendell Phillips and Gough; but The General is the greatest master of assemblies I ever met. He played on those vast audiences of judges, lawyers, ministers, business and working men as Ole Bull played on the violin. They laughed, they wept, they hung their heads with conviction, their bosoms heaved with emotions, they were convinced, convicted, and a multitude were converted. I think at one time there could not have been less than 3,000 eyes brimming with tears. He uncovered sin and made it appear as it is, utterly without excuse, and utterly loathsome; and then he revealed the love and sympathy and helpfulness of Christ, till many could not resist, but had to yield.

"A lawyer said to me the next day that the sermons and lecture were the most wonderful he had ever heard. Another lawyer who had been to each Meeting stayed in his place till the very close on Sunday night, saying that he could not tear himself away.

"The common people heard him gladly, and the uncommon people were overwhelmed with admiration, and conviction. A young lady, belonging to one of the best families in the city, just home from Paris, where she had been studying art, heard him and could not refrain from leaving the box in which she sat and going to the Penitent-Form. She went home truly converted.

"The wave of power and conviction did not cease when The General left; and during the next four days we saw fifty-eight persons at the Penitent-Form."

The special value of all these American testimonies to the effect of The General's brief visits, lies in the fact that they show the triumph of the War plan of God, just in the circumstances where weaklings are tempted to yield to public opinion, substitute orations for real righting for souls, and to press nobody to an immediate decision, or change of heart and life.

There can be no doubt that The Army's invariable fight against the drink has helped to make its General so highly honoured amongst American statesmen. But in that, as in everything else, the important fact to note is that it was by establishing an absolute authority that he secured the faithful carrying on of the campaign against drink and every other evil at every spot where our Flag flies.

The eyes of the whole world have, in our day, been more or less opened to the ruinous character of the drink traffic, and The General and his forces, whilst keeping out of the political arena, have mightily helped the agitations that have ended in the exclusion of the drink traffic altogether from many states and cities, and its limitation, in many ways.

But much less notice has been taken of other evils, which have no less absorbed the attention, and spoiled the means, the minds, and the souls of the masses. The sight daily in every great English-reading city when the sporting editions of the newspapers appear, ought indeed to arouse every follower of Christ. But the habit of irresponsibility that has grown up in most "Christian" circles has still to be fought against everywhere, and The General's persistent testimony against it, indeed the whole theory of a Divine Army and of War, must remain for ever one of the strongest features of his life's work. The old song:—

> Arm me with jealous care,
>   As in Thy sight to live;
> And, Oh, Thy servant, Lord, prepare
>   A strict account to give,

has expressed the thought behind all the arrangements of our Army. And it is remarkable how, in the midst of the general indifference, so large a measure of this "jealous care" for God and souls has been awakened and maintained.

Nowhere, alas! does the theory of irresponsibility find a more congenial soil than in the very places and services where God is most feared, honoured, and obeyed. His doors are indeed opened to the world; but whether anybody enters them or no is the care of but sadly too few. Hymns are so announced as to make it easy for all to join in singing them, if they choose. But whether the words are sung by many, or only by a proficient few, and above all, whether hearts as well as voices are raised in prayer and praise to God, is too often a matter of absolute indifference to almost every one.

How The General altered all that, wherever his influence was felt! He made all his people understand that not merely are they responsible for understanding and heeding God's commands themselves, but for enforcing attention to them, as those who must give account of their success or failure.

The sister leader of some little Meeting in the far-away Outpost of a Corps, thousands of miles from the centre, when she insists upon having a verse sung for the third time because "I'm sure some of you lads were not half singing," has little idea of the religious revolution she represents. That the dislike of so many for any "such innovations" continues, may help to convince any one who thinks of the urgent need there was, and is still, for the substitution of responsible for irresponsible leadership in "Divine Service."

During his visit to the United States in 1907 The General had a severe illness which seriously threatened to cut short his career. His death was indeed cabled as an item of news from Chicago. But the report was, as Mark Twain would have said, "grossly exaggerated." Nobody will wonder, however, at his having been ill when they read Commissioner Lawley's report. He writes:—

> "We have calculated that in the thirteen meetings of his New York Campaign the General was on his feet speaking about twenty-six and three-quarters hours.
>
> "He spent less than six weeks in the Country, travelled about 3,700 miles by train, spoke about eighty-five hours to fifty audiences, before conferring many hours with leading Officers, and talking to the Newspaper Reporters in each town he visited."

An Officer describing his illness wrote:—

> "I never shall forget his effort to ascend the staircase of the Commissioner's house on Friday morning after his victory at Milwaukee the night before. The veteran Warrior had to rest his head and hands on the rail and pray 'My Lord.' It was clear to me that the chill he had sustained days before, and which he fought in vain against would make him a prisoner for days."

What that meant to him when he was already announced for a number of other cities can be imagined.

His symptoms the following day were very serious, and one cannot but be glad that he had at his side at the time his daughter—Commander Eva Booth. Under her loving care, and with all the help of Doctors and Masters that could be got in Chicago, The General recovered so as to be able to go on after a few days with his interrupted tour, after which he wrote in his farewell letter to his American Troops:—

"I have been impressed with the great improvement in the devotion, spirituality and Blood and Fire character of the forces already in existence. I have also most pleasantly gratified by a conviction of the possibility of raising a force in the United States that shall not only be equal to the demand made upon it by the conditions of the country but of supplying me with powerful reinforcements of men and money for the mighty task of bringing the whole world to the feet of Jesus."

During this visit, The General and the Commander were received by President Roosevelt at the White House. The General was presented with the freedom of the City of Philadelphia, and after going through the gigantic final week described alone in New York was able to sail direct to Germany for his usual great Repentance Day in Berlin, and he was already seventy-eight years old.

Need it be said that whilst in this book little mention is made of any one but The General himself, it not having been his habit in his journals to refer to those with whom he was for the time associating, we are not to suppose that at any rate in recent years he was anywhere fighting alone. In Heaven no doubt the victory won in many a crowded building was put down to the credit of someone whom few if any of those occupying the front of the platform would have mentioned; but as a result of whose prayers, faith and effort the audience was gathered or the results attained.

It would have been very unfair to the great majority of his Officers to have called frequent or special attention to the small English Staff who usually accompanied him, for not only the Commissioners and Chief Secretaries but the Officers of every nationality laboured systematically to make the most of his visits to any particular place and to render to the largest possible extent the results of each visit permanent.

This may possibly seem specially and curiously unfair in the United States and Denmark, yet it will only make[1] the principle of this omission from The General's own records and ours the more clear.

It will doubtless be expected that I make some comment upon the painful separation from him of three of his own children which were amongst the saddest events of The General's life, and, yet, I feel it best to say nothing.

It is not within the scope of this book to tell "all about it," and telling part could only cause misunderstanding. So I leave it, and hope everyone else will do the same.

Chapter XII
In Australasia

The entire programme of every tour The General made emphasises so strongly his advocacy of hard work that one really hesitates to pick out any one Campaign as more remarkable than another. What is, however, extraordinary in connexion with one of his far-away Australian journeys is our having letters which so much more than any others give particulars of his doings.

> "I am resting to-night, and well I think my poor body has earned some kind of respite. Such a ten days' work I never did before of sheer hard work. How I have come through it, and come through so well, I cannot understand, except that God has indeed been my Helper."

Here is another side-light on The General's own inner life which we get by the way. We conceal, of course, the identity of the lady in question, except to say that it was a very distinguished hostess with whom he had occasion to spend some hours when travelling.

> "It was perhaps the loveliest journey I ever had. I talked nearly all the time, and, in fact, had no alternative. But I think I ought to have made a more desperate and definite attack on her soul than I did. She is a very intelligent and amiable lady, and I have no doubt I made an impression.

"Good-bye. Go on praying and believing for me. I want to be a flame of fire wherever I go. I thank God for the measure of love and power I have. But I must have more. I am pushing everybody around me up to this--the inward burning love and zeal and purity. I wish our ***best*** men were ***more spiritual***. Give my tenderest love to all."

In each of The General's visits to Australia there was much of the same character; but from the letters to his children which he wrote on one of them, we can extract enough to give some idea of what he saw and felt in passing through those vast regions:—

"What the reception (at Melbourne) would have been had it not been for the torrents of rain I cannot imagine. Although it was known that I could not get in before six or seven o'clock, there was a great mass of several thousand people waiting at three o'clock. As it was we did not get into the Exhibition Building till ten, and a vast crowd had been sitting inside from five, and stayed to hear me talk till 10:45.

"I had an immense Meeting--they say 5,000 were present on the Sunday morning, 7,000 in the afternoon, with as many more turned away.

"The opportunity here is immense beyond conception. The people are delightful, and the Officers also. If they were my own sons and daughters, I don't see how either Officers or Soldiers could have been much more affectionate."

How great was the strain of the Meetings may be guessed from the following remarks as to the final one:—

"I trembled as I rose. You must understand that the Hall down which I spoke is about 400 to 450 feet long, and that on this occasion a partition about ten feet high was drawn across it, some 300 feet from the spot on which I stood, so that my voice had to travel all through the entire length of the building before it met with any obstruction, whilst behind me there was at least another seventy feet. The Press estimate the crowds at 10,000; but, that is an exaggeration. There would be 7,000, at least. I had taken the precaution to send an Officer to the far end to see how far he could or could not hear me, and he brought back word 'excellently.' So I drove ahead, speaking over an hour and a half, and not losing the attention of my audience for a moment. Indeed, I felt I had the whole house from the moment I opened my lips. Of course, it was the greatest physical effort a long way that I ever made, and, considering that it was my seventh address in that 'dreadful' building, and that I commenced with a bad throat, exhausted with the fatigues and miseries of the voyage, and that I had ceaselessly worked at smaller Meetings, etc., all the four days, I do think it very wonderful how I went through it, and I must attribute it to the direct holding up and strengthening of the dear Lord Himself.

"On all hands I think a deep impression was made. To God be the glory, and to my poor constituents, for whom I live and plead, be the benefit.

"I am tired this morning, but shall get a little rest to-day and a little extra sleep in the train. We leave for Bendigo at twelve o'clock, arriving at four for Meeting to-morrow. We go to Geelong next day, coming back here on Friday morning, and leaving at five for Sydney, travelling all night, and arriving there about noon on Saturday.

"You will get tired of hearing of this round of Meetings, and of the very echo of this enthusiasm; but you will, I am sure, rejoice, not merely that the people of this new world have welcomed your father and General with such heartiness, but that there is for The Army such an open door in these parts."

That is indeed what lends such endless importance to the recital which we cannot help reporting ever and anon of The General's Meetings in each country to which he went. It was not the mere coming together of crowds to listen to a speaker, but the enthusiastic acceptance and endorsement of a system, and of demands made by a perfect stranger in which he so delighted. The General never went anywhere merely to preach or lecture. All that he did in that way was always so combined with Salvation Campaigns that at every step he was really recruiting for The Army. Hence his every movement, the reports of his journeys, the conversations he held with all whom he met, everything told in the one great War and helped to create, more and more all over the world, this force of men, women, and children, pledged to devote themselves to the service of Christ and of mankind.

There is a very interesting account of a visit to a State School, especially as it shows The General's keenness to learn, for The Army, anything possible:—

> "At ten o'clock I went by the request of Mrs. McLean, the lady with whom I am staying, to visit one of her State Schools. I was met at the door by the managers and members of the board, who conducted me through the building.
>
> "There were over 1,000 children in ten different classrooms. I was much interested in them, and spoke in each room, so that I began the day with at least ten little sermons.
>
> "I was very much struck with the singing of the children, rendered very effective with some corresponding action with the arms and feet, which gave life and vigour to the thing. I am satisfied that we might follow this plan out with very good effect in our Army singing. The little that is done is always appreciated."

And so whilst the Secular Australian Schools got some little gleam of the heavenly light, the aged General saw and passed on to all his world, a valuable suggestion that has since been taken up and acted upon everywhere in our Children's Meetings and demonstrations.

And then he passes at once to quite another department of his activities. He always exercised the same care in every country, which we have already described as to England to ensure the careful settlement of all property acquired for The Army, so that it may be, as nearly as possible, made certain that nothing given to the one Army should ever be removed out of the control of its central authority. How much of time and care this has demanded will be readily understood by those who have any experience in property matters, and who know how widely laws and legal usages differ in different countries:—

> "I had an interview with Mr. Maddocks, our solicitor out here--a very nice fellow indeed, and I should think capable withal. He seems to grasp the idea of The Army government, and to be anxious to co-operate with us in such a settlement of our property as will be in harmony with it."

Only by means of many such interviews, and all the care they represent, was it possible, under the laws of such thoroughly democratic States, to leave the local holders of authority under The General's complete freedom of aggressive action, and yet to secure that everything they acquired with The Army's funds should remain for all time at the disposal, for The Army only, of a General with his office at the other side of the world.

And then we go on to the journey during which he was hoping "to get some extra sleep"!

> "At twelve, left for Bendigo, arriving about four o'clock. Was very weary on the journey, and had to turn out two or three times to address the crowds waiting to listen to me on station platforms.

"Bendigo is a town of some 30,000 people, entirely made and sustained by the gold-digging industry. An immense amount of the precious metal has been taken here, and sufficient is being secured still to make it a paying concern, although the miners have to go to a considerable depth in order to secure the quartz.

"We had a public reception, and they had made a general holiday of it in the place. People must have come in from miles around to help make up such a crowd. They pulled up at a splendid fountain in the centre of the town, intending to separate with three cheers for The General; but I could not withstand the temptation, and made quite a little sermon about saving their souls, and serving God."

It is this interest both in the everyday occupations and resources of the people, and of the tours they made which, joined with all his intense concern about the soul, constituted The General and all who truly follow him, the true brethren of all mankind. It must ever be remembered, to the credit of Australia, that its leading men were the first to recognise this characteristic of our Officers, and to lend them all the influence of their public as well as private countenance and sympathy. It is this fact which makes it a permanent pleasure to record their kindnesses to The General.

"Came on to Melbourne, on my way to Sydney. Met a body of representative men to lunch, amongst them Sir James McBain, President of the Upper Chamber, Mr. Deakin, an ex-Cabinet Minister, a very nice fellow indeed, a man who appears to me to have more capacity than any one I have yet met in the Colonies. He made a speech, and at the close drew me on one side, and said he wanted to do something for us, and if I could only tell him what it should be on my return to Melbourne, he would be very glad to do it.

"I am sure he is prepared to be a good friend. He is a coming Prime Minister, I should think."

(The General had no idea then that all Australasia would, so soon, be united into one Commonwealth, much less that Mr. Deakin would, for so many of the next ten years, be Premier of the whole.)

But a remark he once made respecting the reported scepticism of some highly-placed Colonials might be made with regard, alas! to many "statesmen" of Christian lands nowadays, and we cannot but see in that fact, and in the friendliness of so many such persons with us, a token of the meaning both of the scepticism, and The Army's position. In how many instances have men, moving in influential circles, met with a Christianity manifestly formal and carrying with it no impress of reality! How natural for them to sink into scepticism! But the moment they encounter men who convince them instantly that they believe the Bible they carry, scepticism retires in favour of joyous surprise, and without any desire to discuss doctrines, they become our lifelong friends.

The General's ability in securing the assistance of all sorts of men, including those whose religious opinions widely differed from his own, or who had got none at all, was remarkable. When reproached, as he was sometimes, for taking the money even of sporting men, he would always say that he only regretted that he had not got a larger amount, and that he reckoned the tears of the poor creatures that would be relieved would wash the money clean enough in the sight of God for it to be acceptable in His sight.

> "Met Mr.----. He is interested in our Maternity work, and promised some time back to assist us with the Hospital we are proposing to erect. He is a multi-millionaire. He promised L2,500 right away--L1,500 when the sum of L23,500 had been raised, making thereby a total of L25,000 with which building operations could be commenced.
>
> "He is a young man; sprightly and generous, I should think. I wanted him to make his promise L5,000 in round figures. But he simply said, 'I cannot promise.' We shall see!"

The following description of one Australian night ride may give some idea both of the eagerness of the people to hear him, and of the amount of fatigue The General was able to endure:—

> "We left at 5 P.M. The journey was certainly unique in my history. Six or seven times in that night, or early morning, was I fetched out of my carriage to deliver addresses. The Mayors of two of the towns were there to receive me, with crowds all placed in orderly fashion, with torches burning, everything quiet as death while I spoke, and finishing up only with the ringing of the departing bell of the train and the hurrahs of the people.
>
> "At two in the morning, at Wagga-Wagga, of Tichborne fame, they fairly bombarded my carriage shouting, 'General Booth, won't you speak to us? Won't you come out?' But I thought you could really have too much of a good thing.
>
> "At another station, after speaking for the twenty minutes allowed for breakfast, a lady put through the window a really superb English breakfast, as good as ever I had in my life, with everything necessary for eating it, and as we went off she added, 'Mind, I am a Roman Catholic.'
>
> "The reception at Sydney was enormous, they say never surpassed, and only equalled once at the burial of some celebrated oarsman who died on the way from England. They had arranged a great reception for him, and they gave it to his corpse. The enthusiasm of the Meetings is Melbourne over again."

The General's almost invariable escape from illness during so many years of travelling, in so many varying climates and seasons, can only be attributed to God's special guidance and care. In Melbourne, influenza raged in the home where he was billeted, and seized upon one of the Officers travelling with him. And yet he escaped, and could resume his journey undelayed. In South Africa, when he was seventy-nine, another of his companions in travel was separated from him for days by severe illness; but The General, in spite of a milder attack of the same sort, was able to fulfil every appointment made for him.

Best of all, however, was the peculiarly blessed inward experience which he enjoyed amidst all the outward rush of the Australian tour. It has been so often suggested by truly excellent men that the soul cannot enjoy all the fulness of fellowship with God without a great deal of retirement from men, that we should like to have The General's inner life fairly exhibited, if it were only in order for ever to bury this monstrous and, we might also say blasphemous, superstition, which has so often been supported by one or two quotations from the Gospel, though in defiance of the whole story of Christ, and of every promise He ever made.

Of what value could a Saviour be who drew back from helping His own messengers upon the ridiculous pretence that they were too busy doing His bidding, and did not spend enough time "seeking Him for themselves"?

> "Just a P.S. to say that God is wonderfully with me. I don't think that I ever in the midst of a great Revival had a more powerful time than last night. It was nothing short of a miracle. I had no definite line ready, and had no time to get one. I preached an old sermon at Melbourne, just because I must have something straight before me that I could shout out to that immense crowd, and I had a wonderful time; but last night God helped me in every way. The power upon the people was really wonderful at times."

Little did most of his own Soldiers guess the extreme strain of inward weight and struggle under which The General was often labouring just when in some great assembly he appeared to every one to be overflowing with youthful gaiety and self-confidence.

The following letter to his youngest daughter, and some entries in his diary, will give some idea of the inner victory he really gained on many such occasions.

Commissioner Lawley, mentioned in this letter, was The General's almost constant companion and helper in many years' travel in many lands, leading the singing, soloing, managing the Prayer Meetings, and generally aiding in every arrangement, a true armour-bearer and comrade at every turn:—

"Fair night; might have been better. Plenty of weakness; still, better than it often is.

"Lawley just been in; he is not over well; says we have got the biggest theatre (The Empire). He is not quite sure whether its suitability for talking is beyond the Coliseum at Glasgow, but he thinks the Meetings are rather heavy for a sick man, whom four doctors have been conjuring during the week to 'settle down' and take things quietly, under pain and penalties of the sufferings described.

"However, I am going on with faith that God won't forsake me. It is very probable that Mr. MacDougal said something of the same kind when he retired to rest on his last sleep, and failing to appear in the morning was found by his son with life extinct, gone to live by sight; anyway, to have some further assistance to sight through his faith in the Better Land.

"This has been one of the most remarkable of the many remarkable days of my history.

"I passed a weary night, and felt altogether unfit for the task before me. The natural force seemed to have passed out of me, both mentally and physically. In fact, my heart failed me, and there seemed nothing before me but the prospect of slackening down. I was only kept going by the memory of so many deliverances brought out for me in the past.

"We had one of the largest audiences, and the biggest crowd I ever addressed in a single day. In the morning it appeared that Satan sat at my door, suggesting all sorts of discouraging things. He tried to make me believe that my public work was done, and especially suggesting that I should renounce the subject on which I was talking, and wait for better days before I attempted to talk again. The Prayer Meeting that followed was certainly encouraging. We had twenty-seven out. Still, I came away with very much the same feeling that had been aroused while I was talking. I took a little refreshment, and tried to get a little sleep, but my mind was too much agitated to allow of it. I woke up and called for the notes of my lecture. My mind could not put two and two together hardly, and so I gave up in despair and left myself to my fate. On my way to the Meeting, however, a strange feeling came over me. It was like the sun through a rift in the black clouds, and all at once a spirit of tenderness, hope, and faith came over me. A voice in my soul seemed to say, 'Go and do the Lord's work, and the people will gather; go for their souls, and all will be well.' I accepted the command, my fears vanished, a spirit of confidence took possession of me, I rose, I addressed the crowd for an hour and twenty minutes with all the physical vigour and mental liberty I could desire.

"Night. A terrific crowd. I talked for an hour and ten minutes with the same force and fervour as in my most successful efforts; 147 came on to the stage in the After Meeting."

It was thus in the smaller matters of personal strength and health, as in the greatest affairs, that The General struggled, believed, and triumphed all through his career.

Australasia has gone farther than most countries towards State socialism. But it was well remarked by some statesman many years ago, "We are all socialists now."

No man within his times was more intensely devoted to the cause of the poor than William Booth. He was indifferent to no practical scheme or effort for the improvement of the people's condition in any land. But for that very reason he loathed, with uncommon vigour, such socialism as would spurn and crush out of the world the man who is no longer in first-class physical condition or desirous of earning an honest living by hard work, instead of going about to create hatred between man and man, and would prevent those who will not submit to any man's dictation from leaving their families to starve when work is to be obtained.

The General's indignation was specially aroused when "socialist" spouters tried to block all his plans of beneficence with their foul misrepresentations. He fought every such attempt with the utmost determination, and by the help of God and the more intelligent of his fellow-countrymen, crushed every such attack more completely than the public sometimes knew, for he resolutely kept out of any political or social agitation and went calmly on his way, even when his quietude led the enemy to imagine that he was yielding. In later years, when all the pressmen of a city came together to meet him, the Social Democratic paper representative would, of course, come with the rest. On the occasion of such an interview once in Denmark, he writes:—

> "The Social Democrat usually contents himself by compassionating the inadequacy of my efforts for dealing with the miseries which they contemplate, with the remark that I don't go deep enough, that mine is a superficial operation, whereas they destroy poverty by dragging it up by the roots!
>
> "My notion is that the principles upon which my efforts are founded carry me to the lowest roots of all, namely, the selfishness of human nature. Their notion is that capital is the root of the misery. Destroy the capital, or rather I expect they mean divide it up, or let everybody have the benefits that flow out of its possession. My notion is that the roots of the selfishness are to be found in human nature itself."

Chapter XIII
Women And Scandinavia

For a number of years it was The General's custom to conduct the annual review of our Swedish troops at Sodertelge, a beautiful seaside spot, near enough to Stockholm to make it easily accessible, and yet far enough down the Fjord to make the journey thither a very delightful excursion.

The sight of from fifteen to twenty steamers crowded with Salvationists making their way, with streaming banners, music and song, to the camp ground, was almost like a glimpse of the coming glory when the whole earth should rejoice before the Lord. But, of course, there came always to that great gathering a sufficient number of the unconverted to furnish abundant opportunity for conquests to be made, and the great Meetings, lasting throughout the day, never broke up without the ingathering of many souls.

The Councils for Officers which followed during the next few days in Stockholm and elsewhere, gave The General great opportunities to confirm and extend the influence of his teachings throughout the whole of these Northern countries.

Some of The General's earlier visits to Sweden were, however, still more interesting, and perhaps even more permanently effective, because, as we shall see, they helped the newly-rising force, enlisted under their first leader—a devoted woman—to gain some liberty for demonstrations and other work outside their own buildings such as they had not had before, and strengthened them in their resolution to fight, whilst almost all their fellow-countrymen still looked down upon them with disdain if not with hatred. It is difficult to realise now what a dreadful thing The Army in those days must have appeared. Huge crowds gathered from the very first to the Meetings, convened in theatres and other public buildings by Major, now Commissioner Ouchterlony, a Swedish lady who had been appointed by The

General to inaugurate the Work in her own land; but the bulk of the population seemed to regard her as though she was a suffragette, advocating window-breaking or something worse. This will explain some of the facts The General records in his diary of his visit seven years later. The journey began with a great Meeting at Hull, after which the traveller went on board his steamer for a miserable two days' voyage to Gothenburg. After Meetings there he proceeded to Sundsvall, a city from which point his Journal reads:—

> "At the conclusion of the evening Meeting the dear Soldiers flocked to the station, crowding the platform and expressing, as far as opportunity served them, their love for me, and their desire that God should bless me. I spoke to them for a few minutes; then came the signal and the start, and then as we slowly moved off handkerchiefs were waved, volleys of 'Amens' were fired, the Band played, and away we were borne out into the darkness. All this was like a dream to my comrades, as neither the railway officials nor the police had hitherto allowed a word to be spoken or a note of music to be played outside our Halls.

> "All that night and all the following day we travelled to Stockholm, which we reached at 6 p.m. Crowds awaited our arrival. The Soldiers had come down in force, wearing sashes on which the words, 'God bless The General,' 'Welcome,' and other devices had been worked. The police had come too. There were 200 of them--some mounted and some on foot. Our people had been formed into an avenue down which I passed to an open space. Every face wore a smile, but there was comparative silence. The Police Master had insisted that there should be no volley firing or shouting. But hands and handkerchiefs were waved, and every one appeared delighted. We were soon in a carriage, galloping off to the Headquarters where we were to stay."

If all that The General has done for the attainment of a larger liberty by the peoples of every land were recorded, one might easily make him appear as a great political reformer. But whilst consistently aiming at the one great purpose of all his journeys and Meetings, the Salvation of souls, he has, incidentally, done more to stir the humblest and least capable to great nation-rousing efforts than any mere political reformer can hope to do.

During this first visit of twelve days to Sweden, he travelled by rail over 3,000 kilometres (say 2,000 miles), held twenty-eight public Meetings, besides a number of private ones with press interviews, and wayside gatherings at railway stations. Five nights were spent in the trains, mostly in crowded compartments, for the days of comfortable "sleepers" on all lines had not yet come. He had, besides his interpreter, a young English companion, who paid his own expenses, and he could seldom be persuaded to take any refreshment whilst travelling that could not be got in the carriage. It must not be forgotten that in winning and retaining the enthusiastic affection of such multitudes of persons, The General has had to face the difficulty of only being able to speak through an interpreter, and that he has had to endure campaigns of opposition and slander, of which we can say very little, but which, founded so largely as they have been upon his being "a foreigner," have had so good a chance to build up walls of difficulty before him.

After this tremendous journey and reception, The General continues:—

> "In the night Meeting I felt a little nervous. The Riding School was nearly full, another 100 persons would have filled every seat, although a charge had been made for admission, in order to help with the heavy expenses.
>
> "Many had stayed away for fear of the crush. The audience, which was most respectable, included the Police Master. I was very tired, and no particular topic had been announced. However, I spoke an hour and a half, and all seemed intensely interested.
>
> "Sunday.--The Riding School was full for the morning Holiness Meeting. Much power. About 100 stood up to make a full surrender of themselves to God.

"In the afternoon the Hall was again full. The police, of whom there were twenty present, would only allow persons to stand in the end aisles. Spoke an hour or more.

"Night. Full an hour before the time. Many convicted. About twelve pressed forward.

"Monday.--Inspected new Hall and Training Home--building to cost L5,000. Also visited present Training Home and attended to correspondence.

"At night the Riding School was full long before we arrived. Spoke two hours. Immense impression seemed to be produced.

"Tuesday.--Morning, addressed Officers and Cadets. One o'clock, Meeting of Clergy and Evangelistic workers, at which 300 were present. Spoke an hour, and answered questions for an hour. Was enabled, I think, to answer all objections, putting every one to silence.

"Dined with Lieutenant Lagercrantz of the King's army. He is a dear fellow, and he has a dear wife. They are in deep sympathy with us. She put on a bonnet and riband that night.

"I was determined to have a free Meeting for the poorest, a charge for admission having been made for all the Meetings yet held in Stockholm. So called one at 6 p.m. in our own Hall in the south of the city. At six we were quite full. I spoke an hour or more, and some twenty or more came out for a clean heart. Closed at 8.15 p.m.

"At 8.30 p.m. Soldiers' Meeting. Some 500 were present. Spoke for nearly two hours. At the close cleared the front as a Mercy Seat, and nearly all in the place--Officers, Cadets, and Soldiers--went down in company after company. The wonderful Meeting closed about midnight.

"Wednesday.--Rose at 6 a.m., not having had much sleep. Away in Norrkoeping at 7.30 a.m. Arrived at 2.30 p.m. Meeting at 3.30 p.m. in a great church, where 800 were present. Good time. Very tired.

"Night. I,500 present. Talked two hours. Afterwards, at 10.30 p.m., had a Meeting for Soldiers. Got home about 11.45 p.m.

"Thursday.--Meeting at 10 a.m. to say 'Farewell.' Spoke about an hour, and left at one o'clock for Lynkoeping, arriving at 2.30 p.m. Meeting in our beautiful Theatre at 2.30 p.m. Fine audience."

Mere lack of space forbids further quotation. But surely enough has been said to show with what marvellous exertion The General managed in one brief journey to do so much for all classes, and so much not merely in the way of Meetings but of organisation and administration in every way.

And the diary tells us nothing of his talks with Officers between Meetings, which have formed so important a part of all his travels. By means of such conversations, especially in the case of Officers who are not English, The General has gained a close knowledge of them and their difficulties as they have of his thoughts and wishes.

Between his arrival at Gothenburg and his Sundsvall Meetings came a rough journey to Norway, where we had as yet no Officers, yet where, nevertheless, a great Meeting had been arranged for by friends, who later helped in the establishment of our work in their country! The General passed on to Denmark, where our work was in its first year.

On the afternoon of his arrival he tells us he rested, wrote up correspondence and journal, and had some little thought about the coming Meetings.

"Night. Welcome Meeting in the Methodist Church. Packed. There must have been nearly 1,300 people present. The admission was free, and there were many Philistines, some socialists, and some lads bent on mischief. To add to our difficulties, my interpreter did his work so miserably that we had some confusion and restlessness. After an hour's talk, I paused for the collection to be taken, and changed interpreters. The second one did very much better. His voice, however, was feeble and his manner very quiet, so that things were not very much better for a time. Then we had a little quiet, and a decent finish. It was a considerable disappointment, however, and next door to a defeat. I retired to rest very sad, and with awkward forebodings about the coming Meetings.

"The great funereal vault of a church, the interpreting, the mocking young fellows void of any sense of honour or conscience to appeal to, or any respect for a stranger, the intense anxiety of the Officer in command to have good Meetings, and above all my longings to meet the needs of the hungry crowd, only wanting to hear, and many of them equally willing to obey: these and other troubling thoughts haunted my mind and spoiled my night's sleep. But I fell back on my old remedy, and, comforting myself in the Lord, resolved to do what could be done and left myself in His hands.

"Sunday.--11 a.m. Had a local minister to translate; he did well. Some fifty or sixty stood up at the close as seekers for a clean heart.

"Afternoon. The great church packed. Interpretation went fairly well. Began at 3 p.m. and went on till 5.20 p.m.

"Night. Police sent up word soon after six that the street was filling up, and the doors must be opened. When this was done the young fellows who had made so much trouble on Saturday night--or at least some hundreds of this class--forced their way in through all else, leaving hundreds more outside. They talked and laughed, and although now and then a policeman marched a row of them out, their game went on, spoiling everything.

"The voice of the interpreter was weak, and the confusion flustered him. So my dreams of a smash and of a hundred seekers were not realised, and we terminated with some six or seven gathered out of the crowd immediately near to the platform.

"It was a great disappointment. I felt beaten, and went home confessing it. And yet what could be done? My tongue was all but tied. I was helpless without an interpreter capable of conveying my meaning to the people. Such a man was wanting. Commending the whole matter and the anxious crowds of people so eager to hear to my Master, I retired at midnight.

"Monday.--Breakfast, 8.30 a.m. 9 a.m., spoke with a gentleman from Kiel, who is anxious to see The Army open there, and is building us a Hall. Saw his plans and arranged terms.

"9.30 a.m., saw the Officer from Stuttgart. He has a heavy struggle. 12 noon, drove round the city. In summer time it must be a very pleasant place.

"3.30 p.m., Meeting. Fine audience, very nearly filling the church. Commenced with a new interpreter, a student--execrable! I soon had to fall back on one of the others.

"7 p.m., as full as the police would allow. Continued till 10 p.m. And then had a Soldiers' Meeting till 11.30 p.m.

"Left Copenhagen the next morning at 8.30 a.m."

We who have since seen some of The General's greatest triumphs in that city, and have watched the steady growth of The Army in Denmark till it has won the sympathy of the Royal Family and of every other decent family in the country, must rejoice in this record of his first desperate battles there, and can guess how much of all the subsequent victory is due to what his people learned in those days.

But the record has a far wider interest, for it lets us see, as we have little opportunity ordinarily, the inward conflicts through which The General passed in so many places where, out of his weakness, or the weakness of his forces, he, or they, were "made strong."

Few achievements of The General's lifetime will, I fancy, impress future generations more than his establishment of The Army in Finland at the very time when all the former liberties of that country were gradually being taken away.

Formerly recognised by treaties as a Grand Duchy of the Russian Empire, with its own Parliament and laws, which were supposed to be permanently guaranteed, Finland found itself looked upon with a growing jealousy just when a new constitution was slowly changing the governmental arrangements of Russia. It is, as yet, too early for outsiders to understand how it came to pass that the country was regarded as a centre of disaffection, or why, ever and anon some new step was taken to nullify its Parliament, and to place it more and more under military control. What we are concerned with is the simple fact that these things interfered but little with the steady progress of The Army, and that this proved at every step the soundness of The General's principles, the completeness with which he succeeded in planting them in the hearts of his most distant followers, and the marvellous way in which God guided, protected, and blessed his work, just where he could do the least for its development.

The very beginning of the Work was due entirely to one of his most daring decisions, for it may well be doubted whether any attempt, under the leadership of a foreigner, would have been tolerated at that time. But when a young lady, who had become acquainted with The Army in Stockholm, devoted herself to its service, and after passing some time in Training in London, was sent back with two or three subordinates to begin work in Helsingfors, who could look upon her with suspicion?

The moment she succeeded, however, in inducing a few of her first Converts to put on our uniform or insignia, the police came down upon them, took away all their badges, and declared that the formation of a Corps there must be regarded as for ever prohibited. Even when the Converts were provided with a second supply of badges, they were called to the police-station, and again deprived of them. But the leader had learnt from The General too well the lessons of patient endurance and continuance to give way. And when the police saw her followers supplied a third time with the signs of union with us, having in the meantime had so many opportunities to learn more both of the leader and of her people, they concluded that it would be, after all, the best for the public interest to let them alone.

Two newspapers in the two languages of the country were issued and sold in all the public-houses. Congregations were gathered in all the cities, and even small towns, and everywhere the authorities could see that no spirit of discontent with anything but sin and evil habits was being created, but that the police would find their tasks lightened, and the life of the poorest of the people brightened and bettered, if they let the work go on.

Chapter XIV
Children Conquerors in Holland and Elsewhere

The General's own personal experience, as well as numberless instances that came under his observation in his own and other families, gave him the same assurance as to the need and possibility of the Salvation of children as he had with regard to adults.

If human beings cannot hope to please God until they are born again of His Spirit, what folly it would be to give up the best years of life to mere outside instruction, instead of aiming first of all at this first and greatest need. This law he always laid down as the guiding line with regard to all work amongst children, instead of the ordinary Sunday School idea "first teach, and then try to lead the children to Christ."

In his first publication, ***How to Reach the Masses with the Gospel***, he wrote in 1871:—

> "Great pains are taken, we know, to make the children acquainted with the history and theory of Christianity; but their conversion, which is the main thing, seems to us to be sadly and sorely overlooked. That the immediate gathering of the children to Christ is the teacher's work, is recognised, we fear, in very few schools. It is not the aim of the present moment; and, consequently, little effort is made to bring it about. Feeling all this, we resolved that, if ever opportunity offered, we would try services as much adapted for the conversion and instruction of children as our other services are for adults.

> "On the first Sunday afternoon in April, 1869, we held our first 'Children's Salvation Service,' in our late Hall in the old Bethnal Green Road, and five children professed to find the Saviour."

But of all The General's revolutionary tasks this has, perhaps, proved to be the toughest. His eldest son—now General Bramwell Booth—made the children's work his earliest care, and in later years held annually Councils for all Officers engaged in it in England.

But, although God has wrought wonders amongst the children in every land, so that we have now thousands of Officers who have been won in their early years by that Junior work, the spectre of the Sunday School ever and anon rises to threaten with a peaceful death, this Divine undertaking. Only the most persistent watchfulness can prevent the narrow idea of instruction, and unbelief as to children's Salvation which is its foundation, from gaining the upper hand. It is so easy to get a thousand children drilled into pretty attention, pretty performances, pretty recitations and singing, and even into some degree of knowledge of the killing letter, but so hard to get any one child really to submit to the one great Teacher of mankind, and be saved!

Therefore we take special pleasure in dwelling upon the fact that The General's theory has been proved, on trial, to result in producing heroes and heroines, capable, almost in infancy, of daring battle for God, and becoming, before they reach their majority, thoroughly experienced and intelligent conquerors.

In that earliest record we read:—

> "Although the services are strictly for children, it is not an unusual thing to see adults sitting by the side of the little ones, and sometimes to see parent and child kneeling together seeking 'to know Him whom to know is life eternal.' One Sunday evening a woman brought her young son, who a short time previously had been detected in an act of dishonesty. During the service God's Spirit strove with both. The mother saw that she would have to give an account of her doings, as well as the boy, and so, side by side, they knelt, sought and professed to find pardon.

> "A young lad who had been a source of great annoyance at our Meetings, and a dreadful swearer, a short time ago died triumphant in the faith. When lying in the London Hospital, evidently dying, he sent a request that I would tell the children that he was 'going Home'; 'but tell them I'm not afraid; and, Oh, tell them not to swear.'"

Many of our leading Officers of to-day were truly converted before they were ten years old, so that, at thirty, they were already veterans in the Fight. Two Colonels, who were later most frequently seen closely associated with The General's Campaigns, like him were converted at fifteen—one of them being at that time almost overlooked by the Sergeant, who was counting the Penitents. "Captain," said he, "there are seventy-one; or seventy-two, if you count this lad."

The General has not only counted his young lads and lasses whenever they were true Penitents, but has dared to set them at once to work to bring others to Christ and that with such effect that whole countries have felt the result.

Our first Dutch Officer was a young teacher, dismissed from his employment because he would persist in seeking the Salvation, as well as the instruction, of his young pupils. After spending a few months in England in order to be able to translate for us, he became the Lieutenant and general helper of our pioneer Officer there. The way had been prepared before us by a retired Major of the Dutch Army, who had for some time been carrying on mission work in the city of Amsterdam, and who, having seen something of The Army in England, turned over his Mission Hall to us and gave us all possible help. He was rewarded by seeing all his own children converted.

Holland has suffered, perhaps, more than any country in the world, from the substitution of head knowledge for real heart acquaintance with God. The refuge of true believers in days of terrible persecution, it has seen its Churches either paralysed with the narrowest and coldest orthodoxy, proclaiming the impossibility of Salvation for any but the few elect, or the natural reaction, a wild "liberalism," which doubts everything. How far the two million Catholics of the country hold fast their old faith is doubtful; but it is admitted that very few of the other four millions profess to be "born again."

But The General never sought to trim his sails to catch any "modern" breeze. Upon his every visit to the country he spoke out with the same simple liberty as in England. Of the fisherman leader he sent to represent him in Holland, knowing "only a handful" of Dutch words, a lady said, "He prays just like a man who is drowning." Such praying, and corresponding effort, for "the perishing" soon brought thousands to kneel in penitence before God.

The General has visited the country repeatedly, presiding over the Annual Reviews, which have generally been held on some great land proprietor's estate, or holding "Days with God" in its largest theatres. Of one such visit, in 1906, he writes:—

> "I have just had a wonderful campaign in Holland--Meetings, enthusiasm, collections, and souls far beyond anything that has preceded it in my experience. Praise the dear Lord."

The simple old Gospel that any child can understand, has indeed made The Army triumphant all over Holland, and the following extracts from The General's diary, during his visit of 1908, will show how childlike a faith and devotion our people there have:—

> "Rotterdam, Saturday, *March 14th*.—Soldiers' and ex-Soldiers' Meeting fine—three-fourths men. A great improvement on anything I have seen in the way of Soldiers' Meetings in this place. I got the truth out, and thirty-seven of them fell at the Penitent-Form to seek power to walk in its light.

> "Sunday.--The Doelen Hall (one of the largest auditoriums in the city) full in the morning, and crowds shut out afternoon and night. People hard at first; but twenty-two came to the Penitent-Form in the morning, and fifty-eight at night. Never saw men weep more freely. L212 given during the day.

> "Monday.--Came on to Amsterdam and commenced Officers' Councils.

"Tuesday.--A tired, restless night for some reason or other. Sleep flew. Occupied with many matters, but not very anxious. Still, did not get much refreshment or invigoration for the day's work, and felt accordingly. On the whole, the three Meetings were interesting, and, I think, useful to the Officers present, although nothing remarkable.

"Wednesday.--What I said of the Councils yesterday may be repeated to-day. I had a great deal more material than I could possibly introduce into two days, and on leaving out some topics, on the spur of the moment, some were left out that might have been of great benefit. However, everybody was pleased, and, I think, profited. The only question in my mind, similar to the one that haunts me in every Officers' Council, is whether I am making the most of the opportunity.

"There is no doubt that we have here a powerful body of men and women, good, devoted, and loyal to the principles of The Army, proud to be connected with it, and ready to receive instructions, and to carry them out. The great lack appears to be a want of energy, enterprise, and daring, the being content with a little success instead of reaching out to all that is possible and promising. However, they are wonderfully improved, and I hope the present Commissioner's health will allow of his carrying them a long way farther in the direction of enthusiasm than they have reached before.

"Lieut.-Colonel Schoch (our original friend before referred to) was with us at all the Meetings. He is very cordial, and in making the closing speech, described his oneness with The Army in every direction.
"My correspondence with London is somewhat heavy.

"Thursday.--Fair night's sleep, but feeling rather tired, which must be expected. We are away to Den Helder at 9.42 a.m., so must be stirring. Den Helder is a naval port, the headquarters of the Dutch navy. We were billeted with Rear-Admiral van den Bosch, who is in command of the port, fleet, dockyards, and many other things. We were received at the station in a formal but hearty manner by the leading people of the town, in the large waiting-room (decorated for the occasion), by the minister of the State Church, who made a really eloquent address. The great point of his speech was the work of the Holy Spirit--God working through us to the benefit of mankind. As he stood there talking in that circle of sixty or seventy of the leading inhabitants of the place, including naval officers of rank, professionals of various classes, and prominent people, I could not help feeling, as I often feel now, what a change has come over the people, not only with respect to The Army, but towards myself.

"I answered in a few words that I trust were useful and beneficial to all present. The whole thing, from the moment of my being received at the door of my railway carriage, until I left next morning, had been prearranged through the instrumentality of one of our Local Officers, to his great credit, to the credit of his town, and to the satisfaction of his General.

"The mail brought me a request to take over a certain county council's lodging-house for poor men, on which they are losing a large sum, also another to take over an inebriates' home, which cost L40,000 and is an utter failure. In such exploits people will not have The Salvation Army at the onset, otherwise they might save a good deal of expense, etc.

> "Friday.--Arriving at Amsterdam, the mail brought confirmation of my agreement of yesterday to postpone my South African visit to September, and to begin my Motor Tour at Dundee, and finish at the Crystal Palace. In all these things the maxim is ever present to my mind, 'Man proposes, but God disposes.' Closed the night at the desk, which is becoming more and more a difficult task from the failure of my eyes.
>
> "Saturday.--Good night's sleep. That is for me, anyway, a great improvement on recent nights. So now for a good day's work, of which there is plenty lying before me.
>
> "7.30 p.m., Soldiers' Meeting. We have always been crowded out before, so this time the Palace Theatre was taken, as an experiment, and it justified my reckonings for several years gone by, namely, that we could fill any reasonable place on Saturday night here, and yet keep the Meeting select; that is, confine it to Soldiers and ex-Soldiers, adherents, and those concerned about religion. We were more than full, and the place holds 1,500. I had much liberty in speaking, the After Meeting went with a swing seldom known on the Continent or elsewhere, and we had eighty-four at the Penitent-Form, some of them remarkable cases."

No wonder this octogenarian Leader finds his young Dutchmen wanting in enterprise!

> "Sunday.--The theatre again in the morning at ten. An excellent plan. Oh, that it could be adopted the world over! The senseless system of beginning at eleven makes you feel it is time to close almost before you have had time to get well started. We were crowded, large numbers outside clamouring for admission, so much so that the police called out their reserves, and fifty men guarded

the entrance. We had an excellent service inside, and forty at the Mercy-Seat. It was a beautiful Meeting, and made a mark for ever on my heart, and on the hearts of many more.

"Afternoon. The large Hall of the People's Palace had been arranged for this as well as the Night Meeting. We were full, and many were turned away. I lectured on 'The Duty of the Community.' Great satisfaction among my own people, and a good impression made upon the minds of a good many of the leading people of the city.

"Night, 7.30. Again full. It is a building erected for an Exhibition, and made suitable for a Meeting only by putting up a great screen across the centre. I suppose we could have filled the entire space; but whether my interpreter could then have been heard, I am not sure. I preached with point and power--more breathless attention I never had in my life. I reckoned on an easy conquest, but we had one of the hardest fights I ever remember before we got a soul out. I left at 10.30, completely played out. A wall of policemen on either side kept the people back while I got into the carriage, the crowd having waited a long time to catch a glimpse of me. Had long, restless, and sleepless spells during the night; but still I have not done amiss on the whole. I must now prepare myself for the coming Berlin Staff Congress."

So much for the general effect upon a largely unbelieving people of simple, childlike faith!

But The General was, of course, always just as earnest about instructing all who came to him, old or young, in the way of life, as about getting them into it. In the midst of these tremendous Campaigns, he repeatedly prepared Lesson-books for both children and adults. To a lady who had tried to help him by sending him a number of catechisms for children, on such an occasion, he wrote:—

"Thanks for your letter, and your catechisms sent here.

> "The particular catechisms you send I already had--not that the church affair could be of any advantage to me, and I should imagine it would not be of much use to any one else, especially to children.
>
> "I am trying to produce something that will be a boon to The Army by being blessed to hundreds of thousands of children for years to come. You do not seem to think it is a very important task. I count it the most important work I have had my hands on for years.
>
> "I had a proper day at----. I got at the peasantry for once, although I have often had that privilege before, and we had a mighty day. Oh, the joy of leading those simple souls into the light and power and freedom of the Kingdom! I am keeping better. Praise the Lord!"

Whether The General's hopes for the use of his writings to the good of children will be fully realised, remains to be seen; but it is a great thing to have established even the purpose of making the way to Heaven plain enough for the youngest feet to find.

The other day I heard a Captain explaining how he was "conscripted" into The Army at ten years of age. He was standing outside the door of one of our Halls on an evening when children were not admitted. He had tried, in vain, boylike, to dodge through the doorkeeper's legs—but a drunken woman came up and not only insisted on getting in, but on dragging him in "to keep her company." Once inside, she went right up to the Penitent-Form with her prisoner, and made him kneel with her there. He had never seen so many grown-up people kneeling before, and, as they prayed, he felt what a naughty boy he had been, and began both to weep and pray. However little any older people might think of him that night, God heard and saved him, and he is now fighting under our Flag in the West Indies.

And others, who in their early years came to Christ, are now occupying leading positions all over the world. One of them remembers, when a lad of fifteen, hearing The General, whilst giving out the verse, "Sure, I must fight, if I would reign;

Increase my courage, Lord," say, "I would like to alter it, to—'Sure, I will fight, and I shall reign.'" The lad shouted, "Hallelujah!" and, as he was on the front seat in the theatre, The General both heard and noticed him, and remarked: "I hope you will make as good a fighter as you are a shouter." Thirty-three years of faithful warfare have replied to The General's encouraging challenge.

And we have no means as yet of calculating how many such youthful disciples have been equally helped by The General into a conquering life. May this record help to multiply the number, for it is the will of God to make all His children "strong in the power of His might."

It is, indeed, this bringing all, whether old or young, forward, in the development of all their powers for God, which constitutes everywhere a great part of The Army's work.

The enlarging influence of a close contact with Christ has hardly yet been fully realised even by ourselves. The peasant, whose whole circle of thought was so limited and stereotyped that his life only rose by few degrees above that of the animals he drove before him, is taught by The Army to pray and sing to the Maker and Saviour of the world:—

> Give me a heart like Thine;
> By Thy wonderful power,
> By Thy grace every hour,
> Give me a heart like Thine.

In a few years' time you will find that man capable of directing the War over a wide stretch of country—dealing not merely with as many Meetings in a week as some men would be content to hold in a year, and with the diversified needs of thousands of souls; but taking his share in any business transactions, or councils with civic authorities, as ably as any city-born man.

What has so enlarged his capacity, broadened his sympathies, and turned him into the polite and valued associate of any one, high or low, with whom he comes in contact? His library, if, indeed he has any, beyond the few Army publications he needs for his work, is still scanty enough to make his removal at a few hours' notice remarkably easy, and he will not be found much in public reading-rooms either. He has very little time for fellowship with any of the intelligent friends who, for The Army's sake, might now be willing to help him on.

He has simply had that oft-repeated prayer answered, and with the heart of a saviour of all men comes an interest in men's thoughts and ways which leads the man ever onward, overcoming all his own ignorance and incapacities, for the sake of helping on the War.

Thus The General's declaration at an early moment, that he would get his preachers out of the public-houses, has not merely been justified with regard to the first elementary lines of recruiting; but the grace of God has proved capable of developing, out of the most limited and despoiled human material, the most able and large-hearted of organisers and leaders, without building up any artificial or educational barriers between them and their former associates.

How, indeed, could it be otherwise? Those who are ignorant of God may well doubt the possibility of any mental improvement by means of prayer. But those who believe that it is possible for the poorest to dwell on earth with their Saviour, and to hold continual intercourse with Him, will perfectly understand how enlightening, how elevating, how inspiring such fellowship must ever be. Alas! how few there are yet in the world who can truly say, "Our fellowship is with the Father, and with His Son, Jesus Christ".

Chapter XV
India and Devotees

Nowhere has The Army shown its marvellous power to unite men of all races and classes so rapidly and completely as in India. With its Headquarters in Simla, and its leader, formerly a magistrate under the Indian Government, looked upon almost as a felon, and imprisoned when he first began leading Open-Air Meetings in Bombay, but now honoured by the highest both of British and Indian rulers and by the lowest of its outcasts equally, The Army has become the fully-recognised friend of Governors and governed alike.

When The General decided upon issuing a weekly paper called *The War Cry*, it was to be as nearly as possible The Salvation Army in print, and Mr. Booth-Tucker, then an Indian official, at once got the idea, from the copy he read, that such a force as it described was exactly what was wanted in that country—a set of Christians determined to fight for the establishment of Christ's Kingdom by every method love could devise; but loving especially the poorest and weakest, and proving their love by working continually amongst them. After visiting England, to see The Army and its leaders for himself, he had no hesitation in abandoning his Government appointment, and giving himself up for life to this War.

Such was the devotion of our Officers, and especially of the first Indians they won, that The General, far from having to urge them forward, had rather to check the tendency needlessly to sacrifice health and life. He gladly gave, at later dates, two of his own daughters to the Work; and, perfectly informed by his own repeated visits to the country, and by what he learnt from the actualities of the War, he was the better able to correct mistakes, and so to utilise to the uttermost the forces that were raised in various parts of the vast peninsula. Nobody would hesitate to acknowledge how much his counsels helped to prevent an excessive zeal from sacrificing precious lives.

He divided the country into six Territories, each under a separate Commander, realising that India could not be treated as one country, but that its diverse people must be dealt with according to their several needs, and that unless those using different languages were trained to act independently enough of each other they could never form strong enough forces to cope with the vast enterprises required. But the following account, written to his children, of his first visit to the country gives a photographic view, both of his own activities and successes, and of the attitude of the high and mighty generally towards him at that remote date. He writes from Benares, January 13, 1892, just ten years after our beginning in India:—

"Benares, *January* 13, 1892.
"My Dear Children,—

"Wednesday and Thursday, 6th and 7th, were consumed in travelling to Calcutta, and, all things considered, I got through the journey very well. Nevertheless, I was exceedingly weary on being roused at five o'clock to prepare for the arrival.

"It was early, 5.35 a.m., and Colonel Ajeet Singh did not expect any reception beyond that of our own Officers.

"To our surprise, however, we found the platform crowded with our own enthusiastic little party (who raised some music from a scratch Band), some native Christians, and a very large number of Hindu gentlemen.

"I was taken by surprise, and, unaware of the extent of the demonstration, allowed them to leave by only shaking hands.

"Interview upon interview followed during the morning, but in the afternoon I was down for the Town Hall Meeting. I scarcely ever remember in my life feeling more thoroughly weary than on that day.

Three times I laid down to try to sleep, and each time failed to get a wink, and my brain was benumbed and bewildered when I entered that immense building and was called upon by General Merrill, the American Consul, who presided, to address that crowd.

"I don't know whether Commissioner Booth-Tucker ever had a Meeting at the Town Hall. It is a long building, 120 feet long, with the most clumsy pillars down the sides shutting out almost the side seats from view.

"There was quite as large an audience as I expected, although it was not what it might have been. There were a few Europeans present and a few native Christians, and the remainder were composed of the non-Christian element.

"Amongst others who interviewed me during the day, or were introduced to me before the Meeting, was the successor to Chunder Singh and the two most prominent teachers of the Brahmo Samaj, and a number of other leading people. On the platform was the Judge of the Supreme Court and Vice-Chancellor of the University, and one of the few Hindus who are strict observers of every principle and usage of their sect. Near to me was the Nawal Abdool Luteef (Mohammedan), and just behind me was a boy of about fourteen, a son and heir of a Maharajah whose father had intended to have been at the Meeting, but was prevented, and so sent his son, a bright-eyed youth who paid every attention to what was said.

"General Merrill had consented to preside at the last moment, being induced to do so very largely from the fact that every one of the English of any note had refused.

"Bombay, *January 16th*.

"I broke off at the beginning of my Calcutta Campaign as above, not having had a moment's space to resume. Never had I such a crush of engagements before, and it was really all I could possibly do to keep pace with them, and that I only did to some extent in a poorish way.

"The detail of them I must leave to another day.

"I may say, however, that Calcutta in interest exceeded anything I have seen since I left England. From the rush of welcome at the railway station at six in the morning, to the pack who came to say farewell (in which the papers say there were 3,000 people), it was one series of surprises. Although the Town Hall Meeting was stiff, and the Europeans were conspicuous by their absence, still there was sufficient indication of the high esteem in which The Army was held in general, and myself in particular, to make it a matter of great interest and encouragement.

"Of the welcomes that followed from individuals of note, such as Mr. Bannerjee and Mr. Bhose (representing the Brahmo Samaj); and the Successor of Chunderssing, Mr. Chuckervetty, the lay reader of the Yogal Samaj, His Highness the Maharajah Sir Joteendro Mohun, of Tanjore, one of the most princely men of the city; the Nawab Abdool Luteef, the most distinguished leader of the Mohammedans, etc.; and of the several missionaries who came up, all was really complimentary and respectful--nay affectionate.

"Then there were the crowds, perhaps the greatest in the Emerald Theatre, in which there must have been nearly 3,000 people, inside and out, listening through the doorways. It was certainly the most remarkable audience I ever addressed. Exclusively native. I only saw one white face in the crowd beyond our own people. Nothing more hearty could have been conceived. Then came Meeting upon Meeting; but the Circus on Sunday night outdid almost anything in some respects, that I have ever witnessed in my life. It came upon me quite by surprise. The hour fixed was the same as the churches, and it had been predicted that we should not get an audience. It was right away outside the city, in a park in the swellest part of the suburbs. Consequently, it was not at all attractive to the native, who doesn't like to get outside his own quarter.

"The Emerald Theatre had been a great success because it was in the midst of his quarter; the Europeans would not come there, and now it was fair to assume that the native would not come to the European centre.

"As to any attendance of English people, that was hardly to be expected. They had cold-shouldered me at the Town Hall, the Lieutenant-Governor had even refused to see one of our Officers when she called, although he had the reputation of being a Christian man. The Viceroy had been civil to me--he could not have been otherwise; in fact, he verged on friendliness before we parted--but that was all. His Military Secretary had been as stiff as military etiquette could possibly make him. There seemed to be, therefore, nothing much to expect as to audience from them.

"Then I was tired out--a more wearying morning and afternoon I had seldom experienced--and I bargained in my own mind, and even mentioned it to Ajeet Singh, that if there was not much of an audience I should leave them to bear the brunt of the burden.

"As we drove up the appearance of things seemed to confirm my anticipations. Everything was silent. They had been afraid of the roaring of the wild beasts disturbing the Meetings, but there was not a growl to be heard, nor a carriage to be seen, nor even a pedestrian. It is true we were at the back part of the Circus.

"Hoe came to meet us, however, at the gates, and when asked about the audience very coolly announced, to our amazement, that they were _full_. Without any delay, therefore, I mounted the platform, and the sight that met me certainly was sufficiently surprising to be actually bewildering. They say the place seated 3,500; it appeared to be full. It was a simple circle, with a ring set in the centre. At one end was a little platform seating myself and my Staff, opposite me was the entrance for the horses, which was packed by the crowd, while the remaining space, on circle upon circle, tier upon tier, the audience was to be seen. On the right hand we had row after row of Queen's soldiers in their red jackets, lower down the Eurasian and middle-class Europeans, with a few natives. In the centre we had a very fair proportion of the _elite_ of Calcutta: there was the Lieut.-Governor, the Chief Commissioner of Police, the Consuls of America and two or three other countries, some great native swells, ladies bespangled with jewellery and finery, while on the left was one mass of dark faces reaching right up to the canvas sky. It was the most picturesque audience I ever addressed, to say the least of it.

"Our singing of 'Grace is flowing like a river,' was very weak, still everybody listened, nobody more so than the swell Europeans.

"The solo, 'On Calvary,' was sung with good effect, and then I rose to do my best. The opportunity put new life into me. I was announced to speak on 'The Religion of Humanity,' but this did not seem to me to be the hour for argument of any description; there was no time for dissertation. I felt I must have something that went straight to the point. I had been talking to these Brahmo Samaj and other people upon Social Work, alluring them on afterwards by indirect arguments long enough. Now I felt that I must go as straight to the point as it was possible to do. So I took 'What must I do with Jesus?' and made it fit into 'The Religion of Humanity' as best I could.

"I never hit out straighter in my life, and was never listened to with more breathless attention--except for the few wretched natives in the top seats, who would go out, I guessed, because they did not know the language, and came perhaps expecting I should be translated, and after sitting an hour felt that was enough. However, they soon cleared out, the audience taking no notice of the process.

"Once done, however, a general movement took place; a Prayer Meeting was impossible. We retired feeling that a victory had been gained so far.

"I cannot stop here to speak of the Meeting at which the Brahmo Samaj presented me with an Address of Welcome the next day.

"All I know is, that nothing surprised me more than to hear some of the priests and laymen declare that they had gone with me in every word I had said the night before.

"Other Meetings followed, interviews, visits to the houses of the leading natives, and with blessings without stint poured upon my head, and hand-shaking that almost threatened to lame me, the train tore me away from the packed platform, and I left Calcutta with unfeigned regret.

"I stayed a night at Benares, and had the Town Hall crowded, with a leading Hindu in the chair. Quiet Meeting. Landed here (Bombay) six this morning with a hearty welcome, and, I think, with the promise of good Meetings, although anything equal to Calcutta is not to be expected; and the news of the death of the Prince has come in our way, the news of which we have only just received.

"This will be my last letter, I presume, and I send with it, as ever, my undiminished affection to you all.

"For THE GENERAL,

"J. C. R.

"Written in a terrible haste."

This was immediately followed by the following final days:--

"Saturday:--
   Noon. Interview with Governor.

  5.0 p.m. Interview with native Christian Committee.
  5.30 p.m. Welcome in pandal; a large temporary structure capable of holding people, no seating being needed.

"Sunday:--
  10.30 a.m. Meeting in pandal.
  3.0 p.m. Interview with Indian Judge.
  6.0 p.m. Meeting in pandal.

"Monday:--
  10.0 a.m. Visit to our Institutions.
  3.0 p.m. Visit to General Assembly Institute.
  5.30 p.m. Drawing-room Meeting.
  8.45 p.m. Meeting of gentlemen at Town Hall.

The Bombay programme further included:--

"Tuesday:--
    7.0 a.m. Visit to the Leper Asylum.
    Midday. Visit to the Gaekwar of Baroda.
    3.0 p.m. Meeting in a pandal.
    Evening. Meeting with native Christians.

"Wednesday:--
    8.0 a.m. An assembly at the Institute.
    8.15 a.m. Interview with a solicitor.
    8.30 a.m. Interview with a Parsee engineer.
    9.30 a.m. Interview with Pressmen, who took him to see hospital for animals.
    2.0 p.m. Interview with gentleman, who took him to see the Victoria Jubilee Technical Institute.
    4.30 p.m. Reception at Mr. Jamsetjee Tatas.
    5.30 p.m. Meeting in the pandal.
    9.0 p.m. Lecture in the Framjee Cowasjee Institute to Indian gentlemen.

"Thursday:--
    8.30 a.m. Officers' Meeting.
    3.45 p.m. Officers' Meeting.
    4.30 p.m. Farewell procession.
    5.30 p.m. Farewell Meeting in pandal.

"Friday:--
    8.0 a.m. Staff Council.
    5.0 p.m. Reception at Mr. Cowasjee Jehangiers. (This was, however, abandoned on account of Prince Albert Victor's death.)

"Saturday: Sailed for Europe."

Remembering that The General was already nearly sixty-three years old, such programmes in India might well, fatigue him. But these were easy days, compared with many country ones of this journey, during which he traversed Ceylon, visited South India, spoke to some 8,000 Syrian Christians, and, calling at Madras and Calcutta, went on to the Punjab and Guzerat. His final days in Bombay were, as we have seen, clouded by a bereavement of the Royal House. But to his telegram to the Prince and Princess of Wales (now King George and Queen Mary), he got the cabled reply:—

"Their Royal Highnesses' thanks for your prayers and sympathy."

It had thus already been seen that The General's plans for India were answering their purpose. It became possible first to march large parties through various tracts of country, so impressing thousands in a few days more than the isolated labours of the best individuals could have done in the course of years, and then it came to learn later from Officers placed amongst them. All this The General knew could not mean all that it would have meant amongst peoples who understood more perfectly our teachings; but he saw no reason for not making the most of such incidents. Why not abandon, so far as such people were concerned, our system elsewhere, and recognise them as "Adherents," leaving them to learn after, from Officers placed amongst them, all that was necessary for them to become Salvation Soldiers. By this plan we avoided any watering-down of our teachings or requirements, and yet those who were not fit to be enrolled in our ranks were able, so far as they chose, to abandon idolatry and every evil practice, to get the advantages of Christian schooling for their children, and generally to improve themselves, under our influence.

Famines, epidemics of cholera and plague, and other general calamities really helped us to increase our influence in various districts. We gathered many orphans and abandoned children and brought them up as our own, whilst over wide tracts of country the people learnt to look upon us as a family of "brothers born for adversity," whose help could be relied upon not merely with regard to heavenly but to earthly things.

The barriers of caste, which bind Indians to treat each other to so large an extent as if they were enemies are naturally a constant and serious hindrance to us, especially as most of our people naturally belong to the lower castes, or are even outcasts. And our plan of organisation has helped us wonderfully in this matter, for the villager of Guzerat, or Ceylon, who might be very greatly hampered amongst his own natural surroundings, may be placed in an infinitely better position in some other part of the country. Indians are marvellously quick at learning languages, so that we need seldom hesitate about their usefulness in any new appointment on account of difference of language.

And thus it has come about that we have already, after some thirty years' work, nearly 2,000 Indian Officers, as absolutely devoted to the service of Christ as any of their comrades of any other land. And the forces under their command have shown already that they can deal effectively with peoples utterly inaccessible to the ordinary Europeans.

The Bheels, when we first went amongst them, were all armed with bows and arrows, living entirely by the chase, and so terrified at any sign of officialism that our Officers had to avoid taking a scrap of paper with them when visiting their districts. But we have now many Bheel villages entirely under our teaching, and quite a number of Bheel Officers who have learnt to read their own language, and to lead their countrymen as fully to follow Christ as they do themselves.

So many of our people in Guzerat were weavers that one Officer set himself specially to the task of improving their loom. He was soon able to make one with which they could double their daily product. The making of these looms created a new industry, also, so that we have been able thus to help many. In India we have also commenced in three of our Territories medical work, making it, after first cost of buildings, equipment, and Staff, largely self-supporting, as we found that the people really appreciated help more for which they were called upon to make ever so small a return.

In the same way, respecting all our work, The General has always urged the importance of applying, as far as possible, our general rule of self-support; for though the people may have very little to give, the very least they can do helps to protect us from the prejudice created by the term "rice Christians," applied to those who are believed to have made professions of Christianity for the sake of the food they hope to receive.

And now the Government, having seen the practical effect of our work, are beginning to give us opportunities such as we never had before. The Doms, a tribe systematically trained to live by thieving, were placed under our special care, and the result was such as to lead to our having other unmanageables likewise given over to us. In fact, we are barely now beginning to reap in India what in twenty-eight arduous years had been sown.

Does some one ask, Where does The General's own hand appear in much of this? Is it not all rather due to his having from the beginning, had so able a helper, acquainted with the languages and mental habits of the country, and other exceptionally able Officers both here and there?

Even if it were so, I should ask how all these people of ability placed themselves so absolutely at The General's disposal as to wish to spend all their lives under his direction in the greatest poverty in that far-away land? And I should inquire, further, how it came to pass that British, French, American, Swedish, Swiss, Dutch, and others could be got to submit, not only to work in union under the same "iron" regulations, but often under the leadership of women, and often under that of Indian Staff Officers? Who else but General Booth has ever attempted to place under command of a woman a missionary work, carried on largely by men, over a territory larger and more populous than the United Kingdom? Yet, undoubtedly, nothing has more contributed to the success of our work in a country where women have been so largely repressed, as the fact that The Army has thus demonstrated its confidence in God's power to lift up the weakest to the uttermost degree.

Nobody who reflects on these things will dispute that whatever The Army has done for India has been due most of all to its first General. And so surely as the knowledge of what is already done grows, shall we be allowed to do more and more to show India what Christ really desires, and so to capture it for Him.

In connexion with all our Indian work, one vastly important part of The General's work comes ever before us, whether we think of Commissioner Booth-Tucker or of one of his humblest native helpers.

Commonly enough in recent times The General was honoured because he had won from the path of vice to that of virtue some notorious sinner. But did he not even more remarkably earn the general gratitude by changing the comparatively helpless and uninfluential, though well-meaning, into enterprising and widely useful leaders in good work? How many millions of people he has taught or urged to sing:—

> Were the whole realm of nature mine,
>   That were a present far too small;
> Love so amazing, so divine,
>   Demands my soul, my life, my all.

That grand verse was well known in this country, and widely sung, of course, long before he was born. But alas! how many sing it even now "with the understanding"?

How many thousands of choice spirits first learnt, under The General's direction, to look fairly at the immensity of their responsibility to God, as they sang that and similar verses? And how many only found out, as ever-widening responsibilities were pressed upon them, how great their "all" really could become. The humble labourer, without any great speaking ability, and often involved in a struggle to earn the barest livelihood for himself and family, was taught how to share in seeking the Salvation of men. To-day he has become a well-known benefactor in one way or another to thousands of his fellow-townsmen, and his children, in the Far East or West, are helping to realise his grandest thoughts of winning the whole world for God.

This result would never have come about simply by the reading and singing of the most beautiful words. But the man who was first of all made responsible, perhaps, only for the keeping of a Hall door, learnt with astonishing rapidity how much our common life could accomplish for God, and went on expanding in thought and purpose, as his responsibilities were increased, until he became not merely a local leader in every form of Salvationist effort, but a foreman or tradesman exercising a widespread influence amongst his fellow-townsmen for all that is good, and urging thousands of a younger generation forward in every way, to the glory of God and the advancement of their country.

Such development, when it comes to be applied, say, to an educated lady, produces one of those wise mothers of mankind whose practical counsels and help are being sought by the greatest cities in these days, when men have found out what largeness of both heart and understanding are often to be found under a Salvation Army bonnet.

Chapter XVI
South Africa and Colonisation

The General visited South Africa three times—in 1891, 1895, and 1908. His visits were very largely dominated, as will be seen, by the idea that in South Africa good and abundant space could be found for Over-Sea Colonies; enough space, in fact, to accommodate all the surplus population of England.

The following extract from the record of his first journey is taken, in the main, from one of his "letters to my children," dated from Kimberley:—

"The afternoon Meeting was a select gathering, with the Mayor in the chair. Most of the ministers of the district were present. I talked with freedom, questions were proposed, and I carried the audience with me.

"At night we had a Social Meeting in the amphitheatre, which was well filled. The ex-Mayor presided. I do not know how long I talked, but they say two hours. Everybody was much interested. The doctor with whom I was staying, and a brother physician, came into the house and thanked me for my 'magnificent speech,' giving L5 to the fund for which we were collecting.

"I was very glad to get to bed, and to find that I had not taken a serious cold, for everything was open behind me in the theatre, and the night was piercingly cold, whilst I perspired with the exertion of speaking, and felt the wind blowing at my back, striking me like a wet blanket. I was very tired.

"Tuesday.--Officers' Meetings all day. If I had been pleased with what I saw of the Officers before, I was more so to-day. Their eagerness to hear, and quickness to understand, the readiness with which they assented to every call and everything laid before them, was delightful. No body of men more simple or apparently ready for action ever sat before me.

"At night I endeavoured to deal with their hearts, making clear what a full consecration to the War included, and appealing to them for it. I don't think I ever gave a more heart-searching address, and it awoke a solemn feeling, almost amounting to gloom, which settled down upon every soul. You could see it in their faces. The knife of conviction pierced them through and through, as I called up the particulars in which they came short of that life of love, sacrifice, and service which the War demanded. We then cleared the decks, inviting those who felt condemned in regard to the past, and who were willing to make the surrender, to come out. The first to roll up was about as handsome a fellow as I ever saw, a Cornish-man, who fell down and began to cry out aloud to God. Others followed, and before we finished I suppose we should have nearly seventy down, row after row, sincere, beautiful cases. Some of the testimonies that followed were delightful. T. was one of the first to come out, and he confessed down to the ground, and wept like a child, the whole audience being much moved. It was ten o'clock when I got home, having talked nearly seven hours, and I was glad to get to bed.

"Wednesday.--Officers' Meeting in the morning. A very precious time on matters of detail, which I believe helped the Officers very much."

Only those who thoroughly take in the meaning of these Officers' Meetings can hope to understand The General's hold upon The Army, or the value of his various journeys, for such Meetings had far more to do with the success of his work than any of his great public gatherings. He frequently uses the word "simple" in describing Officers, meaning men who have not got so much puffed up by applause as to be incapable of seeing their defects, and learning how to do better.

Can it be necessary to remind the reader that in The Army no distinctions of race, country, age or colour exist, so far as Officers are concerned? When it is inevitable to have together in one Officers' Meeting groups who do not speak the language chiefly employed, some one of their number is so placed amongst the group as to be able to translate to them The General's addresses.

Here we have a gathering of men and women from near and far, most of whom must needs carry on their work amidst small communities living very widely apart, and where they could very rarely see another Officer, or be visited by any leader. To bring all these up before the tribunal of their own consciences as to the extent to which they had discharged all the obligations they took upon them when they first engaged to form and lead on the forces whose duties, in so vast a territory, must be too varied and too difficult to prescribe by any fixed routine, could not but be of priceless value. Would to God that all persons engaged in missionary work were periodically passed through such examinations, by fire! How easily may any one in such solitary spheres yield to discouragement, or to some ill-feeling towards a predecessor in the same appointment, or towards some leader who has not seemed sympathetic enough!

Remembering that each of these has to go back to some position of lonely toil, with no guarantee of salary, and no prospect of improving circumstances, in a country whose large towns could be counted on the fingers of one hand, you can understand the supreme importance and the after-effect of such Meetings. The letter goes on:—

> "On this and the previous day, my host, the Doctor, had invited guests to meet me at luncheon. Yesterday we had the ministers, who were mostly very friendly and sympathetic. As the Doctor put it, 'To-day we had the sinners,' who he reckoned were by far the most enjoyable--Judges, Commisioners of Crown Lands, etc. All were very respectful, and, to say the least of it, were in sympathy with my Social scheme, if not actually having strong faith in its success.

"I had some further conversation with a member of the South African Cabinet, who said he was on the most intimate terms both with the leaders of the Afrikander Bund, and with Mr. Rhodes. He was quite sure that however any one from political motives, might disguise their feelings, they were equally in sympathy with me. We had some conversation as to the co-operation of the authorities, supposing lazy people turned out unwilling to carry out the engagements they might sign in England. He said he felt sure if anything were wanting in present law to ensure authority being respected, that it would readily be remedied."

This has reference to the scheme of an Over-Sea Colony in South Africa with which The General had been occupied ever since 1890. He, of course, always foresaw the risk that persons, who were sent out in connexion with such a plan, might see in the colonies an easier career than that of the cultivation of land, and that there must needs be some assurance of their being held to their agreement in any such case. He goes on:—

"At night, Farewell Meeting in the amphitheatre. It was a considerable strain on me, as I hadn't a minute to prepare. I had promised myself a couple of hours in the afternoon, when some Dutch ministers came down upon me to open a Y.W.C.A. building that they had just converted from a low public-house at Beaconsfield a suburb of Kimberley. If I would only go for half an hour they would be so grateful. I couldn't refuse, so my bit of leisure was seized upon.

"However, we had a very good Meeting. We were nearly full. I made a new speech which went, I thought, with considerable power, and then commissioned separate detachments for operations amongst the Zulus and Swazis--outriders for the Orange Free State, and Officers for various branches of Social Work. The leaders of each detachment spoke very well indeed. Promising fellows, all of them.

> "At the close of the public Meeting I had to have another for Soldiers, Officers, and Auxiliaries. This I was compelled to conclude earlier than I should otherwise have done by the announcement that the electric light would soon give out. However, we had a very nice finish, and I got to bed about 11.30.
>
> "Thursday.--Breakfast with the Staff Officers at 8. An hour and three-quarters' good straight talk afterwards with beautiful influence, everybody so tender. At the close I said, 'Now let us kneel down,' and after a little prayer asked them to link hands with me, and let us give ourselves up again to Jesus for the service of God and The Army."

Such tender-hearted linkings together of those who have the leadership of The Army's various departments have alone prevented the separations of heart that must inevitably be threatened wherever a number of very strong-willed men and women are engaged in labours into which they throw their whole soul, and in which they cannot, perhaps should not, avoid the feeling that their own department is, after all, the most important in the world. But any one who thinks will understand how men and women so blended together in fellowship with God and each other have been able to override all contrary influences in every country.

> "E. (the leader of our Work in South Africa) then turned to me" (the letter goes on) "and made a few appropriate remarks about his own devotion to The Army, and on behalf of every Officer, present and absent, assured me that they loved The Army as it was, and did not want any alterations in _Orders_ or _Regulations_, and were prepared to live and die in the War. I don't remember anything more tender and affecting on the conclusion of a Council.
>
> "I shook hands all round and we parted. God bless them. I made a hasty call at the Rescue Home, and was very pleased with it--a really nice little place.

"The platform at the station was crowded. A passage was made for me; but I readily reached the compartment, and having five minutes or so made a little speech, which was received with volley after volley, and cheer after cheer. There was a good deal of handshaking, any number of 'God bless you's,' and the train bore me away from a people with whom I have certainly had a really hearty and happy fellowship.

"I should have said that, by request of my host, I went through a kind of board school, in a very commodious and suitable building. I saw room after room so far as I could judge of the happiest, healthiest, and I might say, most beautiful lot of children it was ever my privilege to see. They ought to make a splendid body of men and women for the future.

"Friday.--I did not get on very well last night with the 'plank bed' or shelf which was dignified with the name of a sleeping berth. There was very little spring and no cushion. Moreover, I had heartburn. It was a cold night, and altogether I was glad when daylight came. The sun came out, and it was just as hot by noon as it had been cold at night.

"We stopped at Cradock a little time, where a gentleman interviewed me with regard to 80,000 acres of land possessed by some syndicate of the town at Prieska, up beyond Kimberley. This kind of thing happens almost every day.

"At a station a little further on quite a crowd of Salvationists and others had gathered. I could not see any sign of a town beyond two or three shanties. I used to think some of the places that had been dignified by the name of 'cities' in Canada were rather grotesque; but here it is carried to a greater extreme. However, they must have some method of distinguishing the place of ingress and egress from the train, and perhaps they are named in the hope of becoming what they are said to be--things that are spoken of as if they were.

"Well, on the platform was as picturesque and motley a crowd as well could be imagined. I only wished at the moment the pencil of some artist had been there to have painted the Kafirs in their showy turbans and half-naked bodies, the women with babies on their backs, and the whites of various ranks and conditions, all mixed up with Salvationists. Among others was a Salvationist old woman, half-caste, who had trudged over the mountain fourteen miles from Somerset East, with a big drum over her shoulders, travelling during the night in order to get a glimpse of The General. All at once, whilst the people stared, she struck up a lively chorus, leading the singing, and beating the drum most vigorously. Then followed the choruses: 'No, we never, never, never will give in,' 'Never say die,' and 'Steadily keep advancing,' etc. I beckoned to her, shook hands with her, wrote her name in a copy of _Aggressive Christianity_ in the presence of the crowd, and gave it to her, all of which was interpreted to her, as she spoke only Dutch. Then she wound up in good English with 'Victory for me, through the Blood of Christ my Saviour.' The little scene altogether was very striking."

Yes, surely that scene was striking for every one, and for evermore. That union of races and languages to the glory of Christ, and for the highest well-being of the whole world; that valuing of the humblest true Soldier of the Cross above all the great ones of this world, accounts for the creation, maintenance, and spread of The Army wherever they are seen.

The following report of one of his Meetings with the natives fairly represents one of them:—

"The room could not contain the people who wished to listen to the General. Dark faces were to be seen at every window. The General did not talk at them, but he talked into them, and their close attention and many 'Amen!' showed that he was well understood. No sooner had he ceased talking than the mercy-seat was filled, and at least a hundred came to Christ to seek deliverance from sin, and the supplying of their hearts' needs. Amongst the number were eight or nine women from Central Africa; they had been brought down for immoral purposes, but the Army had got hold of them and rescued them.

"Ere the General turned away he gave them still further advice as follows:

"'My heart is drawn out to you. I am going a long way off, but I want you to think of me, and when you think of me, I want you to pray for me. Be decided to fight for Jesus. God will be on your side. Go in and get all your people saved, and be the friends of all. Before I go I should like to know who have made up their minds to trust God,'--and up went a hundred hands. 'That's right. Now all who have made up their minds to meet me in Heaven raise their hands again'--and once more every hand went up, this time accompanied by a tremendous shout."

These journeys to South Africa were, indeed, taken together, amongst the most painful lessons of The General's life as to the smallness of hope from the great ones of this world. The first visit, paid on the swell of the first admiration for the "Darkest England" Scheme, filled him with great expectations; and no wonder, for everywhere at that time Governments, municipalities, and wealthy magnates talked as if they were ready to assist him immediately to place the deserving, though poor, crowds of the Old Country on the magnificent tracts of land he saw everywhere unoccupied, or very slightly used.

But "Governments" of the elected type come and go, making the most lavish promises and denouncing "the other party," who, on turning them out, do ditto.

MRS. BRAMWELL BOOTH

And so it came to pass that The General made his third journey to South Africa, in 1908, when seventy-nine years of age. His life ran serious risk, because his going to Rhodesia himself was considered indispensable in order so to impress some British or South African "statesmen" that they might give him the needed help to establish an Over-Sea Colony there. And, then, all the "statesmen" denounced to Colonel Kitching by one of themselves as "a set of ——fools" say that "nothing can be done at present." And the old man returns to die with his great dream unrealised.

The following account of one journey taken by Colonel Kitching alone, who was not only his Secretary but his representative in many directions throughout his latest years, shows the loving willingness of an Army Secretary to do and bear anything for Christ's sake, and, what our Staff Officers generally understand by the words "indefatigable," and "unconquerable":—

> "After a long journey of thirty hours I reached ---- railway station, expecting, in the virgin simplicity of my youthful mind, to find his place within sight--perhaps across a couple of stiles--instead of which I found that it was thirty-six miles or more--four hours' drive in a Cape cart. The only 'boy' at the station with a vehicle was engaged, so I bade him come back again for me as soon as he had got rid of his fare, which he did in something over an hour, although he had said he should be 'back in a second.' When he did come he was unwilling to take me without his baas' leave, so we set off to find the baas; he was not at his house nor at his stable; he might be at church. I went and routed him out of his devotions, finally bargaining with him to take me there and back for L3!

> "Now Mr. ----'s 'farm' comprises some eighteen or twenty different farms, of which about 160,000 acres are in one block, and some 80,000 acres more in three or four separate pieces. Each of these farms is managed by a farmer who is responsible to the top manager, who also has charge of one of the individual farms. My destination was a farm where Mr. ---- was believed by the railway people to be that day.

"The first half of the ride we were cooked in the sun; then darkness came on--black darkness; then some ominous drops of rain, which were soon _sheets_ instead of _drops_, and such thunder and lightning as I never want to hear or see again in this life.

"I was afraid we should get lost in the dark; for, although it was called a 'main road,' it was in reality merely a _track_--not that in many places--with any amount of 1 ft., 2 ft., 3 ft., and 4 ft. holes (no, I draw the line at the 3 ft. holes, upon consideration); but my driver, who dignified himself with the title of 'mail contractor,' was sure that his horses could find the way in the darkest darkness, as they do the journey each way twice every week. But when the darkness got so dense that we could not even see the horses except when it lightened, even he grew doubtful, remembered that he _himself_ had not driven them along that road for more than eight months (though his boy had done), and he thought that we had better stand still where we were till the storm was over and the moon rose; but I knew the moon would not rise till 10.30, and we were already about eighteen miles from anywhere!

"My entreaties that he should proceed met with success, and the result that we lost the road twice, got into a deep hole and capsized--the whole caboose.

"When at last we reached the farm, it was to be met with the announcement that Mr. ---- had left there the previous day, and was believed now to be about twenty-six miles (three hours nearly) further on.

"I was soaked to the skin, as hungry as a hunter, and dead beat into the bargain. The farm manager insisted that I must stay the night--it was imposible to go on in that storm--and go on in the morning.

"This is a little world. Mr. ---- had mentioned my name in speaking to him of The General's visit to Johannesburg, and he had remembered it as that of the only Salvation Army Officer from whom he had ever received a letter. Ten years ago or more he had addressed some inquiry or other to Headquarters, and I had written him in reply.

"The next morning I drove on to -----, and found Mr. ----in his orchard. He had not received The General's wire saying I was coming for the simple reason that, not wanting to be bothered with mails or telegrams for a couple of days, he had instructed the post office people to forward all his dispatches to a place which he did not intend to go until the next day!"

If public receptions at railway stations, speeches and addresses by Governors, Mayors, and Ministers, and Press eulogies could have satisfied him, The General could not but have been delighted with South Africa, as the following extracts may show. In *The Ladysmith Gazette* we read:—

"General Booth has flashed past Ladysmith like a meteor, but I am inclined to think he has left a trail of light behind him. It is fifteen years since I last saw the Leader of The Salvation Army. Those fifteen years have made but little alteration in the man. There is the same old Saxon profile, the same storm-defying, weather-beaten, almost eagle-eyed features, and the same slightly rasping, but intensely interesting in its earnestness, voice.

"There is plenty of strength still in that patriarchal figure, and with the exception of a slight stoop The General is as vigorous as he was fifteen years ago. In appearance, The General reminded myself of Canon Kingsley. They have the same Anglo-Saxon,

falcon-like features, and the same indomitable energy and courage. Canon Kingsley was not so well provided with hair as The General; but, on the contrary, he could boast of a more prominent nasal organ. Both men had flashing eyes, deeply-set and overhanging eyebrows, giving force and determination to the face.

"Both the late Canon and General Booth were equally sturdy specimens of Saxon descent, and both worked for the masses. Canon Kingsley, as he would admit to-day, was before his time, and in aiding the Chartist movement made a fatal mistake. Canon Kingsley, as shown in _Alton Locke_, endeavoured to raise the masses to heights attainable only by men of education and men of thought, and to-day the recoil of that pernicious doctrine is being felt.

"General Booth places a man in the position God intended him to occupy, and if the man can raise himself higher by strenuous effort then well and good.

"The Salvation of General Booth is the true Salvation--the Salvation of regeneration, and the world's thinkers are surely recognising the fact that The Salvation Army is a factor to be reckoned with. General Booth and his people have succeeded when all others have failed."

The Rhodesia Herald, of Salisbury, said:—

"General Booth has well been called the Grand Old Man of The Salvation Army, for undoubtedly it is his remarkable personality and fierce energy which has made The Army what it is to-day, and has enabled it to do a work which no other religious organisation has attempted to do on anything like the same scale, and to reach a section of the people who remained untouched by the more orthodox methods of other bodies. It is not so very many years ago that branches of The Army in many towns in the United Kingdom were striving to make headway against most determined opposition--opposition employing methods of which the authors soon became heartily ashamed. Yet to-day, the different branches of The Army are doing their work, not only unmolested, but helped and encouraged by all classes of the community. And this because The Army has wrung recognition by transparent honesty of purpose, and unceasing efforts to help those most in need of help and encouragement. As the aged General put it on his arrival in Johannesburg, the Organisation of which he is the mainspring has set before itself the task of giving a helping hand to the very poor, those who are without friends, and those who have fallen in the battle of life."

The members of the Cape Town and district Evangelical Church Council in their address to General William Booth, D.C.L., said:—

"We have been deeply touched by the energy, the wisdom, and the consecration with which you carry on your work at a period of life when most men have retired from active service.

"We would join with our brethren of the Christian Churches throughout the world in assuring you of our admiration, mixed with our wonder, at the success which has attended your labours for the Salvation of the most helpless and degraded members of our race.

"Hand in hand with your efforts for the Salvation of the souls of the fallen have gone a true Christlike care for the bodies of the unfortunate, and an attempt to stem the current of social evil and degeneracy.

"We are deeply interested in your experiments in colonising those parts of our Empire which are at present sparsely populated, and thus relieving the tension of social problems in the larger cities of Great Britain, and that congestion of population which is a fruitful source of individual and of social degradation.

"We trust your visit to South Africa may result in the settlement in the rich lands now untilled of a population, which by its industry, thrift, and character will compare with those of Canada, New Zealand, and Australia.

"We rejoice that the great Captain of Salvation continues to lead the Organisation, of which you are the head and heart in one, to great victories over the forces of evil, and assure you that in this land we recognise The Salvation Army as a powerful force for the spiritual and social uplift of the people. It is always a pleasure for the Churches we represent to render any aid in our power to an Organisation for whose members and whose work we have the deepest regard.

"It is the earnest prayer of the Council that your visit may be full of blessing to your community, that it may result in a fresh infusion of hope and enthusiasm into the hearts of your fellow-workers, and that God may abundantly fill you with spiritual and physical energy in the fulfilment of the great enterprise on which you have entered.

"*August 26*, 1908."

The address of the Bloemfontein Town Council very carefully avoids any reference to the proposed Over-Sea Colony. Perhaps the whole secret of South Africa's indifference to it is revealed in the following extract from a paper, whose name we omit, lest any appearance of hostility to any locality or any element in that enormous country should seem to have crept into our feelings here.

After half a column of compliments as to his good work and intentions the editorial gentleman, not of Bloemfontein, goes on with his great "But" as follows:—

> "But the social elevation, or the spiritual conversion of the boozy scum of a European nation may not be advanced at the cost of the well-being of our own people. We protest most earnestly against that at once. It does not matter whether he has fixed his eye upon Rhodesia or the Kalahari desert--these lands belong geographically to South Africa, and we need it for its own peoples. True, we have plenty of territory, even for others who may wish to come and settle amongst us, and wish to be of us.
>
> "But we have no room for the 'submerged tenth' of any other nation whatever."

In vain did The General keep explaining in every land he visited that he had never thought of, or made any plan for, "dumping" crowds of wastrels on any country, but only such people as had been tested and proved fit for such an opportunity as they could not get in overcrowded countries. There was always the same loud and continued applause for "his noble work," and, then, almost everywhere—not often with the honest outspokenness of that newspaper—the same "I pray thee have *me* (my country) excused from receiving this Colony."

And then the old man would give the tiny handfuls who, thanks to insane constitutionalism, have been left to monopolise vast areas of the earth, warnings of the future that may be remembered by generations to come. Whilst in South Africa he was gladdened by receiving the following report as to the multitudes he was sending out to Canada:—

"Emigrated from October, 1903, to July 31, 1908, 36,308; of whom were assisted by loan, 9,400; total amounts advanced, L38,375; total amounts repaid (within first five years *already*!), L5,112."

But as to South Africa, he grasped the main feature of the situation there; and thus wrote, in words that may be remembered, **not only in that country,** when, for the British Empire, it is for ever too late:—

"The more I see of this country, the more I am convinced of the folly of the controversy that prevails in some minds, and of the fears that are entertained about the predominance of the Dutch element. Before many years have passed the question will not be as to what nation of whites shall have the mastery, but whether the whites will have any mastery at all; not whether it shall be Dutch land or British land, but whether it shall be a white man's land. The undisputed growth in intelligence of the African and Indian combined will soon give them so great a preponderance that they will capture the agriculture and trade generally.

"What is to hinder them from the capture of the mineral production, and the mastery of the country in general? There is only one way for the white man, and that is to add to his numbers such as will join him in the struggle, and to convert the coloured element to righteousness and truth and honesty and industry.

"I want to help them, but they cannot see far enough.

"These are the sentiments that ought to be pressed upon the attention of our government."

Here is another letter which is valuable especially for the light it gives with regard to The General's careful examination during his journeys into all that concerned the efficiency of The Army and of every leading Officer in it:—

"I have not said much about the character and condition of the work generally, having reserved my ideas for the closing of my correspondence.

"In a general way, however, I will make a few observations:—

"1. The Territory must certainly be in better form than it has ever been before. This, considering the havoc made by the war, is saying a good deal. There are more Corps, more Officers, more Soldiers, plenty of money to meet their requirements, and as much favourable public opinion as is good for them, perhaps a little more.

"2. So far as we have had opportunity for observation, the Officers and Soldiers appear to be in good spirits.

"3. Some important advances are under consideration, or in progress, in the direction of properties, both Social and Spiritual.

"4. Several very remarkable Revivals have taken place.

"5. The Commissioner appears to be much improved.

"6. The more I see of —— the more I like him, and my impression is confirmed that he is a long way the best man in the country for dealing with the natives.

"7. The Commissioner thinks that what there is to be known as to cattle, land, products, etc., is known to ——. I love him very much.

"8. The same applies very largely to ——. What he does know he may know better than ——, though I am not sure whether his knowledge is so extensive.

"9. I have seen little of ——; but he is said to be very successful in his present appointment. Two gentlemen who have been inspecting his place say they could not have believed that such wonderful results could have been achieved in so unlikely a place.

"10. This man, ——, has sat on the platform, and prayed when he has been called upon to pray; but he has done nothing more. I shall instruct K., I think, to ask him a few questions, one of which will be whether he is willing to take a position in another part of the world."

Of course, I am only snatching such sentences as convey the main ideas, without their fuller development, which would risk indicating the persons referred to.

Will it be believed that, whilst this octogenarian was toiling in the heat to prepare if he could a brighter future for some of the poor, a syndicate of slanderers in London, some well educated, some of the Trafalgar Square bawler type, were seeking to bless "the British public" by enlightening them as to his selfish and foolish designs upon them? According to their theories his every new scheme was only brought forth to turn aside attention from his entire failure, and ensure a continuous flow of money into his coffers!

Perhaps, the best feature of all about his "dreams" was that they never became less cheery for all that, and their continuously increasing infection of the world, despite every attack.

The General writes, after his great Meeting with some of our native comrades as reported in connexion with his final Congress:—

"I have been much occupied, as I have already told you I expected to be, with the ***Native Question***; and I am satisfied that one of the greatest things ever done in the history of the world can be done here, and I am determined to make an attempt to do it.

"I do not say that our chance is ***greater*** than it is in India—though I am not sure whether it does not equal it in many ways. Anyway, it appears to me that it is open to us to realise a mighty success."

Chapter XVII
Japanese Heroism

Japan, amidst all the records of its modern progress, must certainly count the honour of having properly recognised the value of The General and his Army before the old "Christian" countries of Europe did so.

The Army's beginning in Japan was almost laughable in its feebleness. The little company of Officers sent out by The General, in 1895, were indeed truly devoted, and in their anxiety to be from the first "as Japanese to the Japanese," were so taken in whilst halting in Hong Kong that they landed in the most extraordinary garments—and it was a long time before they seemed likely to make any impression upon the non-Christian Japanese. But upon the Christians they, undoubtedly, made, from the first, an excellent mark.

With all their lack of knowledge of the language, there could be no mistake about their willingness to learn, and to be the servants of all men. It was clear that they possessed those two great qualifications for Apostolic success, an unlimited readiness for hard work, and an unbounded faith in the will and power of Christ to save. Their first interpreter, a student anxious to do his uttermost for Christ and his country, was speedily won over completely to their side, and as he was already known amongst the Pressmen, this became a very great help to the progress of their work generally.

Yet, under several successive leaders, they toiled on for some years with but little prospect. The language is one of the most difficult imaginable for foreigners to learn, and, although there was from the first great liberty as to Open-Air Meetings, and congregations were gathered outdoors and into the little Halls that were contrived out of shops and dwelling-houses, it seemed likely to prove slow work to raise a Japanese force.

But all at once, in 1902, God gave the little company a great opportunity. For years already some faithful Japanese under missionary influences, had been lamenting the position of the girls given over to immorality, who were severed for life from the rest of the community, and kept under police supervision, in a special quarter called the Yoshiwara of each city, as well as cut off from all the hopes of the Gospel. A law had indeed been passed allowing such girls as might wish to abandon their awful calling to do so; but it was so administered as practically to remain a dead letter.

"Why," thought our leaders, "should we not issue a special edition of our *War Cry*, explaining Christ's love and power to save the deepest sunken in sin, and our Rescue Work, and then go and sell it in the Yoshiwara?"

The idea was carried out, and, to all appearance, the first day, with wonderful success. The great companies of pleasure-seekers saw in the "Paper" a novelty of interest and bought and read it eagerly. But it was far too great a success to please the brothel keepers, who at once hired men to attack *The War Cry* sellers, should they repeat their invasion. When it became known that our Officers had thus been attacked, reporters of the Tokio and Yokohama papers hurried to see the, for Japan, unusual sight, and then the whole Press of the country came out strongly on our side. We were fully recognised as the loving friends of the friendless and oppressed, and from that day our standing in the country was assured.

Not many girls were gathered into our little Rescue Home; but thousands learnt the way of escape from their houses of bondage, and within a few years many thousands returned to their old homes all over the country. It should be explained that the brothels were really supplied as a result of the heroic devotion of the girls to their parents and homes. It was common for a girl, in any time of extra want or destitution, to suggest or consent to her sale to one of the bad houses for the relief of her family. This fact, however, of course increased both the national sympathy for the victims, and the high appreciation of our care for them.

But the main thing, after all, in all this action was the revelation of an Army, unable as yet to make itself well understood in words but capable of thus manifesting its resolution to fight for the liberation of all men from the power of sin.

We had issued already a *Common People's Gospel*, written by our Chief Secretary, Colonel Vamamuro, which gave a very clear explanation of our teachings and system. This book was not only a sort of harmony of the Gospels, but explained how we understand and teach the Salvation Christ bought for us all. This Gospel came to be appreciated and utilised by almost all the missions in the country, and greatly helped us also in making clear our meaning to the nation. By its sale, as well as that of *The War Cry,* throughout the country very many, even of those who were too far off for it to be possible for them to attend any of our Meetings, were led to Christ.

And thus steadily, though slowly, we made our way, until we had Corps in most of the great cities, and became known generally wherever there were thinking and reading people. Our Halls were, and still are, very small, it being almost impossible to find either large ones hireable, or large spaces available for building upon, in the great cities. Yet marvellous were the displays of God's power to save in the little rooms, which were packed to the doors night after night, and in the Open-Air Meetings. Our leaders in the country, for several years, were Officers who, amidst the multitudes of India, or of the slums of London had seen how souls could be won, in spite of every outward disadvantage, by the irresistible power of the Holy Ghost. And thus the numbers of our Japanese Soldiers and Officers steadily grew. Just as in England, men who had been notorious in sin became equally notorious witnesses for Jesus. Japan is a great country for holiday festivals, when all the streets are by day beflagged and by night illuminated with Chinese lanterns, almost the whole population turning out on such occasions. Our troops naturally made the most of such days, and it became a common thing to see men and even women kneeling in an Open-Air Meeting to seek Salvation.

So when it was announced, in 1907, that The General was coming, Japan resolved to give him a welcome such as he had never had before. That a man should undertake, at seventy-eight years of age, such a journey, was felt to be a tribute both to the country and to the man himself, and there was a desire, if anything more in non-Christian than in Christian circles to hear him, and do him honour.

"Tell him," said a Tokio editor, "that he is coming to a country such as he has never before visited—which can appreciate self-sacrifice, as we have shown in the late war."

And from the moment when his steamer entered Yokohama Harbour to that of his departure, nothing was omitted that could open his way to the ears and hearts of the entire nation. I had the pleasure myself to witness those unforgettable scenes, and to notice The General's own astonishment at the universal interest of the people. In each city he found the railway station decorated. A platform was erected, generally in some public space, whence he could address the multitudes who came out to hear him. The largest public buildings were crowded for his indoor services, and hundreds came out publicly in reply to his appeals for their surrender to Christ.

Not only was he received by the late Emperor in his palace, and welcomed to every provincial centre by the Governors of the Provinces, and the Mayors of the Cities, but again and again the most eminent men gave him opportunities to plead with them for Christ. What a sight it was to see the great platform crowded with all the chief men of a city, singing like the rest of the audience "Stand up, stand up for Jesus." The General was accepted by almost unanimous consent, as representing a life of entire self-abandonment to the glory of God and the Salvation of the lost, and far beyond anything even that at the moment appeared, was his Campaign a general victory for the Saviour.

There could be no mistake as to the message he delivered, for, even to the vast crowds of students gathered in the quadrangle of the University, or in and around the Theatre of Kobe to hear him, he stood and cried in no new terms, although with due adaptation to their ways of thought, just as he might have cried to any English audience, that God demanded and deserved a whole-hearted, life-long service from every one.

"What?" asked the Ambassador of a great power, "Do you really want me to come out on to the stage and confess my sins before everybody?" when a woman-Officer invited him to one of The General's last Meetings. Had His Excellency done so, no Japanese would have thought it anything beneath the highest human dignity, for they all recognised the value of that courage for Christ and His War which The General personified to them.

We are still few in number and struggling hard for victory in Japan, for the very appreciation of all that is excellent tends to create in the people a self-satisfaction that fortifies them against all appeals for repentance. But one of the leading officials of the Japanese Home Office has recently paid a tribute to The General's helpfulness to every people.

Mr. Tomioka says, in his ***Society and Humanity***, after having studied The

Army in England and America, as well as in Japan, that he considers it to be "the greatest and most successful Organisation in the world for dealing with and helping the poor and unfortunate classes of society." He attributes our success to the following reasons:—

1. The great personality of The General, whose character greatly resembled that of his Divine Master—the Founder of Christianity.
2. Our aggressive spirit—ever marching on, like the Japanese soldiers in the last war with Russia.
3. Our adaptation to the circumstances of every country.
4. Our straightforward and practical way of preaching Salvation.
5. Our principle of self-support. Teaching men and women to help themselves.
6. Our scientific and business-like methods, as distinct from mere sentimentality.

Some day, surely, men equally eminent in other countries will begin to speak as heartily and thoughtfully of The General's life work.

That the great Mikado, to whose wisdom and energy Japan owed so much of its great renewal and entry amongst the "civilised" nations, should have passed into eternity only a few months before the Founder of a wider and grander, because spiritual, Empire, is an interesting fact. The Mikado received our General, in spite of every court usage that might have hindered, because he found that all the greatest leaders and heroes of Japan, like their Press, saw in him the personification of the highest and noblest purpose for every land and every people.

The Japanese Government gave our Officers, women as well as men, a liberty of access to their prisoners greater than we as yet possess in this and most other "Christian" countries, because they saw the value of our love for the victims of sin, and our power, by God's grace, to inspire them with hope for themselves. How many more years, I wonder, will it take other nations to follow this common-sense example?

Chapter XVIII
Co-operating With Governments

The Government of the Dutch East Indies, which was in the hands, at the time, of a military man, has won for ever the honour of appreciating and utilising The Army of The General they had never seen, before any of those who had seen him. Certainly, The General never ran after earthly rulers, or showed any disposition to court their favour; but he said constantly, "Here we are; if any Government, municipal or national, likes to use us, we can save them more than half of what they now spend upon their poor and criminal classes, and do for these far more than Christian Government officials, however excellent, ever hope to do. They are invariably so bound to avoid any meddling with religion that they cannot bring to bear upon those most in need of it, the heavenly light and love and power, in which we place all our confidence for dealing with these classes."

"Gentlemen," said a Town Councillor, in a German city, when the question of subsidising The Army was being discussed, "The Army can do for your poor what you never can attempt. You can only deal with them from without. The Army works upon them from within, and produces results that will considerably lighten your burdens."

The General had arranged for the Dutch Indies to be missioned from Australia, that country being our nearest Field and one accustomed to deal with pioneer effort. But when he found that Dutch officialdom dreaded contact with British agents, though ready to welcome Dutch ones, he very quickly changed his plans, and as soon as the Colonial Government found that The Army was as much Dutch as English, and could send them a Dutch leader, they showed themselves ready to use us as fully as possible.

Our Officers in every town and village are supplied with all the medicines and bandages they can use, for the Government has found that they live amongst the poorest all the time, and are always ready to bathe and bandage their wounded limbs and feet, or to give them the few medicines needed to combat the ordinary maladies. Moreover, from some terrible losses by death of Officers, in our earliest years there, it was made only too plain to every one that our Officers would not abandon their people in times of cholera or other epidemics, but would rather suffer and die with them.

More unsanitary surroundings than we have in lovely Java could scarcely be imagined, and no government can hope to alter the habits of an entire people very rapidly. The Chinese and others in the cities have never yet begun to consider dirt in house or street as dangerous, and the entire population has grown up with such a love for bathing in the very same canals which serve largely for drainage and every other purpose, that there cannot, for a long time to come, be great hopes of much sanitary improvement.

But when it was seen that we had Officers not only willing and ready to live and die with the people, but, also capable of lifting them into a new life, and of carrying out any simple administrative duties that might be laid upon them, we had first one and then another of the Government's institutions offered for our care, as well as the provisioning of the hospitals. From daybreak in the morning till the end of their evening Meetings, our Officers may be seen showing the people, old and young, brotherly and sisterly love; and though they may not, as yet, have succeeded in many places in raising up such a native force as we should desire, the Government has found them as persevering as if they had gained the crowd which their toils and endurances have deserved.

The first Leper Institution placed in our charge was so rapidly transformed from a place of despair and misery into a home of Salvation hope and joy, that the Government naturally desired to see more such institutions, adequate to receive the entire leper population of the islands, which is, alas! large.

Our position in Java, and the consequent discussion of us in the Dutch Parliament, led to our first public recognition in the world as a Christian force. Because we do not baptise with water there has been in Java a disposition amongst some Christian teachers to refuse to any of our people burial in a Christian cemetery. But when in the Dutch budget discussion this was made an objection to our receiving any grant, the Colonial Minister simply read out the whole of our Articles of War, and asked how any one could refuse to recognise as Christians those who had signed such declarations.

The Governments of the various Australian Colonies must, however, have the credit of first giving to our Officers public patronage. As has already been mentioned, the Governors, Premiers, and Ministers have, for some twenty-seven years past, been seen presiding over the anniversaries of our Colonial work, speaking in no measured terms of all our activities, and so helping us to get the means to support them.

The Queen Mother and the present Queen of Holland were the first royal personages personally to visit our Institutions, although the present King of Denmark, when Crown Prince, had for years used our Refuges in that country for cases he thought deserving, and his brother, King Haakon, of Norway, attended, as a warm friend, one of The General's Meetings in Christiania.

Canadian and South African Governors and Ministers have acted like the Australian ones in their public expressions of confidence in us, and they have given us very considerable liberty in their prisons, so that most of the criminal population comes more or less under our influence.

The greatest of our governmental victories have, however, been won in Switzerland and Germany, where we were for so many years looked upon as a dangerous, if not harmful, influence, owing chiefly to the gross calumnies of "Christian" teachers and writers. The results of our work upon those whose lives had been a disgrace and burden to the community could not be hidden, however, and there is now scarcely a cantonal government in Switzerland which does not subsidise some one or other of our Institutions. The cities of Hamburg and Elberfeld, in Germany, have led the way in granting to us similar assistance, and it can only be a question of time before we gravitate into an equally honoured position elsewhere. For although we continue to keep as far as possible aloof from all parties, and party feeling, and have not, therefore, the means of influencing and obtaining grants from politicians in the ordinary way, we compel attention by what we do, and have, undoubtedly, done more than any other religious community to create that inclination towards intelligent care for the criminal and outcast which is almost becoming a fashion, in governmental circles, nowadays.

It begins to look as if, had The General lived, some of the South American republics would have been the first, after all, to gladden his heart by a hearty and handsome co-operation. For twenty years he pleaded for an opportunity to show what could be done for those whose life and character have been wrecked amidst the breakers of modern life, if they were removed from their old surroundings and compelled to live under our influence in country air. We have come so far in this direction, in New Zealand, that we have bought islands, where former inebriates and their children can be kept completely severed from their old temptations, and so have every opportunity to begin a new life if they will. Men, as well as young people, are frequently handed over to us by the authorities; but there is not yet anywhere a sufficient power given to detain those who are disinclined to hard work.

And recently, The General was promised, in the course of interviews with authorities, a considerable extension in the United Kingdom of the liberty to deal with prisoners, which we have long enjoyed in America and Canada. The long night, when prisoners were treated only as troublesome animals against whom society needed protection, seems to be passing, and with the new, earnest resolve to try and fit them for a better life, which, without God's help, can never be done, we are looking forward to greatly improved opportunities. In India, as has already been noted, many persons belonging to the criminal tribes are already under our care, and, wherever we have the opportunity to prove what the power of God can do in such hearts, there can be no doubt of the ultimate result.

Upon the question of temperance, there is happily a widespread awakening amongst the nations. So convinced are all Governments and peoples that drinking and crime are closely connected, that much has already been done, with good effect, to lessen the sale of intoxicants in many lands, and more is being promised. Anxious as we are to see the drink-traffic abolished everywhere, it has never appeared to us to be desirable to join in agitations of a political kind on the subject. And the wisdom of this attitude has been shown, on both sides of the Atlantic, by the manner in which this question has been used to embitter party strife. But it was a puzzle at first to know by which course to steer. When a Licensing Bill was before the English House of Commons, The General wrote:—

> "The Licensing Bill has given me much anxiety, mainly because I see so imperfectly what we ought to do. However, we shall do what seems

the best to be done--with what success has to be seen. I am heartily sick of politics and parties, and that, mainly, because they seem to me so insincere.

"What an unsatisfactory thing is life, apart from the real work we do for God and the Salvation of souls! I want more faith, more conquering faith. I must have it.

"I have got work to-day to do that cannot be done without Divine wisdom. I have asked for it. I am asking for it while I write, and, surely, it will be given; and yet it seems as though the Spirit whispers in my ear, 'You will not believe you have it when it is imparted.' But I will. Anyhow, I will make a desperate effort to believe that the Spirit of the living God guides my judgment, however I may feel, or whatever the outcome may be. Pray for me. I cling to life and the work I love so well."

Remarkably enough, the German police, who, more than any other, suspected and watched and restricted us at first, have become the first convinced of the value of our operations, and those in the city of Cologne have been the very first heartily to arrange for our co-operation with them by placing at our disposal a convenient hand-waggon for the transport of helpless drunkards, and by arranging for their officials to call us upon the telephone, whenever such help is needed, instead of taking the poor drunkards to the cells.

This plan was arrived at only after the police had seen the work carried out by our people with an ambulance which required the services of two strong men. But there is reason to suppose that our cordial relationships with the authorities in Cologne and elsewhere are largely due to the good impression made upon them by The General himself. Of his great Meeting in Cologne, attended by many officials, and other persons of influence, he wrote:—

"I had certainly a remarkable Campaign, and my Meeting in Cologne was one of the most remarkable in my history. Oh, it was a moving, hope-inspiring affair. Oh, what wonders the dear Salvation Army may yet accomplish in the Fatherland! I am sure it will be so, whoever lives to see it."

Thank God that he was spared to see another seven years of progress in that direction since this was written.

In Japan, which cannot be supposed to be specially favourable to any Christian Society, we have long had opportunity regularly to visit all persons in custody, and as we have already seen, to invite all girls living an immoral life to come to our Institutions.

Why is there still difficulty in the way of our work for the prisoners, and other needy ones in Christendom? Chiefly, because there are chaplains and others specially appointed to deal with such needs, and who, naturally, do not wish to see others "interfering," as they think, with their parishioners. In very many cases nowadays there is a much better feeling than formerly, and such persons heartily welcome our help, knowing that we never wish to meddle with any one's work, but only to work where others can gain no entrance.

In a certain Australian jail, at the time when men there could be sentenced to death for many crimes other than murder, a condemned man was in such agonies of remorse that none of the warders could get any rest. The help of one of our Officers was greatly desired, but the chaplain would not consent, so that our Officer could not be admitted. In another part of the prison, however, one of our Soldiers was a warder, and those who knew this sought him out and brought him to the distressed sinner, whom he very soon succeeded in leading to the Saviour, who gave him a peace as complete as that which He gave to His companion in crucifixion.

It is by this patience and efficiency that our Officers, wherever they get opportunity, win the favour of authorities, prisoners, and sufferers of every kind. Therefore, we reckon that it can only be a question of time before our way is opened to do far more than ever for the friendless of every land.

In times of special emergency, The General's Officers always find an opportunity to distinguish themselves. Thus, in the last earthquake of Jamaica our Officers in Kingston were said to have been the calmest and readiest to undertake all that needed to be done. In those terrible days, again, of earthquake and fire in San Francisco the Salvationists provided food and shelter for the Chinese, and others of the most despised; and in South Italy such was the impression produced by the way in which our Officers laboured, when Calabria was desolated by earthquake, that our Officer there, Commissioner Cosandey, had the honour of a Knighthood conferred upon him in recognition of the manner in which he had superintended the distribution of blankets and other articles provided out of the Lord Mayor of London's fund, the skill he manifested gaining the approval of both the Italian Government and the British Ambassador there.

We seek neither honours nor rewards, however; but only the opportunity to carry out our first General's plans for the good of all men everywhere.

Chapter XIX
Conquering Death

Only those who have had some experience of a perfect life-partnership—such as existed for thirty-five years between The General and his wife—can form any conception of the sufferings he had to pass through, in connexion with her prolonged illness and death.

She had always been more or less delicate in health, yet had, through nearly all those years, triumphed so completely over weakness and suffering as to be at once one of the happiest of wives and mothers, and the most daring of comrades in the great War.

During much of 1887 she had suffered more than usually, and yet had taken part with him in many great demonstrations; but in February, 1888, new symptoms made their appearance, and she decided upon consulting one of the ablest of London physicians, because she had always dreaded that her end would come, like that of her mother, through cancer, and wished to use every possible care to prolong, as much as might be possible, her days of helpfulness.

When in February, 1888, Sir James Paget told her that she had, undoubtedly, got this disease, and would, probably, not be alive for more than eighteen months or two years, she received the announcement with the greatest calm and fortitude. The General says:—

> "After hearing the verdict of the doctors, she drove home alone. That journey can better be imagined than described. She told me how, as she looked upon the various scenes through the cab windows, it seemed to her as if sentence of death had been passed upon everything; how she had knelt upon the cab floor and wrestled in prayer; and how the realisation of our grief swept over her.

"I shall never forget, in this world or the next, that meeting. I had been watching for the cab, and had run out to meet and help her up the steps. She tried to smile upon me, through her tears; but, drawing me into the room, she unfolded to me gradually the result of her interview. I sat down speechless. She rose from her seat and came and knelt beside me, saying, 'Do you know what was my first thought? That I should not be there to nurse you, at your last hour.'

"I was stunned. I felt as if the whole world was coming to a standstill. She talked like a heroine, like an angel, to me. She talked as she had never talked before. I could say nothing. I could only kneel with her and try to pray.

"I was due in Holland for some large Meetings. I had arranged to travel there that very night. She would not hear of my remaining at home for her sake. Never shall I forget starting out that evening, with the mournful tidings weighing like lead upon my heart. Oh, the conflict of that night journey! I faced two large congregations, and did my best, although it seemed to me that I spoke as one in a dream. Leaving the Meetings to be continued by others, I returned to London the following evening. And then followed, for me, the most painful experience of my life. To go home was anguish. To be away was worse. Life became a burden, almost too heavy to be borne, until God in a very definite manner comforted my heart."

After this, there were two years and a half of such tortures for him to bear! For some time, indeed, Mrs. Booth was still able occasionally to take part with him, even in very large Meetings. But any one can understand how such privileges only increased his sense of coming loss.

Her last address was delivered in the City Temple, on June 21, 1888, and she had to remain for nearly an hour after in the pulpit before she could move.

Nevertheless, she was able to continue her help by writing for our publications, and to individuals, for a long time after this. Before the Self-Denial Week of 1888 she wrote to our Soldiers:—

"Although not able to be at the front of the battle in person, my heart is there, and the greatest pain I suffer arises from my realisation of the vast opportunities of the hour, and of the desperate pressure to which many of my comrades are subject, while I am deprived of the ability to help them, as in days gone by."

In 1889 she wrote:—

"I am now realising, as never before, how much harder it is to suffer than to serve. I can only assure you again, by letter, that my heart is as much with you as ever. Regard no opposition, persecution, or misrepresentation. Millions upon millions wait for us to bring to them the light of life."

To the great Crystal Palace Demonstration of 1889 she sent a message which was displayed in large letters:—

"My place is empty, but my heart is with you. Go forward. Live holy lives. Be true to The Army. God is your strength. Love and seek the lost. God is my salvation and refuge in the storm."

Hers was, indeed, a prolonged storm of suffering, the strain of which upon The General cannot easily be realised. He would go out, time after time, to his great journeys and Meetings with, necessarily, a gnawing uncertainty as to what might occur in his absence, and would be called, again and again, to what he thought might be her last agony, only to see her, after hours of extraordinary pain and weakness, rally again, to suffer more. To the very end her mind continued to be as clear and powerful as of old, so that her intense interest in everything connected with his work made it difficult for The General to realise that she might at any moment be called away from him. Often through the long hours of the night he would watch beside her.

To a party of Officers who visited her in 1889, she said:—

"I feel that at this moment I could put all my children into their graves, and go to a workhouse bed to die, sooner than I could see the principles of The Salvation Army, for which I have lived and struggled, undermined and sacrificed. God will not fail you. Give the children my dear love, and tell them that, if there had been a Salvation Army when I was ten years old, I should have been as good a Soldier then as I am to-day."

To the last she maintained her interest in comrades who were furthest off, as well as in those who were near. To Australians she sent the message:—

"Tell them I look on them and care for them, as for my English children, and that I expect them to gather in many a sorrowing mother's prodigal, who has wandered far from his Father's house."

Of one of those terrible occasions when it seemed as if the end had come, The General writes, in December, 1889:—

"To stand by the side of those you love, and watch the ebbing tide of life, unable to stem it, or to ease the anguish, is an experience of sorrow which words can but poorly describe. There was a strange choking sensation in the throat which threatened suffocation. After several painful struggles there was a great calm, and we felt the end had come."

What a mercy that nobody knew how many months of agony were yet to follow! It was not till October, 1890, that the end really came. She sent that year to The Army for its Self-Denial Week, the message:—

"My Dear Children and Friends,—

"I have loved you much, and in God's strength have helped you a little.

Now, at His call, I am going away from you.

"The War must go on. Self-Denial will prove your love to Christ.

All must do something.

"I send you my blessing. Fight on, and God will be with you.

Victory comes at last. I will meet you in Heaven.

"Catherine Booth."

On October 1st violent haemorrhage set in. The General was telegraphed for, and after days and nights of continual suffering and extreme weakness, she passed away on Saturday afternoon, October 4, 1890.

Writing immediately afterwards, The General said:—

"Ever since our first meeting, now nearly forty years ago, we have been inseparable in spirit; that is, in all the main thoughts and purposes of our lives. Oh, what a loss is mine! It cannot be measured."

And yet, anxious, as in every other case, to make the very best of the funeral for the good of souls, The General rose, by God's grace, so completely above his own feelings as to be able to take part in all the unparalleled services that followed. More than forty thousand people visited the Congress Hall, Clapton, to look upon her remains there, and to pray and give themselves to God in many cases, whilst her favourite hymns were sung by bands of Cadets. The coffin was then removed to the Olympia, the largest covered building we could hire in London, and 30,000 persons passed the turnstiles to attend the funeral service, conducted mostly by signs, according to a printed programme.

The next day, the funeral march was restricted to Officers of whom 3,000 were present; but the crowds which looked on as it passed right through from our Headquarters in the City to the Abney Park Cemetery were beyond all computation. A crowd of 10,000, admitted by ticket, surrounded the grave, where The General spoke, as one newspaper reported, "as a Soldier, who had disciplined his emotion without effort, and straight from the heart." Of his wonderful address, we have only room to quote the final words:—

"What, then, is there left for me to do? Not to count the weeks, the days, and the hours which shall bring me again into her sweet company, seeing that I know not what will be on the morrow, nor what an hour may bring forth. My work is plainly to fill up the weeks, the days, and the hours, and cheer my poor heart as I go along, with the thought that when I have served my Christ and my generation, according to the will of God, which I vow this afternoon I will, to the last drop of my blood, that then she will bid me welcome to the skies, as He bade her. God bless you all! Amen."

And then he knelt and kissed the coffin, and we lowered it into the grave. The Chief of the Staff read a form of Covenant, which thousands repeated, and then we parted.

From that very day The General rose up and went forward, sorrowing, as every one could see, to his last days over his irreparable loss, but never allowing his grief to hinder his labours for those who, amidst their afflictions have no heavenly Comforter.

A still further blow was to fall upon him, only three years later. Mrs. Booth had delighted, especially during her years of suffering, in the fellowship of her second daughter, Emma, who had been married to Commissioner Tucker, in 1890, and who had always seemed to The General to be the nearest representative, in many respects, of her mother. He had gladly given her up to go with her husband to India, and was equally willing for her, later, to go to the United States. But he always kept up a very full correspondence with her. Her last letter to him, written on an American train, said:—

"My Precious General,—

"I am still on the wing. We were at St. Louis on Sunday, where we had, in some respects, a rather remarkable day. The entire feeling of the city has been distinctly different since your visit—the sympathy now is most marked.

"I also spoke for 'fifteen minutes' (stretched a little) in the Merchants Exchange, a huge marble structure. No woman, they say, has ever been heard there before. This was on Saturday at noon, and quite a number of the leading business and money men turned up at Sunday's Meetings.

"Can't write more. How I wonder how you are! Up above us all so high, like a diamond in our sky, though perhaps I ought to say cyclone or race-horse, or—but there is no simile fine enough.

"Good-night! Would that you were here, so that I could say it, and hear all that you would like to say, and then start off again to try and carry out your wishes with better success, as

"Your unfailing Emma."

Alas, alas, for the uncertainties of human life! Little did she imagine that before the letter could reach him she would be gone from another train, for ever from his side.

Her own devotion to the War, from her very childhood, had always been such as to set an example to all who knew her. As head, for ten years, of our Training Home for women Officers, she did more than can ever be known to ensure the purity and excellence of The Army's leaders, so that it may be easily guessed how much her father valued her.

As joint leader with her husband of our forces in India, and afterwards in the United States, she never spared herself, but, in spite of repeated illnesses, and without, in any way, neglecting her duties as mother of six children, she travelled and laboured incessantly.

Starting out at one o'clock in the morning of October 28th, from Colorado, to ride to Chicago, she managed to make a rush-call, between trains, in Kansas

City, to view a new building The Army was about to take as an Industrial Home. Throughout most of the two days' journey, she was in conversation with one or another Officer as to coming extension of the work until, finding that Colonel Addie, whose Province she last passed, had composed a new song, she asked him to sing it over to her, and to repeat three times the last verse, which was as follows:—

> Time and place will cease to know you,
>   Men and things will pass away;
> You'll be moving on to-morrow,
>   You are only here to-day.

Little did either of them imagine how terribly the words were to be verified within four hours of their being sung.

Just as she was leaving her place in one carriage, to go to the sleeping berth prepared for her in another, a tremendous crash announced to all the passengers that the car through which she and one of our Officers were passing had left the rails and been destroyed. Both were buried in the debris. The Colonel (Holland) survived, but Mrs. Booth-Tucker, after lingering in unconsciousness a couple of hours, passed away.

What a blow for The General! He wrote at the end of the year: "This has been, is, and will be, to the end of my earthly chapter, a mysterious and painful dispensation—at least, so it appears at the moment. What God may do for me in the future, and how He may make it work for my good does not at present appear. But He is able to make it mightily helpful to His glory, and the Salvation of souls. With this prospect, God forbid, then, that I should be other than content—nay, filled with praise. I am at present strangely supported and cheered; and not strangely either, for is it not what might have been expected, with so many loving prayers going up to Heaven on my account hour by hour."

Remembering that he had lost not only the most tenderly beloved one left to him, but an Officer holding one of the most important posts he had to fill, we can somewhat estimate the grace that could thus sustain him, and make it possible, even then, to go gladly forward!

Yet again he was to drink the bitter cup of family bereavement, this time affecting his youngest daughter, who had married Commissioner Hellberg, already mentioned as one of our first Swedish Officers.

Not only had he kept all the promise of his first brave and sturdy stand for The Army as a student, but, gaining by every year's experience in various lands, he had shown remarkable ability in many spheres.

With his no less able and devoted wife, he had laboured in India, at International Headquarters, in France and in Switzerland, when consumption, alas! showed itself, and, in spite of all that could be done for him, during years of suffering, in Algiers, and in various resorts of health-seekers, he steadily sank. Though, of course, death had long threatened him, he was caught suddenly at the last, and died in Berlin on the journey homewards to Sweden from South Germany, at a time when his wife could not be with him.

It will be readily understood how much more trying this was to The General than if he had been near to comfort his daughter in all her sorrow. And yet this blow, falling upon him when he was seventy-nine years old, found him no less resolute than ever. He sent this widowed mother out into Denmark, where she was a stranger, to persevere in the fight. She had showed herself, like her father; able to plead at the very grave-side with the crowd, for God.

In connexion with the loss of Mrs. Booth we began a system of special Memorial Services which have been wonderfully blessed. The first one, held on the first anniversary of her death, in the Agricultural Hall—one of the largest buildings in London, was altogether too large for any speaking to be heard. The plan was adopted, therefore, as at the funeral, of a complete form of service, each point of which was indicated on the programme, and by large illuminated signs. By this means the audience, of some 15,000, was able closely and unitedly to join in all the songs and prayers, whilst scenes from Mrs. Booth's life, and messages taken from her writings and from The General's, were also on the great lantern screen passed on to them. Thousands of the most careless and thoughtless were present; but there was no break in the solemnity of the service. Hundreds went as requested, from the Meeting to a room in the stables, to volunteer for life-service as Officers.

What it cost The General to be present on this, and, since then, on similar occasions, specially after his daughter's death, may be imagined; but he never hesitated to endure this, for the sake of the many souls such services have invariably aroused to repentance, faith, and self-sacrifice for the War. Writing, in 1905, to a friend, he says:—

"Were you at the Memorial Service? That was a trying ordeal for me, but I hear that many were benefited. It seems selfish to ask for so many intercessions; but I cannot get on without them. (In all our Memorial Services all present are asked to unite in prayer for the bereaved ones.) The mere fact of my knowing that so large a number of the very elect of the Kingdom are pleading for power and love on my account, helps me forward. God bless and keep and comfort you every day and every hour."

Undoubtedly, these services, whilst blessed to all present, have also served to provoke much prayer and faith for all our bereaved ones, and for The General most of all, and have thus made it easier for him, and for all of us, to triumph over personal sorrows and losses, and press forward to ever-increasing victory.

That The General's example of burying his own sorrows in redoubled effort to cheer and help others has been followed everywhere, may count as large compensation for all he has lost. And yet, all who knew him best, have seen that the wound caused by Mrs. Booth's loss was never healed. With the badge of bereavement, which we have substituted for any costly mourning, ever upon his left arm, just as it was twenty years ago, our first General went onward to the great re-union above, "as sorrowful, yet always rejoicing," his sadness ever touching as many hearts as his merry remarks aroused.

Curiously enough, The General, whilst anxious at all times to remind every one of death and judgment, and to prevent their being so intoxicated by pleasure and passing trivialities as to prevent their thinking of their souls and of eternity, abolished, so far as his followers were concerned, the horrible formalities which, in all countries have come to be thought necessary whenever death and the grave come into view.

Nothing could be more opposed to everything taught by Christ than the usual processes of "Christian burial," and the records of "the departed." He who "brought life and immortality to light" through His Gospel could not wish to see His people's graves surrounded exclusively by signs of mourning, and then plastered over with flattering records of earthly glory, making, as a rule, no mention of His Salvation, and the eternal glories it assures. He manifested, indeed, and always shows the deepest sympathy with our sorrows; but He does so most by teaching us to make them steps to higher life and joy.

This great purpose The General aimed at in all his arrangements as to burials, and thus alleviated sadness, and turned death into victory to a very remarkable extent. No widow or orphan under his Flag will add to all the inevitable costs of nursing the dying those of fashionable "mourning," clothing, flowers, or monuments. The cross and crown badge worn on the left arm by himself and his bereaved ones, sometimes for years, whilst providing a most touching token of abiding affection for lost friends, is, at the same time, a special declaration of faith and hope, and yet obviates entirely the need for any peculiar dress "for the occasion."

Every funeral thus becomes a very valuable opportunity for comforting and strengthening the mourners, and for urging the unsaved to ensure an eternal triumph. It would not be easy to compute the total of crowds thus brought under the sound of the Gospel, in connexion with our losses, every year.

Thus all these occasions for sadness have been turned into fountains of joy, not merely to those most immediately concerned, but to the whole community. We have not yet had time or opportunity, thank God! sufficiently to redeem the grave and the cemetery from the scandal of men-praising expenditure, for any sort of tombstone has generally been too costly for our people. But the small, simple edgestone which marks the resting-place of "Catherine Booth, Mother of The Salvation Army," and which asks every passer-by, "Do you also follow Christ?" has set an example, consistent with all our past and our eternal future.

Surely, the day will come when our General's teaching and practice in this matter will help to lighten the burden of every bereaved family, and make every cemetery the birthplace of crowds of souls. The music and song with which we surround every deathbed and funeral, still too much tinged sometimes with the follies of traditional show, have already been used by God's Spirit to bring life and gladness to many a spiritually dead soul.

Chapter XX
His Social Work

Most erroneously and unfairly it has been widely assumed that the great work of The General was the establishment in the world of some Social Institutions. Happily, we have got a verbatim report of an address to his Social Officers gathered around him a year before his death in which we have a complete statement as to the beginnings and principles of the work, so that we can see exactly how he wished it to be regarded.

1. By the Social Work, I mean those operations of The Salvation Army which have to do with the alleviation, or removal, of the moral and temporal evils which cause so much of the misery of the submerged classes, and which so greatly hinder their Salvation.

2. Our Social Operations, as thus defined, are the natural outcome of Salvationism, or, I might say, of Christianity, as instituted, described, proclaimed, and exemplified in the life, teaching, and sacrifice of Jesus Christ.

Here I would like to say that Social Work, in the spirit and practice which it has assumed with us, has harmonised with my own personal idea of true religion from the hour I promised obedience to the commands of God.

To help the poor, to minister to them in their slums, to sympathise with them in their poverty, afflictions, and irreligion, was the natural outcome of the life that came to my soul through believing in Jesus Christ.

Before many days—nay, before many hours—had passed after my conversion, I was to be found praying in the cottages in the working-class quarters of the town in which I lived, talking in the slums, comforting the dying, and doing, so far as I knew how and had ability, what seemed to me most likely to help the poor and miserable classes, both for this world and the world to come.

3. But Social Work, as a separate entity, or department of the Kingdom of Jesus Christ, recognised, organised, and provided for, had to wait for The Salvation Army.

For many years after the commencement of my public work, during which time I had, as opportunity served, helped the poor in their distress, I was deterred from launching out to any great extent in this direction by the fear so commonly entertained that by relieving their physical necessities I should be helping to create, or at any rate to encourage, religious hypocrisy and pretence.

All this time, nevertheless, I felt, and often keenly felt, that there surely must be some way by which, without any evil consequences, I could legitimately fulfil the cravings of my own heart, as well as comply with the commands of my Lord, who had expressly told me that I was to feed the hungry, clothe the naked, care for the sick, and visit the prisoners. For a long time, however, I failed to see how this work could be done in any organised or extensive manner.

Gradually, however, the way opened, and opened largely, as a result of our determination to make the godless crowds hear the message of Salvation.

I said, "They shall hear; we will make them hear; and if they won't hear in any other way, we will feed them, and accompany the food we give them with the message to which they so determinedly turn a deaf ear." In the very earliest days of The Army, therefore, in order to reach the people whom we could not reach by any other means, we gave the hungry wretches a meal, and then talked to them about God and eternity.

4. Then came the gradual unfolding of our Social methods, which have been so remarkably successful.

My dear wife's heart had been particularly drawn out on behalf of the fallen outcasts of society, who, often more sinned against than sinning, appealed peculiarly to her large and tender sympathies. More than once she found opportunity for extending help to individual cases of misfortune, obtaining homes amongst her friends for some of the children, and assisting the poor mothers to win their way back to virtue.

But it was not until the end of 1883, or thereabouts, that anything like a systematic effort in this direction was organised on their behalf. Touched by the helpless and pitiable condition of some poor girls who had sought Salvation at the Corps at which, with her husband, she fought as a Soldier, a baker's wife, living in one of the most wretched streets in Spitalfields, took the girls, in distress and trouble, into her own home. Before long it was crowded to its utmost capacity, and still other women were clamouring for admission. She implored us to help her, and we engaged and opened a house as our first Rescue Home, placing it under the direction of Mrs. Bramwell Booth.

The breaking forth of the same spirit in different directions in other lands quickly followed.

At about this time our first Prison Rescue Brigade, in the Colony of Victoria, was organised by the late Colonel Barker. So striking was the success attending his effort that, before many months had passed by, magistrates in the city of Melbourne were actually giving delinquents the option of being sent to prison or to our Prison-Gate Home, and the Government placed the former Detective Police Building at our disposal, at a nominal rental.

Not only does the genuine Christian spirit carry the soul out in sympathy with misery, but it often leads it to prefer certain particular classes of sufferers or wrong-doers, on whom to lavish its self-sacrificing love, and restlessly spend itself in efforts for their benefit. In the case of one Salvationist, it will be the dying; in another the daughters of sin and shame; in another the homeless; in another the children, and in yet another the drunkards.

With Colonel Barker, as with other comrades under our Flag to-day, it was the criminals.

This spirit thrives and becomes more effective by what it feeds upon. It must, therefore, be wise to favour its preferences, so far as it is possible to do so without losing sight of the well-being of the whole.

We did this with Colonel Barker, and we are acting on the same principle with others to-day.

Then came our first Women's Rescue Home in Melbourne, to help us in the establishment of which the Colonial Government gave L1,000.

It was upon foundations of this character that our Social Operations in New Zealand, France, South Africa, and several other countries were subsequently built up.

For years past our Officers, men and women, both in the United Kingdom and elsewhere, had carried on what may be spoken of as an unorganised form of Slum

Work; but it fell to the hands of my glorified daughter, the Consul, to institute, in London, what was then and for some time afterwards known as "the Cellar, Gutter, and Garret Brigade"—the forerunner of scores of Slum Posts, which are now such a recognised feature of our operations all over the world.

Our first Men's Shelter was opened in Limehouse, London, during the winter of 1887-8, and was soon followed by the opening of similar Institutions in other countries, far-off and near at hand.

From our earliest days drunkenness had been one of the many foes of God and man against which we had specially taken our stand, and thousands of its slaves had been rescued from its grip, and become valiant Soldiers in our ranks. Our first Inebriates' Home, conducted in the interest of women, was not, however, opened until 1887. This was in Toronto, Canada.

The Social Work in the United States had its birth in 1885, in an effort made on behalf of prisoners at Hartford, Connecticut. Similar efforts followed in other cities, and Rescue and Industrial Homes, Shelters, and Farm Colonies followed on in due course.

All these enterprises and many others, to which I have not time now to refer, were prior to the publication of "In Darkest England and the Way Out," and had, no doubt, a powerful influence in inspiring that volume.

Since then one branch or other of Social Work has been commenced in every country in which our Flag is flying.

Notwithstanding the satisfaction produced by these and kindred efforts in my own mind, and in the minds of those immediately associated with me, and although the results were truly remarkable, and the possibilities seemed to be still more wonderful, the beginnings of these Social enterprises attracted comparatively little notice.

The New Movement—for thus I may describe it—which, with half an eye, thoughtful men might have seen to be pregnant with blessings for the whole world, was almost unnoticed by either the Authorities or the Press; while our supplies of men and money for its conduct and extension were very limited.

Suddenly, however, the scene was changed, and, all at once, everybody was asking, "What is The Salvation Army?" "Who is General Booth?" and "What is this Social Scheme?"

This change was largely brought about by the publication of "In Darkest England and the Way Out," together with the notices of the Scheme in the Press which it brought about.

Judged by the effect produced, the book was certainly a remarkable one. In the first place it had a title which, in a striking manner described its character. Everybody wanted to see it, and, as a result, it was sold, lent, read, thought about, and talked about in every direction. Nearly a quarter of a million copies were sold. The profits from the publication and sale amounted to about L20,000, of which sum I had the privilege of handing over L5,380—which might have been considered rightfully to accrue to me personally as the Author—to the fund devoted to the promotion of the object for which the book was published.

In its pages I propounded those Schemes which I thought would prove most successful in alleviating the terrible misery I had described, and in rescuing some, at least, of the sufferers from the conduct that produced it.

In order to set the Scheme in motion, I asked the public to give me L100,000, and a further L30,000 per annum to maintain it.

I can never forget the morning that directly followed the appearance of the volume. I was, of course, in ignorance of what the nation would think or say about it.

I had made plans for the book to be delivered to the newspapers at one and the same time, and, regarding the Press as being to some extent the voice of the people, I was anxious to hear what that voice would say.

I was not kept long in suspense. As I ascended the stairs at Headquarters that morning, a gentleman with a countenance beaming with kindness and anxiety met me. I do not think he had ever seen me before, and I was certainly in complete ignorance of him.

"General Booth, I believe?" he said.

"Yes, sir," I answered.

"I have been reading the critique in *The Times* of your Darkest England Scheme," he said, "and, believing your plan to be right and good, I want to be the first to express my sympathy and practical assistance in carrying it out, and I wish to give you the first L1,000 towards the sum asked for."

This gentleman proved himself a firm friend of the Scheme, actively co-operating with us so far as he had opportunity.

A short time afterwards our friend was present at the opening of our first London Ex-Prisoners' Home. When I had finished speaking he expressed a wish to say a few words. I invited him forward for that purpose. He came, hurried and excited, began to speak, staggered, reeled, fell into my arms and immediately expired. It may be truly said that he died calling down blessings on the Darkest England Scheme.

After meeting this gentleman on the stairs, I had scarcely sat down at my desk, with his cheque in my hand, before a telegram was handed me, from one of the most influential newspaper proprietors in the city, expressing a similar hope, and promising a similar amount for its realisation.

But along with these cheering expressions of approbation there came the invariable murmuring objections. One of these strove to minimise the value of the effort, by arguing that it was only an attempt to extend The Army's religious influence. People said they would be willing to help if all religious and propagandist motives were eliminated from the Scheme.

One night a gentleman was announced as wishing to see me. He declined to give his name, and the only description of him I could gain was that he was a prominent member of the Stock Exchange.

"I want to ask you one question—only one," he said, upon entering my office, "about this Social Scheme of yours."

"All right," I replied, "as many as you like."

"Well," he continued, "I want to know whether you are going to give religion alongside your other benefits to these people whom you seek to help? I am not a religious man myself. I am not saved, and never shall be—I am a lost soul; but there is no reason why these poor wretches should not have religion; and if you will give them religion, I will help you."

"Yes," I answered, "we will give them religion. While we won't refuse to help them because they are irreligious—but, on the contrary, will take in the vilest and the worst—we will give them all as much religion as we can."

"I will help you," he answered, as he handed me Bank of England notes for L500.

He came to see us again and again, proving for the time being a generous friend. Then he disappeared.

In a very short time, and in the readiest and most kindly manner, L104,000 were subscribed. But, alas! only a very small proportion of the L30,000 that was asked for annually was forthcoming.

In this, as in many other similar cases, I have found that whilst the public will be ready—nay, eager—to embrace a new thing, they soon get tired of it, run after some other novelty, and leave you largely to struggle for its continuance, as best you can.

5. It is enough here to state that the results at the onset were remarkable. Amongst others four, which might have been expected, were immediately realised:—

(a) The first was the bringing into public view the ocean of tears, misery, and evil which was rolling around us in every direction.

(b) Another result was that people everywhere were awakened from their selfish lethargy, to look upon these waters of tribulation, and were amazed to find the depth, the darkness, and the despair with which they rolled forward, as well as the damnation to which they invariably led.

(c) A further effect was that a large number of people were won over to care for the class whom it was proposed to benefit, and to believe in the possibility of the Scheme being realised. Many of these proved permanent friends of our Social Operations.

(d) Yet another effect was that the fountains of compassion broke out in the hearts of large numbers of individuals, and led them to make similar efforts. Everywhere the call was sounded to labour for these poor lost people, and instances were adduced which showed that their humble toil was productive of very striking results.

But until now nothing, or next to nothing, had been done to stop this rolling river, or deliver those perishing in its waters, because everybody had felt helpless in the presence of the enormous evil.

But here, now, were results of sufficient magnitude to convince those who became interested in the matter that, by the employment of the methods set forth in "In Darkest England and the Way Out," something permanently effective might be accomplished.

On the other hand, others, as might have been expected, who had never manifested any particular interest before, either for or against, now came out openly as our enemies, and a stiff fight followed, out of which the Social Operations, although in their infancy, may be said to have emerged victorious.

One of the results of this conflict of opinion was the "Darkest England" Inquiry.

The preparation of "In Darkest England" will for ever remain remarkable in my own memory, as it was mostly written and corrected in the adjoining chamber to that in which my dear wife was suffering those awful agonies associated with the disease which finally carried her away.

The spirit which originated and controlled the Social Work had been, pre-eminently, the spirit of her religion. She certainly was the most practical exponent of the Christianity of which I have been speaking that it was ever my lot to meet. It was her religion; she preached it with natural eloquence and remarkable skill; and, in life and death, she exemplified it.

From that day to this the history of the Social Work has been one of steady progress and of surpassing interest, and I have sometimes wondered whether any movement, based so solidly upon principles of permanence, and so calculated to bless the classes for whose benefit it was, by the Providence of God, called into being, has ever existed within the memory of men.

Now what has come out of this beginning?

1. Here is a list of the various Social enterprises we have in hand. I do not vouch for its completeness; but, anyway, we have here a goodly number of schemes for the benefit of the poor and friendless already in active and useful operation:—

(a) For the Starving, we have— i. Children's Free and Farthing Breakfasts. ii. Midnight Soup and Bread Brigades for the Homeless. iii. Cheap Food Depots. iv. Special Relief Funds for cases of Special Destitution. v. Old Clothes' Depots for Slum Families. vi. Poor Men's Hotels, vii. Cheap Grain Stores. viii. Famine Loan Fund for Destitute Indians.

(b) For the Drunkards, we have— i. Drunkards' Brigades. ii. Midnight Drunkards' Brigades (of use also in any sudden emergency—Fire, Flood, etc.). iii. Drunkards' Advice Bureaux. iv. Homes for Inebriates—Men and Women.

(c) For the Paupers, we have— i. Workhouse Brigades. ii. Salvation Guardians of the Poor. iii. Pauper Colonies. iv. Pauper Transportation. v. Labour Bureaux, vi.

Homes for the Aged.

(d) For the Unemployed, we have— i. Labour Bureaux—Men and Women, ii. Industrial Homes. iii. Labour Wood Yards. iv. City Salvage Brigades. v. Workshops.

(e) For the Homeless, we have— i. Midnight Scouts. ii. Shelters for Men and Women. iii. Metropoles.

(f) For the Criminals, we have— i. Prison Visitation. ii. Police-court Work. iii. Prison-Gate Work. iv. Probationary Police. v. Correspondence Bureaux. vi. Ex-Criminals' Homes. vii. Criminal Settlements

(g) For the Daughters of Shame, we have— i. Visitation of Streets, Brothels, Yoshiwaras, Clubs, etc. ii. Midnight Meetings. iii. Receiving Homes. iv. Rescue Homes. v. Factories, Laundries, etc. vi. "Out of Love" Funds. vii. Service Girls' Brigades. viii. Shepherding Brigades. ix. Maternity Homes. x. Investigation and Detective Department.

(h) Slum Work. We have— i. Visitation. ii. First-Aid Brigades. iii. District Nursing. iv. "Poorest of the Poor" Aid.

(i) For the Sick, we have— i. Visitation. ii. Hospitals. iii. Dispensaries. iv. Village Dispensing, v. Leper Hospitals, vi. Maternity Nursing.

(j) For the Lost, we have— i. Inquiry and Correspondence Bureaux. ii. Legal Assistance.

(k) Prevention and Protective Work for Young Girls. We have— i. Servants' Homes. ii. City Institutes. iii. Theatrical Girls' Home. iv. Registries. v. Students' Homes.

(l) Anti-Suicide Bureaux. We have— i. Advice Department. ii. Loan Department.

(m) The Home League.

(n) Land Schemes. We have—

i. Emigration. ii. Home Colonisation. iii. Colonisation over the Sea. iv. Lands and Farm Colonies. v. Small Holdings.

(o) Deep Sea Brigades. We have—

i. Mission Boats. ii. Life-boat.

(p) Training Colleges.

(q) Students' Homes.

(r) Working-Men's Association.

(s) Village Banks.

The total number of our Social Institutions is now 954.

The value of properties, etc., held for the use of our Social Operations is:—

At Home (U.K.) £ 228,000

In other Countries 747,000

Total £ 975,000

2. In the history of the Social Work, nevertheless, there have been, as you will know, any number of shortcomings. We have not realised all our expectations, nor fulfilled all our dreams. It was not to be expected that we should. This is an imperfect world; the Movement has been imperfect, and the people who have carried it on have been imperfect also. Consequently, it is only natural that we have had imperfect results.

(a) Many things have been calculated to cause these shortcomings. For example:—

i. There has been a great lack of direct aim at the true goal of our Social Work on the part of some Officers who have been engaged in its direction.

Some of our comrades have been content with a "soup-and-blanket" regime. That is to say, they have too often been satisfied with the alleviation of the miseries of the hour, and have stopped short of the removal of the evils that have caused the poverty, vice, and agony from which the sufferings sprang.

Consequently, the work, being superficial, has in some cases only had superficial and temporary results.

You get out of a thing as much as you put in—and no more, and that, not only in quantity, but in quality. If you go in for root-and-branch efforts, you will get root-and-branch results.

ii. Another cause of our shortcomings has been the lamentable fact that some of our Officers have been deficient in personal religion.

Our Social Work is essentially a religious business. It can neither be contemplated, commenced, nor carried on, with any great success, without a heart full of pity, and love, and endued with the power of the Holy Ghost.

iii. Another of our difficulties has been the scarcity of suitable people for carrying the work on. This was also to be expected.

If we had been content with hirelings, and had sought them out from among the philanthropies and Churches, we should have found plenty in number, but it is equally certain we should have had considerably more doleful failures than those we have experienced.

We are not only making but are now training the Social Officers, and we shall doubtless improve in this respect, whilst the work they turn out will be bound to improve proportionately.

iv. Then again a further reason for our shortcomings has been our shortness of money.

This need unfortunately is not passing away, as you will all well know. But I suppose some of you have come from distant lands with bags of francs and dollars to present The General with an ample supply of this requirement. He thanks you beforehand.

(b) Nevertheless, and notwithstanding all our shortcomings, the position now occupied by our Social Operations, and the influence exercised by them on the great and small of the earth, is in evidence in every Continent and on every hand.

There is no doubt that the world, as a whole, feels much of the admiration and gratitude which the Press lavished upon me on my recent Birthday—admiration which was assuredly intended not only for myself, but for The Army as a whole, and not only for The Army as a whole, but for its Social Workers in particular.

1. And now, in conclusion, let me summarise a few of the advantages which have flowed out of the Social Work, and which will continue to flow out of it as long as time rolls on.

(a) The first benefit I will mention is the Salvation of thousands of souls.

(b) The world has been further benefited by the knowledge of Salvation spread throughout every part of the habitable globe.

(c) The world has been further benefited by the Conviction that has been brought to governmental, philanthropic, and religious agencies, as to the duty they owe to the classes we seek to benefit.

(d) The world has been further benefited by the sympathy created in the hearts of royal personages, scientists, literary people, and the Press generally; indeed, in every class and grade of mankind.

(e) The world has been further benefited by the removal of misery on such an extensive scale as had never even been dreamed of as possible.

Think of the multitudes who, by our operations, are daily saved from starvation, vice, crime, disease, death, and a hundred other nameless woes.

In some of the principal cities in Italy, Holland, Germany, and elsewhere, visited during my recent Continental Campaign, I have been looked upon with unspeakable satisfaction and enthusiasm as The General of the Poor, and The Salvation Army has been regarded as their friend.

(f) The world has been further benefited by the help which our Social Operations have afforded to the Field and other Departments of The Army all over the world.

(g) The world has been further benefited by the confidence the Social Work has created in the hearts and minds of our own people—both Officers and Soldiers—as to the truth and righteousness of the principles and practices of The Salvation Army.

(h) The world has been further benefited by the answer which the Social Work constitutes to the infidel's sneers at Christianity and the assertion of its effeteness.

Truly, our future chroniclers will have to record the fact that our Social Operations added a celestial lustre and imparted a Divine dignity to the struggles of the early years of The Salvation Army's history.

To our own eyes in The Army, however, that which has been done in connexion with the Institutions is only a very insignificant part of the whole effect produced. Until the present movement all over the world in favour of the betterment of the social condition of the masses of the people has had time to accomplish definite results, our Institutions may yet have a good work to do.

But the great work The General did in this connexion was the restoration to men's minds of the Saviour's own view, that we owed to every man every care that a truly brotherly heart must needs bestow. That principle, as The General pointed out, had always been acted upon, as best it could be, from the beginning, and is daily acted upon to-day, wherever The Army exists.

Chapter XXI
Motoring Triumphs

During one of his Motor Tours The General remarked:—

"It was here (Banbury) that the idea of a Motor Campaign was conceived. Seven or eight years ago (1900) I held an afternoon Meeting in this place. On that occasion a crowd of my own people and friends came to the station to give me a send-off. Such was the affection shown, and so manifest was the pleasure derived from my visit, that I said to myself:—

"'Why should I not impart this satisfaction to those comrades and friends throughout the country who have never had the satisfaction of seeing my face, or hearing my voice?'

"And then the idea occurred to my mind that the automobile would not only be the readiest means of transit, but the only plan by which I could reach the small towns and outlying hamlets. Moreover, it would perhaps prove the only method by which we could get through the crowds who would be likely to assemble on such a Campaign."

By most men, in their prime, it would be thought an ample filling up of any week to address three large Meetings on the Sunday, and one each week night; but The General, at seventy-four, saw that, travelling by motor, and visiting in the daytime such smaller towns and villages as had never seen him before, or not for many years, he could not only reckon upon three large indoor Meetings every day, but speak, perhaps, to millions of people he had never before addressed. And so in six Motor Tours he passed from end to end and from side to side of Great Britain, gathering crowds from day to day for six weeks at a time.

We have met with people frivolous enough to write of all that as if The General's Motor Tours were luxuries! In one glorious sense they were really so, for, to him, there could never be a greater luxury than to proclaim the Gospel to a crowd. But, as a matter of fact, he found it less expensive to travel in this way than to go as he ordinarily did for a long journey to and from London by train to reach each town separately.

And the economy of Army forces, by means of Motor Tours, has been marvellous, every little Corps and village Outpost on the route on week-days being given an opportunity to gather crowds they never ordinarily reached together, and to unite their own efforts for once with those of their General in trying to lift up Christ more than ever before.

And The General was so alive to the value of inflaming the love of any handful of villagers or children, but especially of his Soldiers and Officers to the Master, that it was to him a continual delight to move about amongst his Soldiery in every land.

The General could rarely venture to plan very far ahead, because his public appearances had all to be made to fit in with other and often even more important engagements, of which only his Staff knew anything. It is, indeed, marvellous how few engagements he made ever had to be broken, and how successful almost every Campaign of his has been, seeing at how short notice most of them were undertaken. In one of his diaries I found a bitter complaint of the waste of time involved in having to wait for three hours between the steamboat and train. "Why," he asks, "could they not have arranged a Meeting for me?"

One who has travelled 8,000 miles with him on four Motor Tours says, though everybody, everywhere, pressmen included, were of necessity impressed with his sincerity and transparency, they could see that he had all the time only one object in view, the glory of God and the Salvation of souls.

And it is the extent to which he led all ranks into the same spirit which made it easy for arrangements to be made and carried out in so few hours for the very largest demonstrations, as to which it was never possible to hold any approach to a rehearsal, those joining in them living usually so widely apart from each other.

An occasional private letter gives, perhaps, the best possible explanation of his own heart in this perpetual motion towards the Cross. Who that saw him in some grand demonstration could imagine that he had been feeling just before it as this letter reveals:—

"My feelings alternate; but my faith is steadfast. Morning, noon, and night I tell God He is my only help. He will not fail me. To-night's Meeting will be, as you say, a great strain; but the memories of God's goodness encourage me to go forward in spite of unutterable sadness and gloom."

And who that heard him on one of those Congresses, in which a great company of his Officers and Soldiers felt themselves to be feasting on heavenly manna for days together, could imagine his writing the week after:—

"If ever I felt my full agreement with my Lord's definition of service as expressed in the parable, I do to-day. After all, I am a poor, unprofitable servant, and I have lost no little sleep since Friday night in criticising regretfully and condemning my share of the wonderful Congress that has certainly taken a large part of the world by storm. Nevertheless, I thank God from the bottom of my heart for the part I have been allowed to have in the matter."

Amongst the incidents of all touring, but especially of motoring, are storms such as the one The General thus triumphed over:—

"We are still rushing on. I had five Meetings yesterday, Friday, and an hour's ride through the most blinding storm I ever encountered. Two of our cars broke down, gave up, and retreated to the nearest town for the night; another got through in a damaged condition, and three with difficulty arrived at our destination. However, we who did get in, were rewarded with a big audience and a big reception. It was very wonderful. I am now reckoning on the closing Meeting which takes place on Wednesday afternoon.

"Everybody continues to bless me and speak well of me. Is it not a little surprising, and, viewed from the Master's Standpoint, a little dangerous? You must keep on praying that my faith fail not. Abundance of trying things await me. I must wait for my rest 'until the Morning.' God bless you!"

Well may a man sometimes long for rest who has experiences like the following:—

"I nearly killed myself on Saturday and Sunday at Birmingham. For some cause or other both throat and head got wrong, and it was with difficulty I could frame my sentences or pronounce my words, and yet I had to meet the great opportunity that was presented. I am paying the price to-day in weariness extreme. There is hardly a bone in my body that does not ache, or a nerve that does not seem overstrung.

"But I shall rally and be myself again; indeed, I must, for things of vast importance have to be attended to before the day is out. Our exchequer is empty, and I have to prepare for my autumn Campaign in Holland, Germany, Italy, etc."

"A mile or two after Penzance, the chauffeur turned to General Booth, and 'Now she's waking up!' he said, with a satisfied sigh, as the great car began to hurry through the open lanes.

"The General nodded his head meditatively. 'Yes,' he said, in his beard, 'people have to wake up before they begin to move. England wants waking up; I'm trying to wake her up myself, just a little, and then we shall move.'

"I asked him what he made of our national apathy.

"He shook his head. 'I don't know how it is," he said, 'but people are somehow afraid to examine themselves, afraid to see facts as facts. There is a spirit in England which is worse than opposition to religion; it's a spirit of—of—of detachment, of separation, a spirit which says, "I don't want you, I can do without you; and so long as you leave me alone I shan't interfere with you." It's a kind of slackness. They want waking up. They want rousing. They want a good shaking. It seems as if they have fallen into a deep slumber—opium-eaters!'

"He is setting out to rouse England once again, make one great final effort for the future of humanity. The future of humanity, he believes, can only be secured by 'conversion.'

"Look at him in his car! There he sits, with a light-coloured overcoat buttoned round his neck, a grey forage cap pressed over his ears, his hands in his pockets, his eyes looking straight ahead, and his lips biting at his beard—an old, old man in the newest of motor-cars.

"Through lanes where Wesley rode his horse, poring over a book as he went, General Booth flies in his beflagged car—on the same errand. These two men, so dissimilar in nature, so opposed in temperament, and separated by nearly two hundred years, the one on horseback, the other in a motor-car, sought and are seeking the same elusive end—the betterment of humanity.

"One feels as one rides along our country roads with General Booth the enormous force of simple Christianity in this work of evolution. One sees why Wesley succeeded, and why The Salvation Army is succeeding.

"'We make too much of sin,' says evolution. 'We don't make half enough of sin!' cries The General. Politicians and men of science seem like scene-shifters in the drama of life, and religion stands out clear and distinct as the only actor.

"'People have taken to The Salvation Army because it's so kind to poor people,' General Booth tells me; 'they know I love the poor, they know I weep bitterly for all the hunger and nakedness and sorrow in the world. People know I'm sincere. That's it! They know The Salvation Army is sincere, that it's doing kind actions, and helping those whom nobody else will help or can help. That's what makes us popular. Sympathy.'

"But the secret of The General is not humaneness. His secret is the reality with which he invests sin. Hear him talk about sin, and you realise the man's spell.

"At one moment he is full of humour and robust talk, a genial, merry, shrewd-eyed old gentleman; at the next—at the mention of real sin—his brows contract, his eyes flash, and his tongue hisses out such hatred and contempt and detestation as no sybarite could find on the tip of his tongue for anything superlatively coarse or ill-flavoured.

"'Sin!' he cries to me. 'Sin is a real thing—a damnable thing! I don't care what science calls it, or what some of the pulpits are calling it. I know what it is. Sin is devilish. It is sin and only sin which is stopping progress. It is sin and only sin which prevents the world from being happy. Sin! Go into the slums of the great cities—pick up little girls of six years of age sold into infamy by their parents; look at the drunken mother murdering her child, the father strapping his cripple son—sin!—that's what I call sin; something beastly and filthy and devilish and nasty—nasty, dreadfully nasty.'

"As you listen and as you realise that The Salvation Army contains numberless men changed in the twinkling of an eye from lives of such sin as this to lives of beneficent activity, you begin to feel that General Booth, right or wrong, has at least hit upon one of the most effective ways for helping evolution.

"He makes sin as real to the individual as only the mystics can imagine for themselves. Perhaps humanity likes to be told how black it is, how far it is from the perfectness after which Nature is blundering and staggering. I know not; but it is manifest that when this grim old man, with the ivory face, the black, flashing eyes, the tangle of white hair and the tangle of beard, leans over the rostrum and calls sin 'beastly' and 'devilish' and 'nasty' the people sit as white and spellbound as the patient of the hypnotist.

"It is a different General Booth whom the villagers flock to see as he drives, smiling and genial, through Cornish villages, whom the band plays into towns, and whom mayors and councillors receive with honour. But the reason of this honour and this popularity is the fact that he is a force, a living, breathing power who has made sin real to the world and has awakened the religious consciousness in thousands of human beings."

William Booth was always very wide awake to the discouraging emptiness of mere demonstrations, and never expressed himself more contemptuously with regard to them than when he thought that any of his Officers, in the midst of some grand display, which was attracting unusual attention, seemed to be likely to be satisfied with the show of what had been done, instead of pressing forward to greater things.

Yet he saw that, in presence of the continual and enthralling exhibitions of the world, there was absolute need for such manifestations of united force as might encourage every little handful, usually toiling out of sight, and convince the world that we were determined fully to overcome all its attractions.

There had been before his time large demonstrations in favour of teetotalism, and in some parts of the country the Sunday Schools were accustomed annually to make displays of more or less fashionably-dressed children and teachers. But The General was alone in his own country and time in organising any such public demonstrations in honour of Christ, and of total abstinence from sin and from worldly-mindedness.

How perfectly The General could always distinguish between the enjoyment of demonstration and of real fighting, was strikingly manifested on one of our great Crystal Palace days. Looking down from the balcony upon the vast display, when some 50,000 Salvationists were taking part in various celebrations, he noticed a comparatively small ring of our converted military and naval men kneeling together on the grass, evidently within hearing of one of the band-stands upon which one Band after another was playing, according to programme.

"Go and stop that Band," said he to one of his A.D.C.'s. "We must not have those praying men hindered in their fight for souls by the music."

And this was only one example of his frequent abandonment of any programme, or practice, or arrangement which seemed to him only to have demonstrative effect, when any more enduring benefit could be otherwise secured.

In short, demonstration in his eyes was only valued at its military worth, and he never wished any one to become so occupied with appearance as to miss enduring victory.

The following description, by a writer in a big London daily, of one of The General's tours might be fairly accepted as a sample of them all, and as giving some idea of the way in which they manifested his care for all that concerned men:—

"'An easy day' was The General's description of that on which we fared to mediaeval Godalming, through the beautiful Hindhead region to Petersfield, and thence in the evening to antiquity and Winchester. He meant that he had only to address three great gatherings (the day's course admitted of scarcely any of the customary wayside and hamlet musters), so his oratory would be merely a matter of five hours or thereabouts. There were solid fact in The General's airy designation; it ***was*** an easier day than most of those of the tour; but it had sundry distinctions of its own, apart from the great, welcoming Meetings.

"It was curious and pleasant to see gipsies salute The General from their wayside Bohemia on the road to Hindhead; it was delightful to see The General himself as he descended and spoke to the church school-children who hailed him by the wayside at Roke, in one of the most charming wayside spots on the journey. They stood with their teachers under the trees in the sunshine, little pictures of bloom and happiness. 'Now wouldn't you like to be running round the country on a motor?' he asked them straight away, and their answer come with hearty directness. In a naive and tender little speech, that had a touch of airiness, he told them of the joy of motoring, turning anon to the many glad and beautiful things within the reach of little people who yet might not go a-motoring, and so in simple little touches appealing to the joy of life and soul that the child-sense could understand.

"'Isn't he like Father Christmas?' a little girl was heard to whisper. Here he charmed those in the morning of life; away at Petersfield in the afternoon the sight of him consoled some in life's evening. One poor old lady, who had lost the use of both limbs, was carried to her door and set in a bath-chair, and there she remained till The General had passed. We noticed the light on her face, and how vehemently she waved her handkerchief. An Army Officer chatted with her before we left the town in the evening. 'I can now die happy,' she said; 'I have seen The General. And when the call comes I know that God will send down the hallelujah motor for me, and the loss of my old limbs won't matter in the least.'

"I have mentioned 'an easy day.' Having now described in a broad way the typical early stages, it may be well, in a somewhat more intimate and personal way, to give an idea of the work, moods, and trend of the average day of the whole tour. The stress and excitement it meant in the long stretch of country from the first town to the last were extraordinary. We mustered, as a rule, at nine in the morning for the day's work and travel, most of the folk of the town where the night had been spent turning out for the send-off.

"The General was on the scene almost invariably to the minute. Nearly always at those starts he looked grave, resigned, and calm, but unexpectedly careworn. It was as if he had wrestled with all his problems, with a hundred world-issues in the watches of the night, and was still in the throes of them, and unable for the moment to concentrate his attention on the immediate town and crowd that hurrah'd around him. But, of course, he stood up and acknowledged the plaudits—though often as one in a dream. But the picturesqueness of his appearance in the morning sunshine—with his white hair, grave face, and green motor garb—took the imagination of the mass, and without a word from him the people were left happy.

"He looked a new personality at the first important stopping-place, reached usually about an hour before noon. His air and mood when he stepped to the platform for the public Meeting had undergone a radiant change; all the more radiant, we noticed, if the children who had hailed him from the waysides had been many and strenuous. There was something of the child in his own face as he stepped to the platform's edge, and replied to the enthusiasm of the house by clapping his own hands to the people. There was always something naive and delightful in The General's preliminary task of applauding the audience.

"Here came his first important address of the day, lasting an hour and a half, or even longer. It had many 'notes,' and displayed The General in many moods. He was apt to be facetious and drily humorous at first. He had racy stories to tell—and none can tell a story for the hundredth time with fresh zest than he—in illustration of the old and bitter prejudices against The Army. A typical one was that of an old woman, arrested for the hundredth time for being drunk and disorderly, who was given the option of going to prison or being passed over to The Salvation Army. Too drunk to realise what she did, she decided for the latter. She was kindly tended, set in a clean cosy bed, and watched over by a sister till the morning. When she woke the sunlight streamed through the window, and the happy, unaccustomed surroundings surprised her. 'Where am I?' she exclaimed in bewilderment. 'You are with The Salvation Army,' said the sister kindly and softly. 'Oh, goodness gracious,' roared the old woman, 'take me away, or I'll lose my reputation!'

"Often in these long and comprehensive addresses The General told how he found the work of his life. He was never so impressive as at this stage. And the tale in its intensity was ever new. His language was nervous, intense, almost Biblical, his figure suggestive of a patriarch's in a tragedy. 'Sixty years ago—sixty years ago—sixty years ago,' each time with a different and a grimmer intonation—'the Spirit of the Living God met me.... I was going down the steep incline when the great God stopped me, and made me think.'

"In the last stage of his address he was the coloniser, the statesman, the social wizard who would recast character and rearrange humanity. He gave an epic sense to the story of emigration and colonisation. But he was invariably clear and lucid in his detail, so that the immediate and practical meaning of it all was never lost on the mayors, and corporation and council worthies, who heard him. Then miles and miles away at the second important stopping-place in the early afternoon, after incidental wayside speeches and idylls, he went over the same ground in a further address of an hour or more. Somehow in the afternoon he appeared to speak with added individuality and passion, as if the wants and woes of the world had been growing upon him since the morning.

"A needed rest, perhaps a little sleep, then away once more by the waysides and through the welcoming hamlets. The third and last great stopping-stage was reached, as a rule, about eight o'clock. He typified serene old age as he stood up in the white car, passing the long lines of cheering humanity. Here in the evening light it was not easy to regard him as a propagandist. He might be a study for Father Christmas, or a philosopher who dealt much in abstractions and knew little of men. The General who, twenty minutes later, proclaimed his spiritual truths and his social ideals to a new audience, seemed, once more, an absolutely different personality. Often at these evening meetings he spoke for the better part of two hours."

Chapter XXII
Our Financial System

The continued strain to raise the money needed for the work was, undoubtedly, to William Booth the greatest part of his burden all the way through life. And it is to this day the puzzle which makes it most difficult to write as to The Army's finances. On the one hand, we have to praise God for having helped him so cheerily to shoulder his cross that he did not seem many times to feel the burden that was almost crushing him to the ground, and hindering all sorts of projects he would gladly have carried out. Yet, on the other hand, we must guard against saying anything that could lead to the impression that The Army has now got to the top of its hill of difficulty, and needs no more of the help, in small sums as well as in big ones, that has been so generously sent to it.

It would be hopeless to attempt to estimate the numbers of appeals The General sent out in any one year, for he not only tried at fixed periods to get for his various funds truly interested subscribers, but was always seeking to link the hearty giver with the deserving receivers.

But perhaps the very extremity of his one need helped him with the most practical wisdom to avoid all unnecessary expenditure, and to cultivate all those habits of economy and systematic effort which alone made it possible to keep up so vast a work mainly by the gifts of the poor. To this very day it is the same old struggle to get each L5 that is wanted together. Yet all of it is precious to us because it so guarantees exemption from indifference, and the pervasion of all our ranks everywhere with the principles of self-help which The General always so inculcated as to make The Army everywhere independent of the wealthy, yet their trusted and skilful almoners.

Rejoicing as we do in all that, we cannot too strongly guard every one against the impression that The Army has become, either at its centre, or anywhere else, so situated that there is not at any given moment extraordinary strain in some financial direction. It has come to be very generally known that the individual Officer can only keep in existence because he has schooled his desires to be content with what others all around would regard as "an impossible pittance."

We hear one day of a great city where the conditions of life are such that a Rescue Home is evidently urgently needed, and the lady who calls our attention to the matter offers at once to find L500 towards the fitting-up of such a Home. But we know that to keep it up requires gifts amounting to some thousands of pounds each year, which, if not subscribed locally, we shall have to provide from Headquarters.

Now what is to be done? Are we to stand still with what seems to us so valuable an offer, not only of money-helps but of opportunity to help? Under the circumstances we know what The General would have done. He would without a moment's hesitation have said: "This ought to be done, and must be done"; and, trusting in God, he would have made the other step forward, though perfectly conscious that it would probably involve him in new cares and anxieties.

"Four shillings and tenpence. Now, really, can't we manage that twopence to make five shillings?"

Such an appeal, heard at a street-corner, where one of our Open-Air Meetings is being closed, is, I fear, the first and last that many people hear of The Salvation Army. They have not been present at the Meeting. All the beautiful speaking and singing of happy men and women, anxious to do anything they can for the good of others—of this the passers-by know nothing. Many of them "would not be seen standing to listen" amidst the crowd, still less when, for want of any considerable crowd, they would be more conspicuous. Hence they have no chance to see or know what really takes place. Had they even seen the whole process of getting that four shillings and tenpence they would have noted that most of the money really came from the Salvationists forming the ring, who threw their pence, or sixpences, gradually, in the hope of inciting others to do likewise.

As it is, I fear, many go their way "disgusted at the whole thing," because of the little scrap of it they have overheard.

But, pray, what is the essential difference between the call for "twopence to make up a shilling," and the colossal call made in the name of some royal personage for "an additional ten thousand pounds" to make up the £25,000 needed for a new hospital wing? Surely, a hospital, whose value and services commend it to the entire population should need no such spurs as subscription lists published in all the papers, or even the memory of a world benefactor to help it to get the needed funds. But it does, and its energetic promoters, be they royal or not, deserve and get universal praise for "stooping"—if it be stooping—to any device of this kind needed to get the cash. Do they get it? is the only question any sensible person asks.

And nobody questions that our "stooping" Officers and "begging Sisters" get the twopences and shillings and pounds needed to keep The Army going, in spite of all its critics—whether of the blatant street-corner, or of the kid-gloved slanderer type.

If we reflect upon the subject we shall see how sound and valuable are the principles on which all our twopenny appeals are based.

From the very beginning The General always set up the standard of local self-support as one of the essentials of any real work. Whilst labouring almost exclusively amongst the poorest of the poor, he wrote, in 1870:—

"The entire cost of carrying on the Mission at present is about £50 per week. The offerings of the people themselves at the various stations are now about £17 per week; indeed, nearly every Station is paying its own working expenses. Thus the poor people themselves do something. This they ought to do. It would be wrong to deprive them of the privilege of giving their mite, and if they prize the instrumentalities that have been blessed to them, and are rightly instructed, they will cheerfully give, however small their contribution may be."

It has only been by clinging to this plan that the little Society, begun in the East of London, has been able to spread itself throughout the world and yet remain independent, everywhere, of local magnates. And The General had the sorry satisfaction of seeing the structure tested by the most cruel winds of slander and suspicion, with the result that the total of contributions to its funds during the last years has been greater than ever before. Part, indeed, of our greatest difficulty with regard to money now is the large total yearly at our disposal, when all the totals in every country and locality are added together. Any one can understand that this must be so, and that it could not help us to publish the amount all together.

EMMA BOOTH-TUCKER
Born January 8th. 1860. Died October 28th. 1903.

If in a hundred places only a thousand pounds were raised, anybody can see that to cry aloud about the hundred thousand in any one of those places could not but make everybody in that place less capable of strenuous struggle such as is needed to get together each thousand.

Therefore, whilst publishing every year the properly audited balance-sheet referring to amounts received and spent in London, and similar balance-sheets, similarly audited, in each other capital, we have always refrained, and always shall refrain, from any such massing of totals, or glorying in any of them, as could help our enemies to check the flow of liberality anywhere.

When, in 1895, there seemed to be a general cry for some special investigation into the use made of the Fund raised as a result of The General's "Darkest England" Appeal, we were able to get a Commission of some of the most eminent men in the country, whose Report effectively disposed of any doubts at the time.

The Commission had for Chairman Earl Onslow, and its members were the Right Hon. Sir Henry James (afterwards Lord James), Messrs. Sydney Buxton, Walter Long, and Mr. Edwin Waterhouse, President of the Institute of Chartered Accountants, the Right Hon. Hobhouse, M.P., acted as Secretary.

The Report of no Commission could, however, still any hostile tongue. The cry for "investigation" has always been simply the cry of enmity or envy, which no amount of investigation could ever satisfy. The General perfectly understood this at the time, and wrote to a friend of the discerning order:—

> "How I feel generally with respect to the future is expressed in one word, or rather two, 'Go forward.' The Red Sea has to be crossed and the people rescued from Hell here and Hell hereafter. We must stick to our post.
>
> "I am quite aware that I may now, probably shall be, more misunderstood than ever. But God and time will fight for me. I must wait, and my comrades must wait with me.
>
> "I need not say that the subject has had, and still has, our fullest consideration; but I cannot say more until I see clearly

what position the country will take up towards me during the next few days."

Need I say that this Report never checked for one day the ferocity of the attacks upon the General or his Army. Had public opinion been deluded by the babblings of our critics in any country we should not only have lost all support, but been consigned to jails as swindlers and robbers. But the fact that we get ever-increasing sums, and are ever more and more aided by grants from Governments and Corporations, or by permissions for street-collecting, is the clearest demonstration that we are notoriously upright in all our dealings.

So many insinuations have been persistently thrown out, year after year, with regard to the integrity of The General's dealings with finance, that I have taken care not merely to consult with comrades, but to give opportunity to some who were said to "have left in disgust" with regard to these matters, to correct my own impression if they could.

Having been so little at Headquarters myself since I left for Germany, in 1890, I knew that my own personal knowledge might be disputed, and my accuracy questioned; therefore, I have been extra careful to ascertain, beyond all possibility of dispute, the correctness of the view I now give.

One who for many years had the direction of financial affairs at the International Headquarters, and who retired through failing health rather than become a burden upon the Army's ever-strained exchequer, wrote me on November 28, 1910:—

> "The General has always taken the keenest interest in all questions bearing upon The Army's financial affairs, and has ever been alive to the necessity for their being so administered as to ensure the contributing public's having the utmost possible value for the money contributed, at the same time rendering a careful account from year to year of his stewardship.

> "Carefully prepared budgets of income and expenditure are submitted to him year by year in connexion with all the central funds, reports are called for from time to time as to the extent to which such estimates have been realised.

> "He was always keen and far-sighted in his consideration of the proposals put before him, and quick to find a flaw or weakness, or to point out any responsibilities which had not been sufficiently taken into account.
>
> "Until recent years, when his world-wide journeyings made it necessary to pass the responsibility on to the Chief of the Staff, he largely initiated his own schemes for raising money, and wrote his own principal appeals.
>
> "Those who refer to The General as 'a puppet in the hands of others,' or as anything but an unselfish, disinterested servant of humanity, only show their ignorance of their subject."

One of the schemes by which our finances have been greatly helped everywhere, and which is now imitated by many Churches and Societies all over the world—the Self-Denial Week, established in 1886—was The General's own invention. It was at a time when, as he writes:—

> "In some Corps half, and in some more than half, of our Soldiers have been for months without any income at all, or at most with just a shilling or two. In addition, many of our regular contributors, as owners of land or of manufacturing houses, have suffered from the depression, and have not been able to assist us further.
>
> "The rapid extension of The Army has necessitated an increased expenditure. Our friends will see that our position is really a serious one.
>
> "What is to be done? Reduction, which means retreat, is impossible. To stand still is equally so.

"We propose that a week be set apart in which every Soldier and friend should deny himself of some article of food or clothing, or some indulgence which can be done without, and that the price gained by this self-denial shall be sent to help us in this emergency.

"Deny yourself of something which brings you pleasure or gratification, and so not only have the blessing of helping us, but the profit which this self-denial will bring to your own soul."

This effort, which in the year of its inauguration only produced 4,280, has in twenty-six years grown till it totalled in Great Britain in 1911, L67,161, and has so taken hold of the people's minds and hearts everywhere as to produce even in poor little Belgium last year 7,500 f.

Perhaps it need hardly be explained that the system of special effort and special begging near the entrance to railway stations, and in all the most prominent places of the cities, which has grown out of this week, with the approval of Governments and Press everywhere, has done more than any one could have dreamt of to increase interest in the needs of others, and holiness and self-denial in attending to them.

And it is, after all, upon that development of practical love for everybody that The Army's finance depends.

Merely to have interested so many rich people in The Army might have been a great credit to The General's influence, but to have raised up everywhere forces of voluntary mendicants who, at any rate, for weeks at a time are not ashamed to be seen begging in the streets for the good of people they have never seen, is an achievement simply boundless in its beneficent value to all mankind, and limitless in the guarantee it provides for the permanent maintenance and extension of our work.

Do let me beg you to realise a little of the intense interest taken in our finances locally by all our Soldiers. Did you ever get to know one of our Corps Treasurers? If not, believe me, that your education is incomplete. Whether he or she be schoolmistress in the mining village of Undergroundby, shopkeeper in Birmingham, or cashier of a London or Parisian bank, you will find an experienced Salvation Army Treasurer generally one of the most fully-developed intelligences living. He or she could easily surpass Judas Iscariot himself, either for ability at bargaining, or for what we call "Salvation cheek." He considers the Duke who owns most of his county, or the Mayor of the city, is "duty bound" to help The Army whenever its Officer thinks a fitting moment has come to him to ask them to do so—and the Treasurer never thinks that they already have helped us enough.

Every farthing his Corps has received or paid, for years past, has passed through his careful fingers. In any city Corps I would accept his judgment about a "doubtful" coin before that of almost any one. And no human being could surpass him in eagerness or care to get the very uttermost possible value for every penny spent. Hours after great Meetings are over you may find him with other officers busy still parcelling coppers, or in some other way "serving tables." His own business or family would very often suffer for his late hours of toil in the cause, if God allowed that sort of thing. But God has seen to it that many such a Treasurer has climbed out of the very gutter into a well-to-do employer's position, **because** he sought first His Kingdom and His righteousness.

These Treasurers, if anybody took the trouble to interview them, would make it impossible for any decent person to believe the lies that have been told about our "not publishing accounts," our "extravagance," etc. They know how carefully even the smallest Corps book or collecting-card is examined, and with what precise and skilful method every account is kept.

Like almost all our Local Officers, they are particularly cheery, friendly men and women. I fear we have but few women Treasurers, as finance, like so many other things, is supposed to be "beyond women's powers," and the sisters really do not, as a rule, like arithmetic. But man or woman, you have only to watch one of them a few moments, when anybody is trying to arrange a joint excursion with various Corps, to see that, with all their kindliness, the interests committed to their charge always command their first sympathy. Treasurer Pitman, of Leatherby, "never could see," and never will, why either Birmingham I or Leamington, or any other Corps, should be more favoured, or more burdened, than his own. Even should his words at times seem rough, or few, he will charm you, almost without exception, if you get out of his wife or the Captain, or somebody, all he does and suffers for Christ's sake. Nobody will ever know how often it was the Treasurer who gave half the "twopence to make up a shilling" in the street-corner collection that, perhaps, made the impression that The Army was "not self-supporting!"

But, in spite of all his jollity, the Treasurer is often a sorely-tried and burdened man. For, Oh, it is a struggle to get the pence together, week after week, especially where the Corps has a "Hall of its own," for ground rent and interest on which it must pay £5 to £10 a week!

The Treasurer's great opportunity comes when he has the joy of harbouring in his own home, for a night or two, the Chief of the Staff, or some other "Special from London." Then he may get a chance to "put a word in" for his Corps.

Does the Chief ask him, "Why do we not get on better in this town?"

"Well, Chief," he will reply, "just look at our Hall. It fairly stinks—always has done, owing to that canal at the back. That has almost made it impossible for us to get a large congregation, especially in warm weather."

"But why don't you get a better place?"

"Well, there is nothing in the town large enough to let, and as for building—any site that would be of use would cost a pile of money, and we have no hope of raising any large sum here."

"Why? Have you no rich friends?"

"There are a few very rich men here. I was seeing one of them myself only last month when we wanted to get some new instruments for our Band. But what do you think he said to me?

"'Why,' said he, 'I have more than enough to do to keep up my own church. We have got to rebuild it, and it will cost us £30,000.'"

"There is not a mill-owner in the place who does not want to get Salvationist workpeople, even to the boys of our Soldiers, because they know they can depend on them. But to help us to get a Hall! Ah! 'that is not in their line.'"

Therefore, the Treasurer and every Officer must go on week after week, with the miserable beg, beg, beg, which afflicts them, perhaps, even more than the most critical listener. And then our great work must suffer both for want of the needed plant to carry it on, and from the appearance of too much begging, which, in so many instances, has undoubtedly hindered our gathering in the very people we most wished to help.

What stories of self-denial, not one week in the year more than another, any such Treasurer could tell! How Officers managed to rear a healthy and promising family upon less than a pound a week: how The General's own granddaughters "made six shillings a week do" for their personal support, for months, because their Corps could not afford more: how the Sergeant-Major's wife did her washing during the night "before Self-Denial Week came on," so as to be able to stand all day long outside the station, in the cold, collecting: how widow Weak "keeps up her cartridges"; that is to say, goes on giving the Corps a regular subscription of sixpence a week since her husband's death, as before, "lest the Corps should go down."

Lately they took me to see a German widow, now suffering in a hospital, who when her whole weekly cash earnings outside only totalled two shillings a week, invariably "put in her cartridge" two pfennigs, say a farthing. No. I gave her nothing, nor did anybody else in my presence, as her needs are now attended to; and I am sure she would rather keep up the fact of never having received anything from, but always having given to, The Army.

Of course we do not pretend that all Treasurers and Soldiers are of the model sort. If they were, many of our bitterest financial struggles would never occur. If everybody who "kept back part" of what they ought to give to God were struck dead for singing such words as—

>   Were the whole realm of nature mine,
>   That were a present far too small.

God would need many a regiment of corpse carriers, I fear.

The General, seventeen years ago, wrote to a wealthy lady who had been excusing somebody's want of liberality to us by some of the slanders they had heard.

"Tell your friends in Gull-town the same that I am telling the public: that nine out of every ten statements in the Press that reflect upon us are either out-and-out *falsehoods* or '*half-lies*,' which are worse still; and that, though not infallible, when in one case out of ten we do make mistakes, there are circumstances which, if known, would excuse them very largely.

"I am having wonderful Meetings—immense crowds, soul-awakening influences all day—Penitent-Forms; back-sliders, sinners and half-and-half saints coming back to God. Never saw anything, anywhere, in any part of my life, much more blessed.

"Read my letter in *The War Cry* about the Two Days—every word as from my heart.

"Money or no money, we must and will have Salvation. If the rich won't help Lazarus through us, then their money must perish. We must do the best we can.

"Join the Light Brigade, and give a halfpenny per week! We shall get through. Is your soul prospering? Cast yourself this morning on your Lord for a supply of ***all your need***."

This "Light Brigade" is another invention of the General's, partly founded upon the Indian habit of taking a handful out of every new supply of food, and laying it aside for the priests.

The "Light Brigade" consists of Soldiers and friends who place on their table a little box, into which all who like can drop a little coin by way of thanksgiving to God and care for the poor before they eat. These are called "Grace-before-Meat" Boxes, and in England alone they produced last year £8,284. 17 *s.* 2 *d.* for the support of our Social Work.

Altogether I venture to say it will be found that for every shilling he ever got anywhere he prompted the giving of at least a thousand shillings to other benevolent enterprises, and that mankind is indebted to him for the stirring up to benevolent action of countless millions who never even heard his name.

At the same time it will be found that by his financial plans he has made The Army so largely dependent upon public opinion that, were its beneficent work to cease, its means of survival would at the same time become extinct, so that it could not continue to exist when it had ceased to be a Salvation Army.

Chapter XXIII
In Germany in Old Age

Though we have had occasion to mention Germany repeatedly, there has been no opportunity to call attention to the great importance which The General attached to our Work in that country. It seemed almost as though we had been premature in our attack upon the country, so little were either Governments or people prepared for our violent urgency, when we began in Stuttgart, in 1886. But The General lived to see his annual visits to Berlin looked forward to by the Press and public as a natural provision for the spiritual wants of those who had practically ceased to be of any religion.

In the following description of him, taken from German papers during one of his last visits to that country, we get not only some idea of his appearance to the people when he was eighty-one years of age, but his sense of the importance of that people in the future of The Army. And it is a remarkable fact that German cities should have been subsidising The Army's work before any English one did so.

We have happily got complete enough accounts of The General's tour in Germany, when eighty-one, to supply not merely a most artistic representation of his own appearance and action at that age, but at the same time to give an almost perfect view of the impressions and teachings his Army has been giving out there for nearly thirty years.

In Duesseldorf, we are told:—

"The old idealist spoke for an hour and a half with the fire of enthusiasm, throwing out every now and then some spark of his humour amidst his stream of eloquence. He did not speak like a dying greybeard, but like a young man ready to take up to-morrow morning the struggle with the misery of the whole world. Out of such material as this old man are made the great men who do great deeds on the battle-field, in the sphere of science, in the province of religion, of humanity, and of society."

The ***Cologne Gazette*** goes more into detail, and says:—

"At his great age the Founder and Leader of The Salvation Army hastens from continent to continent, from land to land, to awaken in Public Meetings love for your neighbour. After a journey through Holland he came into West Germany. In this week he speaks in great cities from Dortmund to Carlsruhe, each day in a new place, and often in several Meetings. Many thousands came together last Sunday from Essen and neighbourhood, so that the great hall of the Soldiers' Home itself was not large enough to hold them at the various Meetings. Here yesterday evening 2,000 people wanted to give him a warm welcome in the Emperor's Hall.

"The eighty-one-year-old philanthropist, who strides so unbendingly along, is full of youthful enthusiasm. His tall figure, with its gleaming eyes, long curved nose, and flowing beard, help him to present himself to the audience, with lively gestures illuminating his thoughts, as at once accuser of our times and gentle judge. He is especially a gentle judge of fallen women and girls, 55,000 of whom, from ten years of age upwards, he tells us, The Army has rescued.

"'The fallen young men are forgiven by their fathers and mothers,' says he. 'Why should not we also forgive the fallen girls? If nobody else will do so, we will.' This sentiment called forth general applause.

"'And then,' The General went on, 'The religion of The Army has three main principles: (1) You must get right with your God. You must be reconciled with Him, and feel the kiss of His forgiving love. (2) You must live righteously in your own private life, in your family, and in holiness of heart. (3) You must give yourself up to the service of your fellow-men—must not wait to be called upon, but must have a fire in yourself—the fire of love.'

"It took mightily hold of the audience as, following upon this definition of the religion of The Army, he told them that he felt himself now nearing the cold stream of death, but fully believed that this religion, which had carried him through so much of care and disappointment up to this day, would also carry him through the dark valley into Paradise, where he, who for so long had known no holiday, would at last find rest."

Everywhere in Germany it is this revelation of a religion, founded on unshakable faith, which impresses even the sceptical journalist. Here and there the tendency to doubt shows itself a little between the lines, and it is suggested that the audience were only for the time being under the spell of this remarkable speaker. But most impressive is always the description of The General's calls to repentance and faith.

In Berlin for a number of years the General held Meetings in the great Circus Busch on the National Buss-tag, Repentance Day; and, as the way in which his name is pronounced by most Germans comes very near one of the two words, it has almost become a Booth Day in the thoughts of many.

"It was evident," says one paper, "again in the two Meetings held yesterday that the personality of the Founder and Leader of The Army still exercises its charm. Both Meetings were crowded; the Circus was filled from arena up to gallery with a pressing multitude. At the close of the evening address there was the call to the Penitent-Form, and 158 men and women, out of the most differing circles of society, obeyed the call. Mr. Booth spoke in both Meetings with the freshest energy and youthful fire, and to-day he travels to Denmark."

The *Frankfort Gazette*, and other papers, having the opportunity for the first time to report The General's Meetings on a whole Sunday, a little later, gave a much completer description of his preaching:—

"The Founder of The Army," says the *Gazette*, "bears his eighty-one years lightly. He is still equal to all the toils of the agitation, and spoke for over five hours in three Meetings in the great hall of the Merchants' Union. The old gentleman keeps up his good humour, and perfectly understands how to intersperse interesting anecdotes in his addresses."

"Last Sunday," says another paper, "was a Booth Day, and certainly a Repentance Day. The General came to win Soldiers for his Army, and ammunition for it, too; but there was plenty of opportunity for repentance given. Everybody knows now the why and wherefore of The Army's Meetings. There is music—then prayer with closed eyes, and then a little sister sings a religious song to a worldly tune. That was so yesterday; but then The General came as chief speaker. He had no need of any other influence; his mere appearance works upon every one.

"The public was composed of all sorts of people. Politicians, Socialists, as well as clergymen and leaders in Church work were there, together with officials and working-men and women."

Nothing could be more impressive as to the ever-widening circles who crowded to listen to The General than the following description of his Meeting in Potsdam, the German Windsor, where the Emperor generally resides. Says the local paper:—

"One could not cease to marvel at the crowded state of the auditorium. The intelligent public, which generally keeps away from popular demonstrations, was there in force. Jurists, state officials, officers in uniform, doctors, and many ladies were amongst the hearers of The General."

But some of the papers in smaller but not less striking reports gave us a far fuller description of what The General's appeals brought home to the hearts of his hearers everywhere.

"No laboured rhetoric," said a Leipzig paper, "distinguished the speech, and applause was not won by catchy phrases. The speaker talks like a plain man to plain people. Everybody listens enthralled as he tells of his life's work, of the unbounded love with which he would like to surround and lead to Salvation every one who lives and moves. One gets to understand how this man could gather around him such masses of disciples, and why, right and left, many a lady deeply touched puts her handkerchief to her eyes and many a man wipes a tear from his cheek."

Best of all, however, comes ever and anon in these reports the testimony that The General has not been a mere talker, like so many others of his day, but has raised up a real fighting force who have, by gradual painstaking labour and endurance, won for him this unbounded confidence in what he says of The Army's religion.

"I remember," writes one reporter, "how in the nineties, in Berlin, no Soldier, much less a Sister, could appear in the street without being laughed at at every step, made fun of, and even abused, and I visited Meetings in which there was great disorder. But how the picture was altered a few years later! Quietly and patiently the Soldiers let scorn and even assaults pass, until the very rowdiest of the Berliners were sick of it. And on the other hand every one soon said that these people, after all, were doing nothing but to go right at the deepest miseries of the great cities—that they fed the hungry, visited the sick, and generally carried out practical Christianity."

"True," writes another, "it is naturally not every one whose taste is pleased with the ceremonies of The Army; but before the world-wide, unending, unselfish work of the Salvationist every one feels like saying, 'Hats off!'

"It was not mere love of sensation that led such a stream of men to the Princes Hall on Tuesday evening. They wished for once to come face to face with the old General whose work they had learnt in the course of time to value. Men of science, clergymen and officials and educated people generally, for once made The Army their rendezvous."

And those who had heard the General before immediately recognised that they had not only to do with the very same resolute Leader, following the one aim with undiminished ardour, but relying upon the same old Gospel to win the world for Christ.

"He speaks," says a Hamburg paper, "mostly with his hands behind his back, swaying gently to and fro. The short, sharp English sentences are translated one by one. It is the old recruiting talk of the chief captain in the fight against the sins of this world, the pressing exhortation to get converted at once, to-day, in this very hour. It is the old entreaty to become a child of God, in spite of all opposition; the old call to purity of heart and life. Whoever has wandered must come back again. He who has fallen a hundred times must get up again for the hundred and first time.

"This General believes in the Salvation of the worst and the most deeply sunken. He preaches the gospel of holding on, of going steadily forwards, of freedom from the lusts of the flesh and from public opinion. He preaches at the same time the gospel of work, of unwearied faithfulness in business, and of love to all mankind.

"When he has finished The Army sings with musical accompaniment and clapping of hands its glad and even merry-sounding songs, not without a mixture of that sudden inrush of enthusiasm which springs from the conviction of having the only faith that can make people blessed, and the consciousness of a resistance hard to be overcome. And then begins that extraordinary urgent exhorting of the sinner from the stage—the ten-and-twenty times repeated 'Come'—come to the Penitent-Form, represented here by a row of twenty chairs. 'In the last Meeting of The General's in Copenhagen thirty-three came out. How many will it be in Hamburg?' cries the leading Officer.

"The first are soon kneeling, sobbing, praying, their hands over their eyes at the chairs. Ever new songs are sung—spiritual songs set to worldly melodies. Ever anew sounds the ringing 'Come' from the stage. Below, the men and women Soldiers go from one to another, speaking to the hesitating ones, laying a hand on the shoulder of the ready ones, and leading them to the front. What a long time it may be since any loving hand was laid on the shoulder of many of those Recruits! Life, the rough, pitiless life of the great city, has always been pushing them along lower and lower down till it got them underfoot. Here they listen to the sound of a voice of sympathy, and feel the pressure of a hand that wishes to lead them. And there above sits The General for a while in an arm-chair, saying: 'The deepest-fallen may rise again. He has only to step out into the ranks of The Army, which is marching upwards to the Land of Grace.' As we left the Hall the thirty-fourth had already come out."

It must be remembered that all these descriptions come from part of a single month's journeys, and that The General was dependent upon translation for nearly every moment of intercourse either in public or private with the people, and that it will be entirely understood how great a power for God in this world a man entirely given up may be after he has passed his eightieth year, and with what clearness witness for God can be borne even in a strange tongue when it is plain and definite.

"From time immemorial it has been customary to class philanthropists amongst the extraordinaries, the marvellous people—who do not pass muster in the common world—exceptions. Nobody thinks of measuring himself with them, for the battle of life belongs to the egotists—each one of whom fights for himself. He who fights for others is smilingly acknowledged by the well-disposed as a stranger in the world. The ordinary man of the street pitilessly calls him a fool, and the mass considers him unworthy of a second thought. He is there, and he is endured so long as he does not bother any one.

"There are three factors against which the old General has had to fight all his life long—against well-meaning hesitation, against hard-hearted egoism, and against the idle indifference born of ignorance. And these three streams that have flowed against him in every part of the world have not been able to hold him back. To those who think he has only become an important man, and to those who measure a man's worth by the outer honours he gains, he became a man of importance when London made him a citizen and Oxford an honorary Doctor. And now men are better inclined to excuse in his case the curious title of General of a curious Army.

"I have often heard the grey-headed General in Public Meetings. For the first time on Saturday evening I got near to him in a more private way. And then it seemed to me like a picture, as when a grey warrior, a commander with snow-white beard and keen profile, stands upright by the mast of a ship and gazes straight before him towards a new country.

"And General Booth, despite his eighty-one years, is looking out towards new land. He does not live on memories like the generality of old men. He does not allow himself any favoured spot by the fireside. Full of fight and always leading, General Booth stands at the centre of a gigantic apparatus. And the old gentleman does not look like allowing men to take the control out of his hands.

"Everything about him displays energy and justifiable self-consciousness. He energetically shook my hand. With the ability of the man of the world he drew the conversation to that which was nearest to his heart. And what his eyes can no longer exactly observe his ears doubly well hear. He arrived on Friday evening from Denmark, holds three Meetings in Hamburg on Sunday, travels on to Potsdam on Monday, and occupies himself with thoughts of a journey of inspection in India.

"The comfortable arm-chair that was offered him he declined almost as if it were an insult.' That is meant for an old man,' he said; and really the remark was justified when one heard the plans of the grey General, for he has plans such as one of the youngest might have. He appears to me like an able business man who constantly thinks how to expand his undertaking and to supply it with all the novelties that a time of progress offers. He has altogether modern views. He does not hold fast with the reluctance of old age to old things, except to the old faith.

"In the Meetings The General seemed to me rather severe; but that disappears when you get at him personally, especially when you have got used to his way of speaking. He almost flings each sentence out. Every phrase, accompanied by some energetic gesture, is like a war cry. 'I will, and I carry out what I will,' seems to breathe in all about him; and who can complain of this will, this iron resoluteness with which he works at the raising up of men. He is in his kingdom an unlimited ruler, but one with a benevolent look who sees for the benefit of the blind. He must be all that for his extraordinary work.

"The General asks us to put questions. I could not manage it. It seemed to me to be so useless in the presence of this important man. So he said, 'We are never satisfied with the progress we make in view of what still remains to be done.' He spoke of the progress made by the Social Work of The Army in Germany, and of his plans.

"I never heard The General speak without his having plans, upon the carrying out of which he was at work with all his might. He puts his whole body and soul into whatever he is engaged in.

"'The Salvation Army is the most interesting thing under the sun,' said The General at the close of this earnest talk, and then added, jokingly, 'next to the Hamburg Press.'

"On the Sunday I saw him again as he spoke to a Meeting of thousands, a curiously mixed public, where there were many of the foremost gentlemen and ladies of society and many very common people. All, however, were equally enthused. I will only mention a couple of sentences out of the speech: 'The Army wants to come into competition with nobody, only to be a friendly helper—nobody's enemy, but the friend of everybody. It will gladly be an inspiration and example. It has become the almsgiver for many Governments. It is not British because it was born in Britain, just as little as Christianity is Jewish because it came into the world in Judea.'"—Else Meerstedt.

Now that we see it all but completed, we think this book singularly wanting in reference to The General's frequent merriness of mood. We have thought it needless to insert any of the amusing anecdotes that could have been so abundantly culled from any of his visits to any country had we not been so anxious to select from the small space at our disposal what was most important.

Nor have we wished to present the reader with the portrait of an infallible genius, or a saint who never said or did anything that he afterwards regretted. A victim almost all his life to extreme indigestion, it is indeed to all who knew him best marvellous that he could endure so much of misery without more frequently expressing in terms of unpleasant frankness his irritation at the faults and mistakes of others. But really after his death as during his life we have been far too busy in trying to help in accomplishing his great lifework to note these details of human frailty.

Chapter XXIV
The End

It seems almost impossible to describe the ending of The General's life, because there was not even the semblance of an end within a week of his death.

The last time I talked with him, just as I was leaving for Canada in January, he for the first time made a remark that indicated a doubt of his continuance in office. He hardly hinted at death; but, referring to the sensations of exhaustion he had felt a few days previously, he said: "I sometimes fancy, you know, that I may be getting to a halt, and then"—with his usual pause when he was going to tease—"we shall have a chance to see what some of you can do!"

We laughed together, and I went off expecting to hear of his fully recovering his activity "after the operation," to which we were always looking forward. Oh, that operation! It was to be the simplest thing in the world, when the eye was just ready for it, as simple and as complete a deliverance from blindness as the other one had seemed, for a few days, to be. But this time he would be fully warned, and most cautious after it, and I really fancied the joy he would have after so long an eclipse.

It seemed to me that he never realised how great his own blindness already was, so strong was his resolution to make the best of it, and so eager his perception, really by other means, of everything he could in any way notice. We had difficulty in remembering that he really could not see when he turned so rapidly towards anybody approaching him or whose voice he recognised!

To Colonel Kitching during this dark period he wrote one day: "Anybody can believe in the sunshine. We, that is you and I and a few more of whom we know, ought to be desperate believers by this time—Saviours of men—against their will, nay, compellers of the Almighty."

And his writing was always so marvellous, both for quantity and quality. His very last letters to several of us consisted of a number of pages all written with perfect clearness and regularity with his own hand. It was, perhaps, the greatest triumph of his own unfailing faith and sunny optimism that he kept even those who were nearest to him full of hope as to his complete recovery of strength till within a few days of his death; and then, gliding down into the valley, surprised all by sinking suddenly into eternal peace without any distinct warning that the end was so near. His youngest daughter, Mrs. Commissioner Booth-Hellberg, was with him during the last days.

But, really, it would be only fair to describe his end as having begun from the day when, during his Sixth Motor Tour, the eye which had been operated upon became blind. Though after having it taken out, he very largely rallied, and passed through grand Campaigns for some years, he was ever looking forward to the operation on the other eye, which was to restore him to partial sight. His cheeriness through those years and his marvellous energy astonished all.

The following notes of his first foreign journey after the loss of sight cannot but be of special interest, showing with what zest and enjoyment he threw himself into all his undertakings for Christ:—

"Saturday, *February* 12, 1910.—The crossing has been quite rough enough. I slept very little, and it was with real difficulty that I shambled through the long railway depot to my train for Rotterdam. At eight o'clock was woke up from a sound sleep with a startling feeling. It is a pity I could not have slept on. Fixed up at the old hotel six floors up (the Mass Hotel). Very fair accommodation, but a little difficult to get anything to eat, that is, such as meet my queer tastes and habits. Nevertheless, on the principle of 'any port in a storm,' I have had much worse accommodation.

"Sunday, *February* 13, 1910.—Had a wonderful day. Far ahead of anything experienced before in this place. My opinion about it is jotted down in *The War Cry*. I had, as I thought, remarkable power on each of the three occasions, and finished off at ten o'clock far less exhausted than I frequently am. Still, I scarcely got into my rooms before the giddiness came on in my head very badly, and continued off and on until ten the next morning. I can't account for it. It may be my stomach, or it may have something to do with the rocking of the steamer on Friday night. It may be what the doctors fear, my overtaxed brain, or it may be something else. Whatever it is, it is very awkward while it lasts. Fifty-seven souls for the day.

"Monday, *February* 14, 1910.—Left by the 12:37 p.m. train for Groningen. Slept a good bit of the way. Arrived about 5:12 p.m. Reception very remarkable, considering the population is only some 78,000. It was one of the most remarkable greetings I have ever had in any part of the world. There must have been getting on for a couple of thousand people in the station itself, who had each paid five cents for a platform ticket, and outside 5,000 is a low estimate. Everybody very friendly.

"Entertained by the Governor's wife's sister. The Meeting was as wonderful as the reception. Immense hall. Could not be less than 1,500 people packed into it on one floor. I talked for an hour and three-quarters. Colonel Palstra, my translator, did splendidly, the people listening spellbound; not a soul moved until the last minute, when three or four went out for some reason or other. It was a wonderful time. Settled to sleep about 11:30 p.m. not feeling any worse.

"Tuesday, *February* 15, 1910.—Had a fair night's sleep. The strange feelings in the head continue off and on, and the fact that they don't pass off, in connexion with the entreaties of the Chief, and those about me, made me consent to give up the Officers' Council I was proposing to hold at Amsterdam next week, putting on Lectures on the evenings of the two days which I would otherwise have used for Councils. I am very loath to do this, from feeling that the Officers are the great need. So far I have been delighted with what I have seen of the Officers in the country. We ought to capture Holland.

"The Governor has sent word to say that he is coming to see me this afternoon.

"I have had a long sleep, and I hope I shall be better for it. The Governor has just come in. He appears a very amiable person, very friendly disposed towards The Army. We had a very nice conversation about matters in general, and at parting he expressed his kindest wishes for my future and for the future of The Army.

"I left at a few minutes before seven. It has been snowing and raining, and freezing and thawing the last few hours, consequently the atmosphere is not very agreeable. However, my carriage was well warmed, and we arrived at Assen in half an hour.

"A very nice hall—packed with a very respectful audience. I spoke on the old subject, 'The Lesson of my Life,' and made it 'better as new' as the Jew says about his second-hand garments. I was very pleased with it and the people were too. I am entertained by Baron and Baroness Van der Velts. The lady speaks English very nicely, and they are evidently very pleased to have me with them.

"I was glad to settle to sleep about eleven, and thankful for the mercies of the day."

It was thus that nearly three years passed away. Then came at last the time when the long-hoped-for operation was to take place.

Rookstone, the house in Hadley Wood, a village on the northern outskirts of London, where The General died, stands almost at the foot of the garden of the present General, so that they could be constantly in touch when at home, and the General's grandchildren greatly enjoyed his love for them.

But in the large three-windowed room, where his left eye was operated upon, and where a few months later he died, his Successor, his youngest daughter, Commissioner Howard, and his Private Secretary, Colonel Kitching, had many valued interviews with him during those last months. I had not that opportunity until it was too late to speak to him, for he had said when it was suggested, full as he had been of the hope of prolonged life almost to the end, "Oh, yes, he'll want to come and get something for my life and that will just finish me."

Of the operaton itself we prefer to let the physician himself speak in the following extract from *The Lancet* of the 19th October, 1912:

"...He was not in very good health in March, 1910; he had occasional giddy attacks and lapses of memory, and from April till June of the same year he had albuminuria, from which, however, he appeared entirely to recover. The vision of his left eye became gradually worse, but I encouraged him to go on without operation as long as he could. He did so until about the end of 1911, when his sight had become so bad that he could barely find his way about; indeed, he met with one or two minor accidents on account of not being able to see. It then appeared to me he had much to gain and very little to lose by an operation, and further, he was in much better health than he had been for some time. I pointed out to him that there was a risk and that if the operation failed he would be totally blind, but that there were very long odds in his favour, and that I was willing to take the risk if he was. He asked one question: 'If you were in my place would you have it done?' I said certainly I would. That quite decided him and all that remained to be done was to fix a time. General Booth at that date had some work which he wanted to finish, and eventually the date for operation was fixed for May 23rd. On that day I operated. I did a simple extraction under cocaine.

"Nothing could have been more satisfactory, as will be seen from the notes, and the bulletin sent to the papers was, 'The operation was entirely successful; the ultimate result depends on The General's recuperative power.' When I covered the eye and bandaged it I thought that success was certain, and was confirmed in that opinion on the following morning when I lifted up the dressing and found all was well, and that the patient, when he partly opened the eye, could see. On the third day Dr. Milne, who was in attendance, at once saw that mischief had occurred, and the sequence of events I have narrated. How the eye became infected I am unable to say. I used every precaution; as I told the patient afterwards, the only omission I could think of was that I had not boiled or roasted myself.... I looked carefully for these before each operation. I regret two things in the case: (1) that the last operation was not done two or three months before when General Booth was in better health; (2) that it was not postponed for another month, in which case I should not have done it, for looking back on the whole history I feel certain that he was not in his best condition on May 23rd when the operation was performed."

The General's own response when he was gently informed that there was no hope of his seeing objects any more was:—

"Well, the Lord's Will be done. If it is to be so I have but to bow my head and accept it."

He subsequently remarked that as he had served God and the people with his eyes he must now try to serve without them. He continued to dictate letters, and even to write occasionally as he had been accustomed to do, with the help of his secretaries, and a frame that had been prepared for the purpose. But the very struggles against depression and to cheer others, together with the sleeplessness that resulted took from his little remaining strength, and it became evident that he was gradually sinking. Yet he was so remarkably cheerful and at times even confident that all around him were kept hoping up to the very last.

To a group of Commissioners who visited him he said:—

"I am hoping speedily to be able to talk to Officers and help them all over the world. I am still hoping to go to America and Canada as I had bargained for. I am hoping for several things whether they come to pass or not."

But on Tuesday, the 20th August, it became evident that the end was very near. There gathered around his bed Mr. and Mrs. Bramwell Booth, Mrs. Commissioner Booth-Hellberg, Commissioner Howard, who had been summoned by telegram from his furlough, Colonel Kitching, Brigadier Cox, Adjutant Catherine Booth, Sergeant Bernard Booth, Captain Taylor, his last Assistant Secretary, Nurse Ada Timson of the London Hospital, and Captain Amelia Hill, his housekeeper.

The heart showed no sign of failure until within half an hour of his death, and the feet remained warm till within twenty minutes of the event. But the heart and pulse became gradually weaker, the breathing faster and shorter and more irregular, and at thirteen minutes past ten o'clock at night it entirely ceased.

London awoke to find in our Headquarters window the notice, "General Booth has laid down his Sword. God is with us."

The day after his death, at a meeting of all the Commissioners present in London, the envelope containing the General's appointment of his successor was produced by the Army's Solicitors, endorsed in the General's own writing and still sealed. Upon being opened, it was found to be dated the 21st August, 1890, and that it appointed the Chief of the Staff, William Bramwell Booth, to succeed him. The new General, in accepting the appointment, and promising by God's help to fulfil its duties, expressed his great pleasure in discovering that it was dated during the lifetime of his mother, so that he could feel sure that her prayers had been joined with his father's for him at the time.

Immediately there began to pour in upon us from every part of the world expressions of admiration and sympathy which were most valuable in their promise for the Army's increased opportunity and usefulness in the future.

His Majesty, the King, who had manifested deep sympathy with The General in his illness, sent the following generous message, which was one of the first to come to hand:—

"Abbeystead Hall.

"I am grieved to hear the sad news of the death of your Father. The nation has lost a great organiser, and the poor a whole-hearted and sincere friend, who devoted his life to helping them in a practical way.

"Only in the future shall we realise the good wrought by him for his fellow-creatures.

"To-day there is universal mourning for him. I join in it, and assure you and your family of my true sympathy in the heavy loss which has befallen you.

"George R. I."

Queen Alexandra telegraphed:—

"I beg you and your family to accept my deepest and most heartfelt sympathy in the irreparable loss you and the nation have sustained in the death of your great, good, and never-to-be-forgotten Father, a loss which will be felt throughout the whole civilised world. But, thank God, his work will live for ever.

"Alexandra."

President Taft wired:—

"Washington.

"To General Bramwell Booth:

"In the death of your good Father the world loses one of the most effective practical philanthropists. His long life and great talents were dedicated to the noble work of helping the poor and weak, and to giving them another chance to attain success and happiness.

"Accept my deep sympathy.

"Wm. H. Taft."

The King of Denmark wired:—

"Express my sincere sympathy.

"Christian R."

The Lord Mayor of London, Sir Thomas B. Crosby, wired:—

"The City of London sincerely mourns the passing away of its distinguished citizen, General Booth, whose grand and good work entitles him to imperishable gratitude."

Whilst the Governors and Premiers of most of the Colonies where the Army is at work cabled in similar terms. The Emperor of Germany, as well as the King and Queen, and Queen Alexandra, sent wreaths to be placed on The General's coffin, and the tributes of the press all over the world will be found in the following chapter.

More than 65,000 persons came to Clapton Congress Hall to look upon his face as he lay in his coffin, and more than 35,000 gathered for the great Memorial Service in the Olympia, the largest obtainable building in London, on the evening before the funeral. All the press commented upon the remarkable joyfulness of our funeral services, and the funeral itself the next day was admitted to have been the most impressive sight the great city has seen in modern times.

In addition to officers, many bands from all parts of the country came to join in it.

The coffin had been brought in the night to Headquarters in Queen Victoria Street. The funeral procession was formed on the Embankment, and whilst it marched through the city all traffic was suspended from 11 till 1 o'clock. The millions who witnessed its passage along the five-mile march to Abney Park Cemetery seemed as generally impressed and sympathetic as the multitude gathered there. It was indeed touching to see not only policemen and ambulance workers; but publicans and numbers of the people offering glasses of water to the sisters who had been on their feet for six or seven hours before the service was ended.

The memorial services held all over the world on the following Sunday were attended by quite unparalleled crowds, of whom very many publicly surrendered their lives to God.

The following letters to members of his own family show the spirit of affection and of cheerfulness which to the very last distinguished him.

To his youngest daughter, the widow of Commissioner Booth-Hellberg, who, though she had been fighting in one post or another in this country, India, America, Sweden, Switzerland, or France for over twenty years, he still regarded as his "baby" and special darling, he wrote:—

"Hadley Wood,

"*May* 3, 1912.

"My very dear Lucy,—

"Your letter is to hand. I am interested in all you say. It was very kind, indeed beautiful, of you to sit by the couch of dear Erickson all those hours. But it will be a recollection of pleasure all through your life, and I have no doubt, after the fading hours of this life have passed out of sight and thought, it will give you satisfaction in the life to come.

"There is a great deal in your suggestion that we should do more in the hospitals. It would be, as you say, beyond question a means of blessing and comfort—indeed, of Salvation to many of the lovely, suffering, dying people whose melancholy lot carries them there. But the old difficulty bars the way—the want of Officers and money for the task. Well, we are doing something in this direction, and we must wait for the power to do more.

"I think much about many of the things you say. Your practical common sense comes out at every turn. Based, as your comments and suggestions usually are, on the ***religion of love***, makes them very precious.

"Go on, my dear girl. God, I feel, is preparing you for something very useful in His Kingdom. I feel quite sure.

"But, oh, do be careful and not overrun your strength.

"Through mercy I am keeping better. I had a very trying day yesterday on the top of my table work, which I find a continuous trial to my nerves, but I came through it—that is, through yesterday's hard pull. It was a visit to my native town. But you will read about it in the ***Cry***.

"I am eating much more, not only in quantity, but am indulging in a little more variety.

"My difficulty at the moment is, that while a good supper helps me to sleep, a scanty supper is agreeable to my brains, and my feelings hinder me from sleeping, as I am so lively after it.

"***Later.***

"I have just had a nice little sleep. Quite refreshing it has been, and very welcome also.

"I am now in for a cup of tea. What a pleasure it would be if you were here to pour it out and chatter to me while I drink it.

"Well, I had anticipated this delight on my visit to Norway and Sweden in this coming July, but that, I am afraid, will not come—that is, my visit to Denmark; but I shall hold on to it (D.V.) in connexion with my Annual Campaign in Berlin and round about. Then I shall expect quite a long stay in your Territory, similar to my last; or better, I hope.

"I am positively working night and day now, and only hope I shall not break down; but I am careful, after all, and seem to be really substantially improved.

"I cannot finish this letter now, and, although it is not worth posting, I think it will be best to send it off. I may put in a P.S. if there is opportunity.

"Anyway, believe me, as ever and for ever,

"Your affectionate father,
"W. B."

At his last public Meeting to celebrate his 83d birthday, at the Royal Albert Hall, on the 9th day of May, the General had said:—

"And now comrades and friends I must say good-bye. I am going into dry dock for repairs, but The Army will not be allowed to suffer, either financially or spiritually, or in any other way by my absence, and in the long future I think it will be seen—I shall not be here to see, but you will, that The Army will answer every doubt and banish every fear and strangle every slander, and by its marvellous success show to the world that it is the work of God and that The General has been His Servant."

In his last letter to the Chief, he wrote two months later:—

"International Headquarters, London, E.C.

"*July 4, 1912*.

"My Dear Chief,—

"I am pleased to hear that you are sticking to your intention of going away for a few days, in spite of my continued affliction, for affliction it can truthfully be called.

"I am very poorly, and the trial of it is that I cannot see any positive prospect of a definite, speedy recovery. But it will come; I have never seriously doubted it. God won't let me finish off in this disheartening manner—disheartening, I mean, to my comrades, and to those I have to leave with the responsibility of keeping the Banner flying. God will still do wonders, in spite of men and devils.

"All will be well. Miriam will get well, Mary will get well, and both be brave warriors. Florrie will flourish more than ever, and you will be stronger; and, although it may require more patience and skill, I shall rally!

"I am in real pain and difficulty while I dictate this. These horrid spasms seem to sit on me like a mountain, but I felt I could not let you go without a longer good-bye and a more affectionate kiss than what is so ordinarily. This is a poor thing, but it speaks of the feeling of my heart, and the most fervent prayer of my soul. Love to all,

"Yours, as ever,
"W. B."

"The Chief of the Staff."

To his second daughter, in command of The Army in the United States, his last letter read as follows:—

"*July 20, 1912*.

"My dear, dear Eva,—

"I had your letter. Bless you a thousand times! You are a lovely correspondent. You don't write your letters with your pen, or with your tongue, you write them with your heart. Hearts are different; some, I suppose, are born sound and musical, others are born uncertain and unmusical, and are at best a mere tinkling cymbal. Yours, I have no doubt, has blessed and cheered and delighted the soul of the mother who bore you from the very first opening of your eyes upon the world, and that dear heart has gone on with that cheering influence from that time to the present, and it will go on cheering everybody around you who have loved you, and it will go on cheering among the rest your loving brother Bramwell and your devoted General right away to the end; nay, will go on endlessly, for there is to be no conclusion to our affection.

"I want it to be so. I want it to be my own experience. Love, to be a blessing, must be ambitious, boundless, and eternal. O Lord, help me! and O Lord, destroy everything in me that interferes with the prosperity, growth, and fruitfulness of this precious, Divine, and everlasting fruit!

"I have been ill—I have been very ill indeed. I have had a return of my indigestion in its most terrible form. This spasmodic feeling of suffocation has so distressed me that at times it has seemed almost impossible for me to exist. Still, I have fought my way through, and the doctors this afternoon have told me, as bluntly and plainly as an opinion could be given to a man, that I must struggle on and not give way, or the consequences will be very serious.

"Then, too, the eye has caused me much pain, but that has very much, if not entirely, passed off, and the oculist tells me that the eye will heal up. But, alas! alas! I am absolutely blind. It is very painful, but I am not the only blind man in the world, and I can easily see how, if I am spared, I shall be able to do a good deal of valuable work.

"So I am going to make another attempt at work. What do you think of that? I have sat down this afternoon, not exactly to the desk, but any way to the duties of the desk, and I am going to strive to stick to them if I possibly can. I have been down to some of my meals; I have had a walk in the garden, and now it is proposed for me to take a drive in a motor, I believe some kind soul is loaning me. Anyhow, I am going to have some machine that will shuffle me along the street, road, and square, and I will see how that acts on my nerves, and then perhaps try something more.

"However, I am going into action once more in the Salvation War, and I believe, feeble as I am, God is going to give me another good turn, and another blessed wave of success.

"You will pray for me. I would like before I die—it has been one of the choicest wishes of my soul—to be able to make The Salvation Army such a power for God and of such benefit to mankind that no wicked people can spoil it.

"Salvation for ever! Salvation—Yellow, Red, and Blue! I am for it, my darling, and so are you.

"I have heard about your Open-Air services with the greatest satisfaction, and praise God with all my heart that in the midst of the difficulties of climate and politics, etc., you have been able to go forward.

"I have the daily papers read to me, and among other things that are very mysterious and puzzling are the particulars that I gather of the dreadful heat that you have had to suffer, both as a people and as individuals.

"You seem to have, indeed, been having lively times with the weather. It must have tried you very much.

"My telling you not to fret about me is the proper thing to do. That is my business in this world very largely, and if I can only comfort your dear heart—well, I shall do good work.

"Good-bye, my darling child. Write to me as often as you can, but not when overburdened. I am with you, and for you, and in you for ever and ever. Love to everybody.

"Your affectionate father and General,
"William Booth."

To an Officer whom he regarded almost as a daughter, and whose hearing had been greatly affected, he wrote:—

My Dear C.,—

"Thanks for your sympathetic letter. It is good of you to think about me now and then. Specially so as you must be much and often exercised about your own affliction.

"Perhaps you will think that it is easier for me to accept mine than it will be for you to accept yours. I have just been thinking that to have any difficulty in the Hearing Organ is not so serious as a difficulty with the Seeing. You can read and write, and with a little contrivance and patience you can hear any communication that may be specially interesting and important. It is true, you are shut out from the pleasure and profit that comes from the general conversation of a company, and from listening to Public Speakers, although a great deal that you miss is no serious loss at all!

"In my case, I can imagine I am worse off. With me, reading is impossible, and writing is so difficult that, although I can scratch a few lines, the work soon becomes so taxing and difficult that I have to relinquish it. So we'll sympathise the one with the other. We will trust in God, take courage, and look forward to brighter days.

"Anyway, God lives, and there are a thousand things we can do for Him, and what we can do we will do, and we will do it with our might."

Every thoughtful reader of this volume will naturally have asked himself many times over, how was it possible for the Leader of a great world-wide Mission to leave his Headquarters, year after year, for weeks and sometimes for months at a time, without involving great risk of disaster to his Army?

The answer, familiar to every one at Headquarters, and, indeed, to many others, lay in the existence, largely out of sight even to the vast majority of the Soldiers of The Army, of a man who, since his very youth, had been The General's unwearyable assistant. It was the present General Bramwell Booth, content to toil mostly at executive or administrative work, whether at Headquarters or elsewhere, unseen and unapplauded, who was ceaselessly watching over every portion of the vast whole, and as ceaselessly preparing for advances, noting defects, stopping mistaken movements, and urging at every turn, upon every one, the importance of prayer and faith, the danger of self-confidence, and, the certainty of God's sufficiency for all who relied wholly upon Him. It was this organiser of victory in the individual and on many fields who made it possible for the Army to march forward whilst its General was receiving from city to city, and from village to village, in motor and other tours, the reward of faithful service to the poorest everywhere, and was also ever advancing on the common foe.

Therefore this book could not be complete without some account of the then Chief of the Staff to explain his construction.

Born in Halifax, in 1856, amidst one of those great Revival Tours in which his parents shared in the tremendous toils that brought, in every place they visited, hundreds of souls into deep conviction of sin and hearty submission to God, the little one must have drunk in, from his very childhood, some of that anxiety for the perishing, and joy in their deliverance, which form the basis of a Salvationist career. Named after one of the greatest Holiness preachers, who accompanied John Wesley in his campaigning, in the express hope to both father and mother, that he should become an apostle of that teaching, the faith of his parents received abundant fulfilment in his after life.

As a boy he shared with them all the vicissitudes of their eight gipsy years, during which they were practically without a home, and the one settled year of (as they thought) half wasted time, amidst the usual formalities, always galling to them both, or ordinary Church life; so that, with his usual acuteness of observation, he must have noted all their horror of routine, and learnt, more than anybody noticed, the reasons why the Churches had become divorced from the crowds and the crowds from the Churches.

In his tenth year, when they settled in London, and began their real life work, he cannot but have partaken fully of the satisfaction this gave to them, whilst they were, as yet, buried amidst the mass of East-End misery. It was shortly before the foundation of the Work that he was converted at one of his mother's own Meetings. The shrinking from publicity, which seems an essential part of every conscientious person, held him long back from resolving to become one of their Officers. But during all the years between his being saved and that great decision, he was constantly helping, first in Children's Meetings, and then in office work, so that at twenty-one he was already a very experienced man, both in the work of saving souls, and in much of the business management for which a great Movement calls.

When I first saw him at seventeen, he was still studying; but he had been, during the previous eighteen months of the General's illness and absence, his mother's mainstay in the managing both the public and the office work of "The Christian

Mission," and the Secretary and, largely, manager of a set of soup kitchens, the precursors, in some ways, of our present Social Wing. For all this to be possible to a lad of seventeen, of delicate health, may give some little indication of the faculties with which God had endowed him.

It was not, however, till five years later, when he had fully conquered his own taste for a medical career that he gave himself fully to the War. Alone, or with one of his sisters, he visited the towns where many of our largest Corps were being raised, holding Meetings in theatres and other popular resorts, so that he gained first-hand all the experiences of Officers, both in the pioneering days and in the after years of struggle against all manner of difficulty, when every sort of problem as to individuals, and Corps, had to be dealt with from hour to hour.

This much to explain how it was possible for a man so young to become at twenty-five the worthy and capable Chief of the Staff of an Army already at work in both hemispheres and on both sides of the world. The reader will also be able to understand how the Chief, travelling by night as often as by day, could visit the General in the midst of any of his Campaigns, and in the course of a brief journey from city to city, or between night and morning confer fully with him, and take decisions upon matters that could not await even the delay of a mail.

The comfort to The General, as he often testified, of the continual faithful service of this slave of a son was one of the most invaluable forces of his life. Whilst, on the one side we may see in such self-renouncing abandonment a certificate to and evidence of the nature of The General's own life, we must read in it, at the same time, some part of the explanation of his boundless activities and influence.

For the Chief of those days, The General of these, to have gone to and come away from his father's daily scenes of triumph without getting the slightest appetite himself for public displays, or yielding in the slightest to the craving after human support or encouragement, to turn him aside from the humdrum of duty, is one proof of those gracious evidences of God's saving and keeping power with which the history of The Salvation Army abounds.

Chapter XXV
Tributes

The great tribute The General received by the vast assemblies in every country at his Funeral and Memorial services, said far more than any words could have expressed of the extent to which he had become recognised everywhere as a true friend of all who were in need, and of the degree to which he had succeeded in prompting all his Officers and people to act up to that ideal.

The following, a small selection of the most prominent testimonies borne to his life by the Press of various countries, will give some idea of what was thought and felt by his contemporaries about him and his work:—

The Christian World, *August 22, 1912*

"No name is graven more deeply in the history of his time than that of William Booth, Founder and General of The Salvation Army, who passed to his rest on Tuesday night. At sixteen, the Nottingham builder's son underwent an 'old-fashioned conversion,' and, as he told a representative of ***The Christian World***, 'within six hours he was going in and out of the cottages in the back streets, preaching the Gospel that had saved himself.' From that day he toiled terribly, and never more terribly than since his sixtieth year, after which the Social Scheme was launched, and The General undertook those evangelistic tours in which he traversed England again and again in every direction, and covered a great part of the Western world. How he kept up is a miracle, for he was a frail-looking figure, and he ate next to nothing—a slice or two of toast or bread and butter or rice pudding and a roasted apple, were his meals for many years past. It was his great heart, his invincible faith, his indomitable courage that kept him going.

"Plutarch would have put William Booth and John Wesley together in his 'Parallel Lives.' Each man 'thought in continents.' 'The world is my parish,' said

Wesley, and Methodism to-day covers the world. So General Booth believed in world conquest for Christ, because he believed in Christ's all-conquering power, and he had the courage of his conviction. He learnt much from Wesley, for he began as a Methodist. He knew what can be done by thorough organisation, and what financial resources there are in the multiplication of small but cheerful givers. Like Wesley, too, he combined the genius for great conceptions with the genius for practical detail, without which great conceptions soon vanish into thin air. He was more masterful than Wesley. When he broke away from the Methodist New Connexion, and founded the Christian Mission of which The Salvation Army was the evolution, he found that committees wasted their time in talk and were distracted in opinion. He read lives of Napoleon, Wellington, and other great commanders, and came to the conclusion that a committee is an excellent thing to receive and carry out instructions from a masterful man who knows what he wants, but otherwise they are worthless. He persuaded those of his colleagues who had unbounded belief in him, and whose sole concern was the progress of the Mission, to accept the military organisation with himself as Commander-in-Chief, and with his driving power and the inspiration of his heroic example, those Officers went to every part of Great Britain and to something like fifty different countries and 'did exploits.' That system may work with a selfless Christian hero who is a born Caesar or Napoleon. The Salvation Army's severe testing time has now come, when it will be seen whether, after all, the more cautious Wellingtonian methods of Wesley laid firmer foundations.

"The secret of General Booth's personal force and commanding power was an open one. To him there were no realities so demonstrable as the realities of the spiritual world—most of all, the reality of Christ's real personal presence and saving power to-day. He found that unquestioning faith in Christ's saving power worked everywhere and under all conditions. We differed from him on theological details, but we gladly recognise that scores of thousands of 'moral miracles,' in the shape of lives remade that were apparently shattered beyond repair and trodden in the mud of dissipation and bold habitual sinning, verified the faith. The burglar who had been forty years in prison and penal servitude, the most shameless of Magdalens, the drinker and gambler brought down to the Embankment at midnight, greedy for a meal of soup and bread, the man or woman determined to end a state of despair and disgust with the world by suicide, these, under the influence of The Salvation Army, became 'new creations.' But the same conviction, and the evidences of its miraculous Operation, captured a large number of men and women of the cultured and refined classes, who were either the victims of moral weakness, or who felt the challenge to service and sacrifice for the sake of others. Kings, Queens, and Royal Princes and Princesses were glad to see General Booth, and gave their encouragement to his work, and it was fitting that, when King Edward died, a Salvation Army band should comfort the widowed lady by playing in the courtyard of Buckingham Palace her husband's favourite hymns.

"The Social Work was an inevitable outcome of the evangelistic work. It had its dangers, and The Salvation Army has not escaped all of them without scathe. But it was found that the difficulty with thousands of the Converts was that of giving them a chance to redeem their past, and to nurse them physically and morally till they were able to stand alone, in a position to take their places again in the ranks of decent and self-respecting citizenship. Then there was the 'Submerged Tenth'—the human wreckage tossed hither and thither by the swirling currents of the social sea. To safeguard the one class, and to save the other from themselves and their circumstances, the Social scheme was launched, and those who estimate its success by moral valuation rather than in terms of finance, will say that it has justified itself, though it never accomplished what The General fondly hoped.

"Now that his worn-out body lies awaiting burial, The General's personal worth and the worth of his work are frankly confessed even by those who were once his bitterest critics. **The Times** had a leader in which it said that he rose from obscurity to be known as the head of a vast organisation 'well known over all the world, and yielding to him an obedience scarcely less complete than that which the Catholic Church yields to the Roman Pontiff.' We wish **The Times** had followed **The Standard** in dropping the invidious quotation marks from the title, General. William Booth was a great leader of men in a world campaign of individual and social Salvation. Why reserve the title only for men skilled in the art of wholesale human slaughter?"

The Times, *August 8, 1912*

"The death of General Booth, which we announce with great regret this morning, closes a strange career, one of the most remarkable that our age has seen, and will set the world meditating on that fervent, forceful character, and that keen, though, as some would say, narrow intelligence. Born of unrecorded parentage, educated anyhow, he had raised himself from a position of friendless obscurity to be the head of a vast Organisation not confined to this country or to the British race, but well known over half the world, and yielding to him an obedience scarcely less complete than that which the Catholic Church yields to the Roman Pontiff. The full memoir which we publish to-day shows how this Salvation Army grew up—the creation of one man, or rather of a pair of human beings, for the late Mrs. Booth was scarcely less important to its early development than was her husband. Both of them belonged to the Wesleyan body, of which William Booth at the time of his marriage was a minister, though a very independent and insubordinate one; and deep ingrained in both was the belief which is a more essential part of the Wesleyan than of any other creed, the belief in conversion as an instantaneous change affecting the whole life. Booth himself had been converted at fifteen, and at sixty he wrote of 'the hour, the place of this glorious transaction' as an undying memory. Out of this idea of conversion, as not only the most powerful motive force in life, but as a force which was, so to speak, waiting to be applied to all, arose the whole Salvation Army Movement. It was not, of course, in any sense a new idea. Christians had been familiar with it in all ages, and both the New Testament and the history of the early saints supply instances in support of it. But Booth was probably more affected by more recent evidence. Imperfect as had been his training for the ministry, he doubtless learnt pretty thoroughly the history of Wesley and Whitefield, and of the astonishing early years of the Methodist movement. In his own youth, too, Revivalism was an active force, and he himself had been strongly moved by an American missionary. His originality lay in carrying down the doctrine not only to the highways and hedges, but to the slums, the homes of the very poor, the haunts of criminals and riff-raff; in getting hold of these people; in using the worst of them—'converted,' as he honestly believed—as a triumphant advertisement; and then in organising his followers into a vast Army, with himself as absolute Chief. On the methods adopted nothing need be added to what is said in the memoir; they are familiar to all, though not so familiar as they were some twenty years ago.

"The root-idea of William Booth's religion, the object of his missionary work, was 'the saving of souls.' Translated into other language, this means the establishment of a conviction in the minds of men, women, and children that they were reconciled to God, saved, and preserved to all eternity from the penalties of sin. We do not propose to enter on the delicate ground of theological discussion, or to argue for or against the truth or value of such a conviction. The interesting point, in relation to General Booth's ideas and personality, is to note how this belief is worked into the system of The Army in the official programme, fantastically called the Articles of War, which has to be signed by every Candidate for enrolment. This curious document, which will greatly interest future social historians, consists of three parts—a creed, as definite as any taught by the Churches; a promise to abstain from drink, bad language, dishonesty, etc.; and a solemn promise to obey the lawful orders of the Officers, and never on any consideration to oppose the interests of The Salvation Army. The last part, the promissory part, is made much stricter in the case of Candidates for the position of Officer; these solemnly promise not only to obey The General, but to report any case they may observe in others of 'neglect or variation from his orders and directions.' Membership of the Organisation thus depends on absolute obedience, and on a profession of faith in Salvation in the definite sense formulated in the Articles of War. The two are inseparably conjoined. When we reflect upon what human nature is, in the class from which so many of the members of The Army have been drawn, when we think how difficult it is to reconcile the hand-to-mouth existence of the casual labourer with any high standard of conduct, let alone of religion, General Booth's success, partial though it has been, is an astonishing fact. It implies a prodigious strength of character, and a genius for seeing what would appeal to large numbers of humble folk.

"Will that success continue now that General Booth is dead? Everywhere we hear that The Army is not bringing in Recruits as fast as of old. Its novelty has worn off; its uniforms are no longer impressive; its street services, though they provoke no opposition, do not seem to attract the wastrel and the 'rough' as they did at first. We can readily believe that the work goes on more or less as before; but the gatherings, we suspect, are mostly composed of those who have long frequented them and of a certain number of new members drawn rather from existing sects than from persons till now untouched by religion. Then, with regard to the other side of The Army's work, the Social Schemes outlined in **In Darkest England** have met with only moderate success, as all cool observers foretold in 1890. They have, at least, provided no panacea for poverty. Probably Mr. Booth felt this during the last years of his life; but he has been spared the sight of the still further decline of his projects, which to most of us seems inevitable. Of course, some persons are more confident: they argue that Napoleon's system did not disappear after Waterloo, nor Wesley's system with the death of its founder, and that the Roman Catholic Church is as strong as ever, though Pope after Pope disappears. That is true, but for the very reason that these systems were elaborate organisations, based on the facts of life. The Code Napoleon and the Methodist Connexion were much too well adapted to human needs to disappear with their authors. On the other hand, movements and systems which depend wholly upon one man do not often prove to be more than ephemeral. But none would deny that there is much to be learnt from The Salvation Army and from the earnest, strenuous, and resourceful personality of the man who made it. Let us hope that, if The Army as an Organisation should ultimately fade away, the great lesson of its even temporary success will not be forgotten: the lesson that any force which is to move mankind must regard man's nature as spiritual as well as material, and that the weak and humble, the poor and the 'submerged,' share in that double nature as much as those who spend their lives in the sunshine of worldly prosperity."

The Daily Chronicle, *August 21, 1912*

"To-day we have the mournful duty of chronicling the passing of William Booth, the Head of that vast Organisation, the Salvation Army. The world has lost its greatest missionary evangelist, one of the supermen of the age. Almost every land on the face of the globe knows this pioneer and his Army, The Army which has waged such long, determined, and successful battle against the world's ramparts of sin and woe. Not one country, but fifty, will feel to-day a severe personal loss. From Lapland to Honolulu heads will be bowed in sorrow at the news that that striking figure who has been responsible for so much of the religious progress of the world of to-day is no more.

"The stupendous crusade which he initiated had the very humblest beginnings. It opened in the slummy purlieus of Nottingham, that city which gave to the world two of the greatest religious leaders of modern times—General Booth and Dr. Paton. It has passed through periods of open enmity, opposition, criticism, but its Leader and his band of devoted helpers have never lost sight of their high aim. They were engaged in 'war on the hosts that keep the underworld submerged,' and they have now long been justified by their unparalleled achievements. The time of scorn and indifference passed, and General Booth lived to receive honour at the hands of kings and princes, and to have their support for his work.

"It is not given to every man who sets out with a great purpose to accomplish his aims. But of General Booth it may be said that he did more. His Movement reached dimensions of which he probably never dreamed in its early days, yet the extraordinary results made him ever hungrier for conquest. In a way the latter years of his life were perhaps the most notable of his whole career. He displayed a vitality and enthusiasm which seemed to increase with the weight of time. At a time when most men seek a greater measure of repose, General Booth worked on with all the freshness of early years. And it can be said that he has died in harness. He did not lift his finger from the pulse of the far-reaching Organisation which he brought into being until death called.

"The story of the growth of The Salvation Army is the most remarkable in the history of the work of the spiritual, social, and material regeneration of the submerged. From the by-ways of all the world human derelicts, which other agencies passed by, have been rescued. No one was too degraded, too repulsive to be neglected. The work is too great to be estimated in a way which can show its extent. It has been achieved mainly by two great factors. The first is perfect organisation. Lord Wolseley once described General Booth as the greatest organiser in the world. The second feature was the wonderful personality of The Army's chief. He impressed it not only upon his colleagues but upon those whom he wished to rescue, and on the public at large. He radiated human sympathy and enthusiasm. His loss will be a heavy one for the world; it will be a severe blow for The Army. But we cannot think that his good work has not been built upon sound foundations, and that the war he directed so ably and so long will be relaxed. Nationally The Army has done magnificent work in fifty countries, and it has, therefore, tended to promote a greater spirit of brotherhood among the nations. To-day the whole world will unite to pay its tribute to a splendid life of devotion to a great cause. To that world he leaves a splendid example, and it will be the highest tribute that can be paid to his memory to keep green that lofty example which he set before all peoples."

The Daily Telegraph, *August 21, 1912*

"It is with no ordinary or conventional regret that we record this morning the death of General Booth. The news will be received by hundreds of thousands of Salvationists with profound and reverential grief, and by many who are not Salvationists, and who never could be, with respectful and sympathetic sorrow. For, whatever we may think of William Booth and of the wonderful Organisation which he so triumphantly established, it is certain that he belonged to the company of saints, and that during the eighty-three years of a strenuous life, he devoted himself, so far as in him lay, to the solemn duty of saving men's souls and extending the Divine Kingdom on earth. That success attended his efforts is, from this point of view, not of so much consequence as that the success was deserved by the patient, devout, and self-sacrificing zeal of the Founder of The Salvation Army. Long ago William Booth prevailed against the easy scepticism of those who found fault with his aims, and the sincere dislike of humble and reverent men, who doubted whether the cause of religion could be advanced by such riotous methods. Not only was The General of The Salvation Army a saint and a mystic, who lived in this world and yet was not of this world, but he also was possessed of much practical ability and common sense, without which the great work of his life could never have been accomplished. We need only refer to that remarkable book which he published in 1890, ***In Darkest England, and the Way Out***, in which will be found proposals to remedy the crying evils of pauperism and vice by such eminently wise expedients as Farm Colonies, Oversea Colonies, and Rescue Homes for Fallen Women; to say nothing of picturesque but also practical devices, such as the Prison-Gate Brigade, the Poor Man's Bank, the Poor Man's Lawyer, and Whitechapel-by-the-Sea. How is it possible to ridicule the objects or character of a man who has proved himself so earnest a worker for God? As a matter of fact, William Booth was nothing less than a genius, and towards the end of the nineteenth century the world at large gave very generous recognition, not only to the spirit and temper, but to the results of an extraordinarily effective, and, indeed, epoch-making Movement. At the instance of King Edward VII The General was officially invited to be present at the Coronation ceremony in 1902. Nothing could have marked more significantly than this single fact the completeness of the change of public feeling; and when, in 1905, William Booth went on a progress through England, he was welcomed in state by the Mayors and Corporations of many towns.

"Is it better to live in this world with no religion at all or with a narrow and violent form of religious belief? People will judge the deceased teacher and chief, in respect of his theological and propagandist work, in accordance with the views which they hold upon this alternative. As regards his social labours, his passionate efforts to help the 'submerged tenth,' his widespread helpfulness of the poor, his shelters and refuges, the feeling must and will be almost universal that he was an energetic and warm-hearted benefactor of his kind, who wrought much good to his times, and helped others to do it, and who had what Sir John Seeley called the 'enthusiasm of humanity' in very honourable, if noisy and demonstrative, form. But, since The General mingled all this with a cult—a distinct theological teaching, a theory of the Divine government and destiny of mankind which was in external form, as Huxley styled it, 'Corybantic'—the question does and must arise whether religion of the Salvationist school does good or harm to the human natures which it addresses. It is not necessary to dwell upon the dislike—we might, indeed, say the repulsion—felt by serious and elevated minds at the paraphernalia, the pious turmoil, the uproar and 'banalite' of much that has developed under the Banners of The Salvation Army. Prayers uttered like volley-firing, hymns roared to the roll of drums and the screaming of fifes, have been features of this remarkable revival which outraged many of the orthodox, and made even the judicious and indulgent ask whether any good could come out of such a Nazareth. Nobody gave utterance to this feeling with greater moderation or kindliness than Cardinal Manning, when, while confessing that the need of spiritual awakening among the English poor was only too well proved by the success of General Booth—that the moral and religious state of East London could alone have rendered possible The Salvation Army—his Eminence added these grave sentences: 'Low words generate low thoughts; words without reverence destroy the veneration of the human mind. When a man ceases to venerate he ceases to worship. Extravagance, exaggeration, and coarseness are dangers incident to all popular teachers, and these things pass easily into a strain which shocks the moral sense and deadens the instinct of piety. Familiarity with God in men of chastened mind produces a more profound veneration; in unchastened minds it runs easily into an irreverence which borders upon impiety. Even the Seraphim cover their faces in the Divine Presence.'

"Yet against what new movement of spiritual awakening in the people—against what form of religious revival might not the same argument of offended culture and decorous holiness be employed? And where would the lower masses of men be to-day if Religion had not stooped out of her celestial heights—from the first chapters of Christendom until the last—to the intellectual and moral levels of the poor and lowly? In the sheet, knit at four corners, and lowered out of Heaven, there was nothing common or unclean. If, as is practically certain, General Booth, by the vast association which he founded and organised, touched with the sense of higher and immortal things countless humble and unenlightened souls; if, in his way, and in their way, he brought home to them the love and power of Heaven, and the duty and destiny of men, then it is not for refined persons who keep aloof from such vulgar tasks to mock at the life and deeds of this remarkable man. The particulars which we give elsewhere of his career show how, like Wesley, Whitefield, and Spurgeon, in this country, and like Savonarola, Peter the Hermit, and the Safi mystics abroad, William Booth, the builder's son of Nottingham, was obviously set apart, and summoned by time, temperament, and circumstances for the labours of his life. Like Luther, his answer to all objections—worldly or unworldly—would always have been, 'I can no other'. Meeting in Miss Catherine Mumford the wife who exactly suited him, and reinforced by many children, all brought up in the temper and vocation of their parents, The General made his family a sort of Headquarters' Staff of The Salvation Army, and celebrated his household marriages or bewept his domestic bereavements with all the eclat and effect of oecumenical events. We saw him buy up and turn into stations for his troops such places as the 'Eagle Tavern' and 'Grecian Theatre,' overcome popular rioting at Bath, Guilford, Eastbourne, and elsewhere; fill the United Kingdom with his *War Cry* and his fighting centres, and invade all Europe, and even the Far East. At home he plunged, insatiable of moral and social conquests, into his crusade for 'Darkest England,' being powerful enough to raise in less than a month as much as all England and the Colonies contributed for the Gordon College at Khartoum in response to another victorious general. For General Booth certainly ended by being victorious. If the evangelical creed he inculcated was rude, crude, and unideal, it was serious, sincere, and stimulating. He waged war against the Devil, as that mysterious personage was understood by him, with the most whole-hearted and relentless zeal. He enjoined, let it be remembered, an absolute temperance, soberness, and chastity upon the Officers and rank and file of his motley host; and, ugly as some may think the uniforms of Salvationists, the police and magistrates know that they cover for the most part honest hearts. Could The General have affected all this—or a tenth part of it—if he had not lent himself to the eternal necessities and weaknesses of the uneducated, and given them his drill, his banners, his drums, his prayer-volleys, his poke-bonnets, and his military tunics? We doubt it, and in contemplating, therefore, the enormous good this dead man did, and sought to do, and the neglected fields of humanity which he tilled for the Common Master, we judge him to be one of the chief and most serviceable figures of the Victorian age; and well deserving from his own followers the ecstasy of grief and veneration which is being manifested, and from contemporary notice the tribute of a hearty recognition of pious and noble objects zealously pursued, and love of God and of humanity made the passion and the purpose of a whole unflinching life."

Daily Chronicle, *August 22, 1912*

By Harold Begbie

"Scarcely could you find a country in the whole world where men and women are not now grieving for the death of General Booth. Among peoples of whom we have never heard, and in languages of which we do not know even the alphabet, this universal grief ascends to Heaven—perhaps the most universal grief ever known in the history of mankind.

"One realises something of the old man's achievement by reflecting on this universal grief. It will not do to dismiss him lightly. More, it will not do to express a casual admiration of his character, an indulgent approbation of his work. The man was unique. In some ways he was the superman of his period. Never before has a man in his own lifetime won so wide a measure of deep and passionate human affection.

"It will not do to say that by adopting vulgar methods and appealing to vulgar people, General Booth established his universal kingdom of emotional religion. Let the person inclined to think in this way dress himself in fantastic garments, take a drum, and march through the streets shouting 'Hallelujah.' There is no shorter cut to humility. Many have tried to do what William Booth did. Many men as earnestly and as tenderly have sought to waken drugged humanity and render the Kingdom of Heaven a reality. Many men have broken their hearts in the effort to save the Christian religion from the paralysis of formalism and the sleeping sickness of philosophy. It is not an easy thing to revivify a religion, nor a small thing to rescue many thousands of the human race from sin and misery.

"Let us be generous and acknowledge, now that it is too late to cheer his heart, that General Booth accomplished a work quite wonderful and quite splendid, a work unique in the records of the human race. Let us be frank and say that we ourselves could have done nothing like it. Let us forget our intellectual superiority, and, instead of criticising, endeavour to see as it stands before us, and as it really is, the immense marvel of his achievement. Our canons of taste, our notions of propriety, will change and cease to be. The saved souls of humanity will persist for ever.

"I remember very well my first impression of General Booth. I was young; I knew little of the sorrow of existence; I was perfectly satisfied with the traditions I had inherited from my ancestors; I was disposed to regard originality as affectation, and great earnestness as a sign of fanaticism. In this mood I sat and talked with General Booth, measured him, judged him, and had the audacity to express in print my opinion about him—my opinion of this huge giant, this Moses of modern times. He offended me. The tone of his voice grated on my ears. His manner to a servant who waited upon him seemed harsh and irritable. I found it impossible to believe that his acquaintance with spirituality was either intimate or real. Saints ought to be gentlemen. He seemed to me a vulgar old man, a clumsy old humourist, an intolerant, fanatical, one idea'd Hebraist.

"Later in my life I met him on several occasions, and at each meeting with him I saw something fresh to admire, something new to love. I think that he himself altered as life advanced; but the main change, of course, was in myself—I was able to see him with truer vision, because I was less sure of my own value to the cosmos, and more interested to discover the value of other men. And I was learning to know the sorrows of the world.

"There is one very common illusion concerning General Booth. The vulgar sneers are forgotten; the scandalous slander that he was a self-seeking charlatan is now ashamed to utter itself except in vile quarters; but men still say—so anxious are they to escape from the miracle, so determined to account for every great thing by little reasons—that his success as revivalist lay only in his powers as an organiser.

Now, nothing is further from the truth. General Booth was not a great organiser, not even a great showman. He would have ruined any business entrusted to his management. He would long ago have ruined the organisation of The Salvation Army if his life had been spent on that side of its operations. Far from being the hard, shrewd, calculating, and statesmanlike genius of The Army's machinery, General Booth has always been its heart and soul, its dreamer and its inspiration. The brains of The Army are to be looked for elsewhere. Bramwell Booth is the man of affairs. Bramwell Booth is the master-mind directing all those world-wide activities. And but for Bramwell Booth The Salvation Army as it now exists, a vast catholic Organisation, would be unknown to mankind.

"General Booth's secret, so far as one may speak about it at all, lay in his perfectly beautiful and most passionate sympathy with suffering and pain. I have met only one other man in my life who so powerfully realised the sorrows of other people. Because General Booth realised these sorrows so very truly and so very actually, he was able to communicate his burning desire for radical reformation to other people. The contagiousness of his enthusiasm was the obvious cause of his extraordinary success, but the hidden cause of this enthusiasm was the living, breathing, heart-beating reality of his sympathy with sorrow. When he spoke to one of the sufferings endured by the children of a drunkard, for instance, it was manifest that he himself felt the very tortures and agonies of those unhappy children—really felt them, really endured them. His face showed it. There was no break in the voice, no pious exclamation, no gesture in the least theatrical or sentimental. One saw in the man's face that he was enduring pain, that the thought was so real to him that he himself actually suffered, and suffered acutely. If we had imagination enough to feel as he felt the dreadful fears and awful deprivation of little children in the godless slums of great cities, we, too, should rush out from our comfortable ease to raise Salvation Armies. It would be torture to sit still. It would be impossible to do nothing.

"This wonderful old man suffered all his life as few have ever suffered. And his suffering arose from the tremendous power of his imagination. At a Meeting he would tell amusing stories, and in the company of several people he would talk with a gaiety that deceived; but with one or two, deeply interested to know why he was a Salvationist, and what he really thought about life, he would open his heart, and show one at least something of its agony. He was afflicted by the sins of the whole world. They hurt him, tore him, wounded him, and broke his heart. He did not merely know that people suffer from starvation; that children run to hide under a bed at the first sound of a drunken parent's step on the stair; that thousands of women are friendless and defaced on the streets; that thousands of boys go to their bodily and spiritual ruin only for want of a little natural parental care; that men and women are locked up like wild beasts in prison who would be good parents and law-abiding citizens were love allowed to enter and plead with them—he did not merely know these things, but he visualised and felt in his own person the actual tortures of all these perishing creatures. He wept for them. He prayed for them. Sometimes he would not sleep for thinking of them.

"I have seen him with suffering face and extended arms walk up and down his room, crying out from the depths of his heart: 'Oh, those poor people, those poor people!—the sad, wretched women, the little, trembling frightened children meant to be so happy!—all cursed with sin, cursed and crushed and tortured by sin!' And he would then open his arms as if to embrace the whole world, and exclaim, 'Why won't they let us save them?'—meaning, 'Why won't society and the State let The Salvation Army save them?'

"His attitude towards suffering and sorrow was, nevertheless, harder in many ways than that of certain humanitarians. He believed in a Devil, he believed in Hell, and he believed in the saying that there are those who would not be persuaded though one rose from the dead. And so he held it the wisdom of statesmanship that when all men have been given a fair opportunity for repentance, and after love has done everything in its power to save and convert the lawless and bad, those who will not accept Salvation should be punished with all the force of a civilisation that must needs defend itself. The word punishment was very often on his lips. I think that he believed in the value of punishment almost as profoundly as he believed in the value of love. He believed that love could save the very worst man and the very worst woman in the world who wanted to be saved; and he also believed that nothing was so just and wise as rigorous punishment for the unrighteous who would not be saved. I think that he would have set up in England, if he had enjoyed the power which we give to politicians, two classes of prison—the reforming prison, controlled only by compassionate Christians who believe in love; and the punishing prison, which isolates the evil and iniquitous from contact with innocence and struggling virtue. In that direction this most merciful man was merciless.

"Why he became a Salvationist is very clear. He knew that the centre of life is the heart. He saw that all efforts of statesmanship to alter the conditions of existence must be fruitless, or, at any rate, that the harvest must be in the far distant future of humanity, while the heart of man remains unchanged. He suspected the mere respectability which satisfies so many reformers. Even virtue seemed to him second-rate and perilous. He was not satisfied with abstention from sin, or with the change from slum to model lodging-house. He held that no man is safe, no man is at the top of his being, no man is fully conscious of life's tremendous greatness until the heart is definitely and rejoicingly given to God. He was like St. Augustine, like Coleridge, and all the supreme saints of the world in this insistence upon the necessity for a cleansed heart and a will devoted to the glory of God; he was different from them all in believing that this message must be shouted, dinned, trumpeted, and drummed into the ears of the world before mankind can awaken to its truth.

"He made a tremendous demand. Towards the end of his life he sometimes wondered, very sadly and pitifully, whether he had not asked too much of his followers. I think, to mention only one particular, that he was wavering as to his ban upon tobacco. He was so certain of the happiness and joy which come from Salvation, that he had no patience with the trivial weaknesses of human flesh, which do not really matter. Let us remember that he had seen thousands of men and women all over the world literally transformed by his method from the most miserable animals into radiant and intelligent creatures conscious of immortality and filled with the spirit of unselfish devotion to humanity. Is it to be wondered at that The General of this enormous Army should scarcely doubt the wisdom of his first terms of service?

"But towards the end he suffered greatly in his own personal life, and suffering loosens the rigidity of the mind. Those of his own household broke away from him, the dearest of his children died, trusted Officers forsook him, some of those whose sins he had forgiven again and again deserted his Flag, and whispered scandal and tittle-tattle into the ears of degraded journalism. He was attacked, vilified, and denounced by the vilest of men in the vilest of manners. Sometimes, sitting alone by himself, blind and powerless, very battleworn and sad, this old man at the end of his life must have suffered in the solitude of his soul a grief almost intolerable. But he became more human and more lovable in these last years of distress.

"We are apt to think that very remarkable men who have risen through opposition and difficulty to places of preeminence, must sometimes look back upon the past and indulge themselves in feelings of self-congratulation. It is not often true. A well-known millionaire told me that the happiest moment in his life was that when he ran as a little boy bareheaded through the rain into his mother's cottage carrying to her in a tight-clenched fist his first week's wage—a sixpenny bit. Mr. Lloyd George told me that he never looks back, never allows himself to dream of his romantic life. 'I haven't time,' he said; 'the present is too obsessing, the fight is too hard and insistent.' Mr. Chamberlain in the early days of Tariff Reform, told me much the same thing. Perhaps we may say that men of action never look back. And so it was with General Booth. He might well have rested during these last few years in a large and grateful peace, counting his victories, measuring his achievement, and comparing the pulpit in Nottingham or the first wind-battered tent in East London with this innumerable Army of Salvation which all over the world has saved thousands of human beings from destruction. Sometimes smaller men are able to save a family from disgrace, or to rescue a friend from some hideous calamity, or to make a crippled child happy for a week or two, and the feelings created by these actions are full of happiness and delight. But this old, rough-tongued, weather-beaten, and heart-tortured prophet, who had saved not tens but thousands, who could see with his own eyes in almost every country of the world thousands of little girls rescued from defamation, thousands of women rescued from the sink of horrid vice, thousands of men new-born from lives of unimaginable crime and iniquity, thousands of homes once dreary with squalor and savagery now happy and full of purest joy; nay, who could see, as I have seen in India, whole tribes of criminal races, numbering millions, and once the despair of the Indian Government, living happy, contented, and industrial lives under the Flag of The Salvation Army—he who could see all this, and who could justly say, 'But for me these things had never been,' was not happy and was not satisfied. He ached and groaned to save all such as are sorrowful.

"In the last letter he ever wrote to me, a letter that broke off pitifully, because of his blindness, from the big, bold, challenging handwriting, and became a dictated typewritten letter, occurred the words, 'I am distressed.' He was chiefly distressed by the over-devotion most of us pay to politics and philosophy, by the struggle for wages, by the clash between master and man, by the frivolity of the rich, the stupor of the poor, by the blindness of the whole world to the necessity for the cleansed heart. He did not want to establish a Salvation Army, but to save the whole world. He did not want to be acclaimed by many nations, but to see suffering and poverty and squalor clean banished from the earth. And he believed that with the power of the State at his back, and with the wealth now squandered in a hundred abortive directions in his hands, he could have given us a glad and unashamed England even in a few years. He knew this and believed it with all his heart. And he held that his dictatorship would have hurt no just man. He suffered because poverty continues and thousands are still unhappy. For such men this world can never suffice. They create eternity.

"Others may criticise him. And no man ever lived, I suppose, easier for every little creature crawling about the earth in self-satisfied futility to criticise and ridicule. For myself, I can do nothing but admire, revere, honour, and love this extraordinary old realist, who saved so many thousands of human beings from utmost misery; who aroused all the Churches of the Christian religion throughout the world; who communicated indirectly to politics a spirit of reality which every year grows more potent for social good; who was so tender and affectionate and cordial, and who felt for suffering and sorrow and unhappiness wherever he found it with a heart entirely selfless and absolutely pure.

"Even if The Salvation Army disappeared from every land where it is now at work—and, though it will not disappear, I anticipate during the next ten years many changes in its organisation—to the end of time the spirit of William Booth will be part of our religious progress. We cannot unthink ourselves out of his realism, out of his boundless pity, out of his consuming earnestness. He has taught us all to know that the very bad man can be changed into the very good man, and he has brought us back, albeit by a violent method, to the first simple and absolute principles of the only faith which purifies and exalts humanity.

"When the dust has blown away, we shall see him as perhaps the greatest of our time."

The Post of Berlin

"What he aimed at, for the solution of the Social question and the uplifting of the lowest classes of people by their own works, assures for him the respect of the entire civilised world."

Berlin Local Gazette

"In the person of General Booth was embodied one part of the Social question, and, if any man succeeded in bringing any part of it even nearer to a solution one must say it was William Booth.

"His plainness as a man, his genial gift as an organiser, his burning zeal, his self-sacrificing devotion to his aim, prepared and levelled the road for him, and no man, friend or foe, will withhold from him their tribute of high respect as he lies on his bed of death."

The Morning Post of Berlin

"General Booth, the ancient blind man, always kept his glad heart. He was able to point his opponents, who brought up their theoretical maxims against him (and who latterly became ever fewer) to his practical work."

The Berlin Evening Paper

"There has hardly ever been a General who in an almost unbroken career of victory subdued so many men and conquered so many countries as William Booth. His person gained the high respect of his contemporaries through his long, priestly life, and he will ever remain an example of how much, even in a time of confusion and division, one man can do who knows what he wants, and keeps a clear conscience."

Berlin Midday Paper

"In General Booth we have, undoubtedly, lost one of the most successful organisers of the day."

Berlin Day Paper (Tageblatt)

"Whoever has seen and heard Booth in a huge Meeting in Circus Busch will never forget him—the snow-white, flowing beard and the great, upright figure in the blue uniform, with the red-figured jersey, the furrowed face of typical English character, and the finely mobile orator's mouth, with the searching eyes under the noble forehead, and the prominent nose that gave him almost the aspect of an eagle."

German Watchman

"With that constant will power which sprang from deep and upright conviction, and with a faculty for organisation which won hearty recognition from all who knew him, he was able to do such great things."

National Gazette, Berlin

"His unselfishness and his zealous devotion to his creation (The Army) was beyond all question."

Berlin Exchange Courier

"Whoever saw and heard him knows that he remained, after all, the simple, unassuming, humble man. The secret of this personality was the embodiment of an unshakable religious devotion. It rang out in his burning, earnest words, it breathed in the deep heartfelt prayers in his Meetings, it expressed itself in wondrous deeds of love, which ignored difficulties and shrank from no sacrifice. This made of him the organising genius who led the world-wide Salvation Army, with all its higher and lower departments, with strength and security. William Booth was as its Founder and General perhaps the most popular man of our day."

Neckar-Journal of Heilsbron

"And so General Booth, who has now died at eighty-three, risen to be one of the greatest benefactors of the murdering industry period. His name is graven in brass in the social history of the nineteenth century.

"He was a man through whose soul the great breath of brotherly love and devotion moved, and, therefore, his example will never be forgotten."

The Baden Press of Carlsruhe

"The Salvation Army is to-day the mightiest free Organisation of Social help in the world, and the man who made it was once a street missionary, despised, and without influence, whom part of the despairing mass of the East of London threw stones at, whilst another part, with alcohol-fevered eyes, hung on his lips. 'If ye have faith like a grain of mustard seed!'"

The General Gazette of Erfurt

"In General Booth, one has closed his eyes who was able to make a visible reality of the faith that can remove mountains. The Bonaparte of free Social help has died."

The Cologne Times

"One of the greatest benefactors of mankind has passed away, and as success is the greatest joy, also one of the happiest of men. The Salvation Army is a good, Christian undertaking, and William Booth was one of the noblest Christians whose name history can record."

Hanover Courier

"Booth was the born orator of the people. He possessed above all the rare gift of keeping always to the level of his hearers, and so to speak about the highest themes that the wayfaring man understood him."

Hamburg Strangers Paper

"To the last he was the living, energising centre of The Army, and to the last breath in the truest sense its General."

Munchen Latest News

"With the decease of General Booth, mankind has to mourn the loss of a willing, self-sacrificing benefactor, a noble philanthropist of the most distinguished purpose."

The Kingdom's Messenger of Berlin

"What he accomplished in the fighting of drunkenness or other evils is too well known to need description. Taken all in all, whatever any one may have to say about any details of The Army's methods, one must agree with *The Daily Chronicle* that the loss of General Booth is a heavy blow, and the whole world will unite with us in applauding such a life of devotion to a great end."

The Cross Gazette of Berlin

"It was seen that he was not merely a preacher of repentance, but a real shepherd of his sheep, who had an open heart, and a good understanding for all in need."

German News of Berlin

"He was no quack, no charlatan, and Carlyle, had he known him, would have certainly put him into his list of heroes as priest and prophet. It is great, what The Army has done in fighting manifold human miseries, such as drunkenness. We have often known learned men and politicians who went over the sea scoffers at it come back its admirers."

Markish People's Paper of Barmen

"Our opposition on principle does not prevent our acknowledging that The Army has done much good to the poorest of the poor."

German Daily Paper of Berlin

"With the greatest pity he combined the most iron discipline, and sacrificed to the happiness of all every personal enjoyment."

Germania of Berlin

"But the light that always led him out of the deepest darkness to the day was his sympathy for his brethren, whose misery in the East End of London so deeply laid hold of him."

Daily Look-round of Berlin

"Perhaps the most remarkable fact about him was that with all his gigantic plans he never lost himself in phantasy, but always knew how to keep himself down to the practical."

Strassburg Post

"Hard upon himself, he exercised the same severity upon others, from the highest of his Officers to the least in his Army."

Schwalish Mercury of Stuttgart

"He made his Army out of the soil of London's misery-quarter, and its present is the work of his unwearyable devotion, the energy sustained by the fire of his zeal for his idea."

Muhlhaus Daily

"His personality grew out of the old Puritan spirit."

Elbing Latest News

"He is the model of a successful business man. But he is a business man who never works for himself, only for others. So wrote one of the man whom death has now taken from what was the creation of his life. In him has passed away one of the characteristic figures of the century's tendency. His many-sidedness, it is not too much to say, had no equal. Bringer of Salvation—social politician—wholesale business man—are only three comparisons which cannot by far exhaust the description of the phenomenon Booth. If ever the word can rightly be used of any one, then of William Booth it can be said he was a benefactor of mankind."

Altona News

"Modern time has few men to show whose spirit had any such world-embracing might, and who, out of so unlikely a beginning, knew how to raise up *so* gigantic a work as compels us to be filled, if not with love to him, at least with the greatest respect for his honourable intentions."

Vogtland Gazette Plauen

"These were the innermost feelings of his whole life which drove him to his marvellous life's work—religious zeal and sympathy."

Frankfurt Gazette

"William Booth had a mighty will, and he strove on for tens of years from promise to fulfilment."

Augsburg Evening Gazette

"His brilliant talent for organisation, and his ability always to strike the right note, which would take with the masses, were the most outstanding specialities of the deceased."

Rhein-Westphalian Gazette

"Here is a work done by an extraordinarily organising genius so great and such a model, socially speaking, as to fill even the opponents of the old philanthropist with respect."

Journal Des Debats, Paris

"Never, perhaps, has a man been the creator of such Social Work as this one who has died after having passed fifty years running all over the world in search of the miserable ones; who had no hope."

Gaulois, Paris

"His life may be thus summarised. He brought back to God and to morality many souls who had gone to materialism and vice. He founded pretty well everywhere 750 Refuges for the unfortunate; he found work for those who had none; he despised human respect in order to do good."

The Little Republican, Paris

"It is a very exalted moral figure which has disappeared from this world, as well as even more than a person singularly famous. If he became a preacher, he was certainly born an apostle. He had the genius of conversion, and wanted no other career here below. There is not a city of the Anglo-Saxon world where his Army has not snatched, by hundreds, men from drunkenness and women from prostitution."

In Charge of the Salvation Army Work in U.S.A.]

The Republic, Paris

"An indefatigable organiser, ceaselessly working for the success of his effort, he created besides numerous groups of Salvationists, night Refuges, popular Restaurants, Workplaces, journals, and reviews."

COMMANDER MISS BOOTH

The Intransigent, Paris

"In General Booth passes away a truly world-personage, whose influence extended to the two hemispheres, and, perhaps, as much amongst the savage as the civilised.

"He discovered, his real path, and founded The Salvation Army, which has recruited millions of faithful ones in the most diverse nations—even in our sceptical France."

The Voltaire, Paris

"We have not to judge his religious efforts, nor even his methods, which often seemed to us from some aspects so very absurd.

"But one must recognise that The Army created Hospitals, Retreats, Refuges without number in all countries of the world, including France, and that the devotion of its Soldiers has been unbounded. From the social point of view General Booth was certainly a benefactor."

Gil Blas, Paris

"Struck by the misery which some quarters of London displayed to him, he conceived the idea of evangelising these masses, and to bring them along with the Christian light, physical comfort, and moral union.

"An intelligent work, humane in its principles, beautiful in its aspirations, it merits that we salute with respect the remains of him who undertook it with all his disinterestedness and all his heart."

General Business Paper of Amsterdam

"The world has to mourn the death of one of the noblest men who ever lived, of a man who undiscouraged by scorn, contempt, and continual mockery, kept on working according to his convictions, conscious that he had a great vocation to fulfil, seeking the welfare of his fellows of no matter what race or class they might belong to.

"With his departure will be mourned a man who accomplished great things, and of whom his most ardent opponents have to admit that he by his example and by his incomparable power to work, and his mighty talent for organisation, has been able to be a blessing to many.

"William Booth has gone to his eternal rest. He has not lived and worked in vain. His name does not belong only to his Fatherland, but to the whole world, for he was a benefactor to every land, to all humanity. If any name shall continue to live, it is his."

The People, Amsterdam

"A man has died whose figure, owing to his career, his self-chosen sphere of labour, his manifested power and talent, and through his success, too, has become a world-figure, who may be variously judged, but awakened sympathy everywhere, and scarcely anywhere enmity.

"Booth was the man for the outcasts of society, for the poorest and most miserable, for those who had no strength left, and were entirely unarmed in the fight for existence."

The Fatherland, Amsterdam

"Yes, truly he was a great idealist. That was why he could not be content to remain an ordinary minister. His ideal went beyond the circle of his communion. He wanted to overcome the world by love and Divine worship, and work for all mankind. And we see the results everywhere just as in this country, so at the other side of the world."

The Amsterdammer

"The saving of souls was the great, all-consuming passion of the Founder of The Salvation Army. To satisfy this heart-moving desire he began his wide-stretched Organisation, and, notwithstanding the great Social Work, which represented a great amount of practical social betterment, he continued in every direction in The Army only to honour the opportunity it gave him to win souls for God and The Army."

The Evening Courier, of Milan

"When he stepped to the front of the platform, he seemed transfigured. His rapid and incisive words poured from his mouth with unrestrained eloquence.

"'All the foundation of all we say,' he cried, 'are the eternal truths of the Gospel, indestructible as the pillars of the throne of God.'

"The Apostle spoke out. In that body, worn with age, was born again something of that unconquerable faith which had made Booth as a lad cry out seventy years before, in a prophetic transport, 'The trumpet has sounded the signal for the fight. Your General assures you of success and a glorious reward. Your crown is ready. Why do you wait and hesitate so? Forward, forward, forward!'

"Booth was not one to be intimidated. He tolerated insults with Olympic patience. He just wiped off the dirt his persecutors threw at him, and smilingly invited them to follow him. Thus, about seventy years of age, he began the beneficent career which accomplished a truly marvellous work of philanthropy and love, and which gained for him not only the esteem and veneration of the poor of East London, and of the choicest citizens, but the personal friendship of his Sovereign."

The Age, of Milan

"The death of Booth causes consternation through all England, because through the vast Organisation, The Salvation Army, he was so well known for his works of humanity and beneficence.

"Indeed, he was one of the most celebrated men in the world. The great humane work he founded during the seventy years of his apostolate is destined to remain as one of the highest expressions of modern philanthropy and charity. The Army is an immense federation of hearts and consciences which was created, guided, and led to triumph by Mr. Booth."

The Press, of Turin

"The Founder and General of The Salvation Army, dead at eighty-three years of age, after seventy years of unwearyable apostolate, was one of the purest and most popular heroes of modern Christianity. He was not content to preach the Gospel only from the parchment—a mystic and a poet, yet a practical man of forethought, he was able, out of nothing, to create a Society of militant propagandists for the social redemption of the lost crowds, and to fight against idleness, alcoholism, and evil habits."

The Halfpenny Paper

"The message that General Booth is dead will cause sorrow not only in his country or in Europe, but all over the world. Now, at his death, the whole world knows his name, and thousands follow in his footsteps."

Social Demokrat

"No free religious movement has ever become so great or laid so strong a hold upon all classes of society.

"General Booth will be named in history as one of the strongest and most remarkable personages that ever lived. He was a product of society, such as it was, and the Movement he raised was born of that state of things, firstly as a reconciler, and then as a protest.

"To accomplish such a work as has been done cannot be without result on the future shaping of society."

The Morning

"To-day The Salvation Army stands as one of the mightiest and most remarkable religious organisations that the world has ever seen."

Jonkoping Post

"One of our times, and perhaps all times, greatest and most remarkable personages, The Salvation Army's Founder and General, William Booth, died in London yesterday evening. Behind him lies a path such as few have ever travelled. Before him lies the rest with his Lord, in whose service he laboured almost all his long life."

Swedish Morning Standard

"The world has lost one of its noblest and most remarkable men. A great benefactor of mankind has been called home. Our times' greatest spiritual General has died at his honourable post. Peace to his brave and worthy memory."

Norkoping News

"Few of the most noted men of the day did anything like as much work as The General. He was the leading spirit in all this world-Organisation's least details. He spent most of his time travelling all round the world."

Gothenburg's Post

"Wherever in the world men's hearts beat for men's sorrows and misery, the message of General Booth's death will be received with sadness and mourning. For with General Booth departed the greatest modern apostle of Christianity, charity, and mercy—a sort of Saviour up to the level of modern machinery and wholesale industrial city life, and one of the most discussed and remarkable of modern personages."

Gothenburg's Evening

"William Booth's life was one in storm and battle—a great man's life, the life of an unwearied fighter. Now the whole world bows before the great man and the great life which will live through all time, and go on bringing help to the suffering."

Smaland's Post

"Booth's blessed and energetic all-world-embracing efforts have, during the last decades, had general recognition, and his native land has in various ways testified its respect for what he has done in the service of mercy."

Upsala News

"William Booth's sleepless energy and restless activity succeeded in forcing his work's recognition, even where people did not approve his methods, and many who before despised him will, now that he is gone, admit that he has done more for his fellows than many whose names have gone down to posterity."

Malmo S. S. Daily

"It is one of the day's strongest personages who is gone—a man with the utmost wealth of energy and power. One could hardly believe he belonged to our times, and yet he had all the qualities of our nervous and restless epoch. There was much in him to remind of the old prophets—the lonely man of God fighting with the mighty and the wrong. Nobody can dispute that The Army did much good."

Stockholm Morning

"It lay in the Leader's extraordinary foresight that The Army had a great and blessed work to fulfil to save the deepest sunken in the community."

Chapter XXVI
Organisation

The high reputation which The General gained as an Organiser seems to make it desirable to explain, as fully as we can, what he aimed at, and by what means he made The Army the remarkable combination it has become. We have, happily, in several of our books his own dissertations on the subject, for he always sought to make clear to all who should follow him, especially in this respect, the reasons for his plans. In his introduction to *Orders and Regulations for Staff Officers*, he writes as follows:—

"Some of the Converts resided in other parts of London, and they soon commenced themselves to hold Meetings afterwards, and to win souls in their localities. I was entreated to care for these also. The Christian Churches, even when they were willing to receive these Converts, were as a result generally so much occupied with the maintenance of their own existence, or so lukewarm in coping with the necessities of the poor people, as to be unequal to the task of caring for them. I soon found that the majority of those who joined the Churches either relapsed again into open backsliding, or became half-hearted professors. I was, therefore, driven to select men and women who I knew to be lovers of souls, and to be living holy lives, for the purpose of caring for these new Converts. These helpers I afterwards directed to hold Meetings in the streets and in cottages, and then in Halls and other Meeting Places. The Lord was with them in great power, and hundreds of wicked and godless people were converted and united together in separate societies.

"These operations were, in course of time, extended to the Provinces, where my late beloved wife, who was my unfailing helper and companion in this work until God took her from me, preached with much acceptance and remarkable results. It soon became difficult, and at length impossible, for me to express my wishes and give my instructions to my helpers by word of mouth, and consequently I had to issue them in the form of correspondence. This I also soon found to be a task beyond my ability. And yet, if unity and harmony were to be preserved among the people God had given me, and if the work were to be carried on successfully, it was evident that they must know my wishes. I was, therefore, compelled to ***print*** such Directions and Rules as I deemed to be necessary.

"This practice has continued to the present day, and been increased by reason of the advance of the Work to an extent I never could have anticipated. Some seventeen years ago I issued a volume of ***Orders and Regulations for Field Officers***. More than once since then this book has been enlarged, and revised to date, and, although some further developments have been made since that time, that volume may be taken as the expression, in general terms, of my present convictions of what a Field Officer of The Salvation Army should be and do, and as such I commend it to the attention of Officers and Soldiers of every rank in The Army throughout the world.

"Soon after the publication of the ***Orders and Regulations for Field Officers***, a volume describing the duties of Divisional Officers was issued. This volume has also been outgrown, by reason of continued developments in the organisation of the Army rendering further enlargements necessary.

"Meanwhile, the ablest and most devoted Officers throughout the world have been contriving, and, with the authority of Headquarters, executing what have seemed the wisest and best methods for attaining the objects we have in view. It now appears to me not only desirable, but absolutely necessary, that these usages should be again examined and classified, and, if found to be in harmony with our principles, corrected, reduced to writing, and then, endorsed by my authority, published for the benefit of The Army throughout the world, and for the advantage also of those who will hereafter be our successors in the responsibility for carrying forward the War. The ***Orders and Regulations*** contained in this volume are the result.

"It was my intention to make this book a complete Compendium of Regulations for Staff Officers of all Departments in all parts of the world; but it became evident that, owing to the multiplication of the different branches of our operations, and the diversity of the Regulations required by their varied character and conditions, such a volume would have been swollen to most inconvenient dimensions, and I therefore determined to omit everything not applying to the Officers under the command of the British Commissioner.

"It must not be inferred from this that the Staff Officers employed at International Headquarters, or of those engaged in the Social Work, do not rank equally with those whose duties are herein described. Further ***Orders and Regulations*** required by them, and for Staff Officers in other Territories, will be issued from time to time as needed. The Regulations contained in Part I of this volume are to be carried out as far as possible in all Territories and Departments.

"The Regulations herein contained must not be regarded as a final authority on the duties and responsibilities to which they refer. Development has been the order of The Army from the beginning, and will, I hope, remain so to the end. Our methods must of necessity be always changing with the ever varying character and circumstances of the people whom we seek to benefit. But our principles remain as unchangeable as the Throne of Jehovah. It is probable that in succeeding years other ***Orders and Regulations*** will be issued by the Central Authority to take the place of these I am now publishing. It is right, and safe, and necessary that it should be so. God will, I believe, continue to make known from time to time, to those who follow His good pleasure, the way in which the War should be carried on, and The Army will, I hope, continue to receive and record in ***Orders and Regulations*** that manifested Will, and, by obedience, continue to go forward from victory unto victory!

"I think I may truthfully say that in no words which it has been my privilege to write in the past, and in no work that it has ever been my lot to undertake, have I been more conscious of the presence and guidance of another Spirit, than in the preparation of these Regulations. That Spirit has been, I believe, the Spirit of Eternal Light. I have asked wisdom of God, and I verily believe that my request has been favourably regarded. Of this, I think, these Regulations will, to those for whom they have been prepared, bear witness.

"These Regulations are not, I repeat, intended as a finality. If any Staff Officer into whose hand this book may come, or may be brought into knowledge of the working of the Regulations contained in it, can suggest any improvement, let him do so. If he can show any plan by which the end aimed at can be more simply, or inexpensively, or effectually gained, either as regards work, or men, or methods, or money, by all means let him make the discovery known to us. God is in no wise confined to any particular person for the revelation of His will. It would be the vainest of vain desires were I so foolish as to wish that it should be so. Let Him speak by whom He will. What I want to see is the work done, souls saved, and the world made to submit at the Saviour's feet.

"I cannot conclude without saying that there has been present with me, all the way through the preparation of this book, a vivid sense of the utter powerlessness of all system, however wisely it may have been framed, which has not in the application of it that Spirit of Life who alone imparts the vital force without which no extensive or permanent good can be effected.

"And now, on the completion of my task, and at the moment of placing it in the hands of my Officers, this conviction is forced upon me in an increasing, I may almost say, a painful, degree.

"No one can deny that the religious world is full of forms which have little or no practical influence on the minds, or hearts, or lives, of those who travel the weary round of their performances day by day. Are the Regulations that I am now issuing at no distant date going to swell the number of these dead and powerless systems? God forbid that it should be so! Nothing could be further from my contemplation than such a result.

"However, there must be Regulations. They are necessary. If work is to be done at all, it must be done after some particular fashion, and if one fashion is better than another—which no one amongst us will question—it must be the wisest course to discover that best fashion, and to describe it in plain language, so that it may be acted upon throughout our borders until some better method is made known. We want certain things done in The Army for the Salvation of souls, for the deliverance of the world from sin and misery, and for the glory of our God; and the Regulations herein set forth represent the best methods at present known either to me, or to those around me, for the accomplishment of these things. Therefore praying for God's blessing upon them I send them forth with the expectation that the Staff Officers whom they concern will render a faithful, conscientious, and believing obedience to all that they enjoin."

All this was only written in 1904, and there has been nothing since materially to change the system set forth in the 350 odd pages which follow, and which explain as fully as was necessary how the plans which are so fully explained in the volume of *Orders and Regulations for Field Officers*, above referred to, were to be carried into effect throughout the whole country.

The opening chapter of these ***Regulations*** explains the Organisation as follows:—

"THE GENERAL DIVISIONS OF THE ARMY

"The divisions of The Army in the Field are at present as follow:—

"Ward, under the charge of a Sergeant.

"Corps, under the charge and command of a Field Officer.

"Section, under the charge and command of a Sectional Officer.

"Division, under the charge and command of a Divisional Commander.

"Province, under the charge and command of a Provincial Commander.

"Territory, under the charge and command of a Territorial Commissioner.

"A Ward is a part of a town or neighbourhood in which a Corps is operating, placed under the charge of Local Officers, whose duty it is to watch over the welfare of the Soldiers and Recruits belonging to it.

"A Corps is that portion of a country in which a separate work is carried on, and for which it is responsible. It may consist of a city, a town, or a particular district of either, and it may include one or more Societies in adjoining places, or it may consist of a number of such Societies grouped together, in which case it is called a Circle Corps.

"A Section is a group of Corps placed under the command of one or more Officers.

"A Division consists of a number of Corps grouped together with that part of a country in which these Corps are situated.

"A Province comprises a number of Divisions.

"A Territory consists of a Country, or part of a Country, or several Countries combined together, as The General may decide."

In ***Orders and Regulations*** for his Territorial Commissioners, that is, those who hold the highest command over whole countries, he writes:—

"The higher the authority with which Officers are entrusted, and the larger the responsibilities resting upon them, the greater is the need for that absolute devotion to the principles of The Army, and that complete abandonment to the purposes of

God which our ***Orders and Regulations*** express and represent, and without which no system, however perfect, and no body of men, however capable, can achieve the great work He has called us to do in establishing the Kingdom of God in the earth."

One of the greatest problems connected with all organisation is the keeping up to the ideal of those who are in danger of forgetting it; and, therefore, the following section will, we think, be found especially interesting to those who may ask, How has it been done, or how is it to be done? It is the section on "The Development of Field Officers," and reads as follows:—

"The Divisional Officer is responsible for seeking to develop the spiritual life of the F.O.'s. No matter what gifts or zeal the Officer may possess, if he is not walking in the light, and living in the favour of God, it is vain to hope that he will be really successful.

"The D.O. must always, therefore, when he comes in contact with Officers under his command, make inquiries with regard to their spiritual life, leading them to acknowledge their faults and heart conflicts, so that he may give suitable counsel and help.

"The D.O. must regard himself as responsible to God for maintaining the ***devotion*** of the Officers under him to the great purpose to which they have already consecrated their lives. He cannot expect to deal faithfully with an Officer on such matters unless he does so, and he must bear in mind how easy it is to draw back from that whole-hearted sacrifice without which no Officer can succeed.

"The D.O. must see that his Officers possess, and live in, the ***spirit*** of The Army. Without it their Officership will be like a body without a soul, or like a locomotive without any power. The D.O. must encourage Officers to cry out to God for this, and must continually explain its importance.

"The D.O. must understand that if Officers under his command decline in their love for souls and become careless about the progress of their work, he will have failed in a very important part of his duty. The D.O. exists for the purpose of helping and saving his F.O.'s.

"The D.O. is responsible for the development of energy and enterprise in his Officers. One great temptation of F.O.'s is to settle down and to be content with a formal discharge of duty, and, what is worse still, to offer all sorts of excuses for their lackadaisical Laodicean condition. Few people have in themselves sufficient force of character, human or Divine, to keep them pushing ahead for any considerable length of time. Officers who when they first enter the Field are like flames of fire, will, if not looked after, get into ruts, and content themselves with holding so many Meetings, doing so many marches, raising the ordinary Corps funds, Meeting the ordinary expenditure, keeping the ordinary number of Soldiers on the Roll, and doing everything in the ordinary day, while the world, undisturbed, is going forward at express speed to Hell. The D.O. should endeavour to prevent this settling down on the part of his Officers by continually stirring up their minds with inducements to labour and encouragements to renewed activity and increased sacrifice for the Salvation of the world.

"The D.O. is also responsible for the improvement of the gifts of his Officers and of their efficiency for the work they have in hand. He must not only show them wherein they fail, but must teach them how they may do better.

"The D.O. must encourage his Officers. If they have gifts and capacities—and none are without some—he should cheer them forward by acknowledging them. He should point out where they do well, at the same time setting before them the higher positions of usefulness they may reach with a little application and perseverance. He may always remind them of Officers who during the early part of their career have had little success, but who, by sticking to the fight have reached positions of great usefulness. There are few Officers who during their early days are not cast down and tempted to think that they do not possess the gifts necessary to success, and that they have missed their vocation in becoming Officers. This class of melancholy feelings should be battled with by the D.O. with all his might, for if allowed to run their course the result will be not only depression, but despair, and perhaps desertion.

"The D.O. should give particular attention to the development of the ability, energy, and religion of the Lieutenants in his Division. Their position in a Corps often makes it difficult for them to exercise their gifts to advantage, and they are often depressed and discouraged. A D.O. should always inquire on his visiting a Corps having a Lieutenant—

"Whether he is happy with his C.O. and in the Work;

"What special work he has to do and for which he is actually responsible.

"Every Division must have its own Officers' Meeting, which should always be conducted by the Divisional Officer, unless the Provincial Commander, or some Officer representing Headquarters be present.

"Every Officer in the Division must be present at, at least, one Officers' Meeting in each month; and where it is possible, in great centres Meetings should be held once a week. The D.O. must be careful that the Officers' Meetings do not involve a financial burden on the Officers, and he must make such plans as will avoid this, and submit the same to the P.C.

"It will sometimes be found convenient to pool the travelling expenses, but this may easily work unfavourably to the smaller Corps instead of in their favour, and in such cases the D.O. must assist his F.O's with part of the travelling expenses incurred in attending Officers' Meetings in all such cases where F.O's are drawing the standard salary or less for their support. Should his Funds be insufficient to meet the whole of the burden in such cases, he must apply to the P.C. for assistance.

"The Officers' Meetings should always be held in a comfortable room of a size proportionate to the number of Officers present. The Officers should be seated directly before the leader.

"Only Field Officers shall be admitted. A D.O. who wishes to meet his Local Officers with his F.O. may announce a Special Meeting for that purpose at any time.

"There shall always be at the beginning of a Meeting some considerable time spent in prayer for—

"The Officers present and the Division in general;

"The universal Army, its Officers and Soldiers, and especially for any portion of it that may be suffering persecution or passing through trial;

"For wisdom for those upon whom the direction of the Army lies;

"The supply of money and all else needed to carry on the War.

"The mightier baptisms of the Holy Ghost, and the Salvation of a large number of souls.

"The D.O., or any other Officer present, shall have the opportunity, if desired, of pouring out his soul in loving exhortation to his comrades, but nothing in the nature of discussion or the expression of opinions on any orders that may be given must be permitted.

"The Officer being most used of God at the time should be asked to urge his fellows to more holy living, greater self-denial, and increased activity.

"There shall be the opportunity for the publication of any great blessing that may have been obtained, or any remarkable work of grace that may have been realised in the souls of the Officers present, or in their Corps, or for the description of any other wonderful work of God that may have been wrought during the week in the Division. When at all possible, every Officer present should pray aloud during the Meeting.

"There should occasionally be a time set apart for the confession of unfaithfulness and for the open reconsecration to God and the War on the part of any Officer.

"There should be a general rededication of all present to the War at every Meeting.

"There must be a time set apart for the statement by the D.O. of any event of general interest to the whole Army, or of any remarkable occurrence in the Division, or any Meetings, Demonstrations, or other services of importance that may be likely soon to take place in the Division or elsewhere.

"There must be an opportunity after the Meeting, to transact business. It is of the greatest importance that there should always be time allowed for personal intercourse between the D.O. and the Officers present. The D.O. should always announce at the commencement of the Meeting that he will be glad to see any Officer present, personally, at its close.

"It will be seen what an enormous power the D.O. possesses in this Meeting for inspiring, directing, and controlling all the forces of his Division; how every week he can spend the greater part of a day, and as much more time as he likes, in making his Officers, who have the leadership of The Army in that neighbourhood, think and feel exactly as he does. How solemnly important, then, must it be that the D.O. should think and feel just as our Lord Jesus Christ would have him think and feel on such an occasion, and in the presence of such an opportunity.

"It is most important that the D.O. should arrange beforehand, with great care, such business as will have to be transacted. For instance, he should have, among other things—

"A list of the matters requiring attention. He will save himself much trouble and correspondence, much loss of time, and much expense in travelling by seeing the Officers about matters that concern their Corps, and themselves personally at the Meeting. If he have no such list, it is probable he will forget some of the most important questions of business he has on hand.

"He should have a list of the Officers he wants to see, together with the business upon which it is necessary that he should confer with them.

"Notes must always be taken by him of the results of these interviews, according to rule. Especially should any engagements the D.O. makes for himself be carefully recorded.

"The D.O. should make some personal spiritual preparation for the Meeting. There must of necessity be many things of a perplexing and trying character in connexion with the Officers whom he will have to meet, and the condition of the Corps concerning which he will have information. He ought, therefore, to make an opportunity beforehand for special prayer for Divine guidance and strength, and so enter the Meeting with his mind calm, and confident in the assurance not only of the Divine favour in his own soul, but that God will sustain and direct him in the Meeting and in all the business that may subsequently come before him.

"The condition of heart and spirit in the D.O. at such times will be instinctively felt by every Officer in the room before the Meeting has been going on for a quarter of an hour, and this will have far more influence—as has been remarked before—on his Command than anything he may say or do. How important is it, then, that he should be as Saul among the prophets—not only head and shoulders above every one present as regards authority, but in the possession of the wisdom and power of the Holy Ghost!"

Chapter XXVII
The Spirit of The Army

As pointed out in the foregoing chapter, The General was always anxious to make clear to all, and to avoid, the possibility of a continuance of organisation and a routine of effort without the spirit in which the work has been begun. We could not better describe that spirit than he did in the following address to his Officers gathered around him in London, in 1904.

He pictured to them the idea of Seven Spirits sent out from Heaven to possess the soul of every Officer, and thus described the action of two of them:—

"The Spirit of Life

"We begin with the good Spirit—the Spirit of Life. What did he say? What were the words he brought to us from the Throne? Let me repeat them: 'O Officers, Officers, I am one of the Seven Spirits whom John saw. I travel up and down the earth on special errands of mercy. I am come from Him that sitteth on the Throne, and reigneth for ever and ever, to tell you that if you are going to succeed in your life-and-death struggle for God and man, the first thing you must possess, in all its full and rich maturity, is the Spirit of Divine Life.'

"Now, before I go to the direct consideration of this message, let me have a word or two about life itself

"Life, as you know, is the opposite principle to death. To be alive is to possess an inward force capable of action without any outside assistance. For instance: anything that has in it the principle by which it is able to act in some way, independent of the will of any other thing or creature outside of itself, may be said to be alive. It has in it the principle of life.

"This principle of life is the mainspring and glory of God's universe.

"We have it in different forms in this world. For instance: We have material life. There is living and dead water, and there is living and dead earth.

"Then there is vegetable life. In the fields, and woods, and gardens, you have living trees, and flowers, and seeds.

"Then there is animal life. Only think of the variety, and usefulness, and instinctive skill of unnumbered members of the animal world.

"Then, rising higher in the scale of being, you have human life. Every man, woman, and child posesses, as it were, a trinity of existence; namely, physical life, mental life, and soul life; each being a marvel in itself.

"Then, rising higher still, we have a life more important, and bringing more glory to God than any of the other forms that I have noticed, and that is *Spiritual Life*.

"On this Spiritual Life let me make one or two remarks.

"Spiritual Life is Divine in its origin. It is a creation of the Holy Spirit. I need not dwell on this truth. Jesus Christ was at great trouble to teach it. 'Marvel not,' He said, 'ye must be born again. That which is born of the flesh is flesh, and that which is born of the Spirit is spirit.' You have gone through this experience yourselves. You must insist on it in your people. Spiritual life proceeds from God. It can be obtained in no other way.

"Spiritual Life not only proceeds from God, but partakes of the nature of God.

"We see this principle, that the life imparted partakes of the nature of the author of being that imparts it, illustrated around us in every direction.

"The tree partakes of the nature of the tree from which it is derived. The animal partakes of the nature of the creature that it begets. The child partakes of the nature of its parents. So the soul, born of God, will possess the nature of its Author. Its life will be divine.

"This is a mystery. We cannot understand it, but the Apostle distinctly affirms it when he says, the Son of God is a partaker of the Divine nature.

"Spiritual Life, like all other life, carries with it the particular powers belonging to its own nature.

"Every kind of life has its own particular powers—senses, instincts, or whatever they may be called.

"Vegetable life has its powers, enabling it to draw nutrition out of the ground.

"Fish life has power adapting it to an existence in the water.

"Animal life has powers or senses suitable to its sphere of existence, such as seeing, hearing, tasting, and the like.

"Human life has faculties, emotions, loves and hatreds, suitable to its manner of existence. And it has its own peculiar destiny. It goes back to God, to be judged as to its conduct when its earthly career terminates.

"And the Spiritual Life of which we are speaking has powers or faculties necessary to the maintenance of its existence, and to the discharge of the duties appropriate to the sphere in which it moves. For instance: it has powers to draw from God the nourishment it requires; it has powers to see or discern spiritual things; it has powers to distinguish holy people; it has powers to love truth, and to hate falsehood; it has powers to suffer and sacrifice for the good of others. It has powers to know, and love, and glorify its Maker.

"Those possessed of this Spiritual Life, like all other beings, act according to their nature.

"For instance: the tree grows in the woods, and bears leaves and fruit after its own nature. The bird flies in the air, builds its nest, and sings its song after its own nature. The wild beasts roam through the forest, and rage and devour according to their own nature. If you are to make these or any other creatures act differently, you must give them a different nature. By distorting the tree, or training the animal, or clipping the wings of the bird, you may make some trifling and temporary alteration in the condition or conduct of these creatures; but when you have done this, left to themselves, they will soon revert to their original nature.

"By way of illustration. A menagerie recently paid a visit to a northern town. Amongst the exhibits was a cage labelled 'The Happy Family,' containing a lion, a tiger, a wolf, and a lamb. When the keeper was asked confidentially how long a time these animals had lived thus peacefully together, he answered, 'About ten months. But,' said he, with a twinkle in his eye, 'the lamb has to be renewed occasionally.'

"As with these forms of life, so with men and women and children. The only way to secure conduct of a lasting character different from its nature is by effecting a change in that nature. Make them new creatures in Christ Jesus and you will have a Christlike life.

"The presence of the powers natural to Spiritual Life constitutes the only true and sufficient evidence of its possession.

"The absence of these powers shows conclusively the absence of the life. If a man does not love God and walk humbly with Him; if he does not long after Holiness, love his comrades, and care for souls, it will be satisfying evidence that he has gone back to the old nature—that is, to spiritual death.

"All Spiritual Life is not only imparted by Jesus Christ, but sustained by direct union with Him.

"'I am the Vine,' He says, 'ye are the branches; he that abideth in Me, and I in him, the same bringeth forth much fruit; for without Me ye can do nothing' (John xv. 6).

"Nothing will make up for the lack of this life.

"This, indeed, applies to every kind of existence. You cannot find a substitute for life in the vegetable kingdom. Try the trees in the garden. Look at that dead apple-tree. As you see it there, it is useless, ugly, fruitless. What will make up for the absence of life? Will the digging, or the manuring of the ground around it do this? No! That will be all in vain. If it is dead, there is only one remedy, and that is to give it life—new life.

"Take the animal world. What can you do to make up for the lack of life in a dog? I read the other day of a lady who had a pet dog. She loved it to distraction. It died. Whatever could she do with it to make up for its loss of life? Well, she might have preserved it, stuffed it, jewelled its eyes, and painted its skin. But had she done so, these things would have been a disappointing substitute. So she buried it, and committed suicide in her grief, and was buried by its side.

"Take the loss of human life. What is the use of a dead man? Go to the death-chamber. Look at that corpse. The loved ones are distracted. What can they do? They may dress it, adorn it, appeal to it. But all that human skill and effort can conceive will be in vain. All that the broken hearts can say or do must soon terminate, as did Abraham's mourning for Sarah, when he said, 'Give me a piece of land that I may bury my dead out of my sight.' Nothing can make up for the lack of life.

"But this is specially true of the Spiritual Life of which we are speaking. Take this in its application to a Corps. If you want an active, generous, fighting, dare-devil Corps, able and willing to drive Hell before it, that Corps must be possessed, and that fully, by this spirit of life. Nothing else can effectively take its place. No education, learning, Bible knowledge, theology, social amusements, or anything of the kind will be a satisfactory substitute. The Corps that seeks to put any of these things in the place of life will find them a mockery, a delusion, and a snare; will find them to be only the wraps and trappings of death itself.

"And if it is so in the Corps, it is so ten thousand times more in the Officer who commands that Corps—in you!

"Spiritual Life is the essential root of every other qualification required by a Salvation Army Officer.

"With it he will be of unspeakable interest.

"He will be a pleasure to himself. There is an unspeakable joy in having healthy, exuberant life.

"He will be of interest to those about him. Who cares about dead things? Dead flowers—throw them out. Dead animals—eat them. Dead men—bury them. Dead and dying Officers—take them away. Give them another Corps.

"If he is living he will be of interest to all about him. Men with humble abilities, if full of this Spiritual Life, will be a charm and a blessing wherever they go. Look at the lives and writings of such humble men as Billy Bray, Carvosso, and Hodgson Casson. Their memory is an ointment poured forth to-day after long years have passed away.

"Without this life an Officer will be of no manner of use. No matter how he may be educated or talented, without life is to be without love; and to be without love, the Apostle tells us, is to be only as 'a sounding brass.' But it is not that of which I want to speak just now.

"Spiritual Life is essential to the preservation of life.

"The first thing life does for its possessor is to lead him to look after its own protection. When the principle of life is strong, you will have health and longevity. When it is weak, you have disease. When it is extinct, you have decay and rottenness.

"Only vigorous Spiritual Life will enable a Salvation Army Officer to effectually discharge the duties connected with his position.

"Life is favorable to activity. It is so with all life. Go into the tropical forests, and see the exuberant growth of everything there. Look at the foliage, the blossom, the fruit. Look at the reptiles crawling at your feet, and take care they do not sting you. Look at the birds chattering and fluttering on the trees, and they will charm you. Look at the animals roving through the woods, and take care they do not devour you.

"Contrast all this movement with the empty, barren, silent, Polar regions, or the dreary, treeless sands of the African desert.

"Go and look at the overflowing, tirelss activity of the children. Why are they never still? It is the life that is in them. Go to the man at work. With what glee, and for what a trifling remuneration, he sweats, and lifts and carries the ponderous weights. Go to the soldier in the military war. How he shouts and sings as he marches to deprivations, and wounds, and death.

"Even so with Spiritual Life. It never rests; it never tires; it always sees something great to do, and is always ready to undertake it. What is the explanation? How can we account for it? The answer is, Life—abundant life.

"It is only by the possession of Life that The Salvation Army Officer can spread this life.

"That is, reproduce himself, multiply himself, or his kind. This reproduction or multiplication of itself is a characteristic of all life.

"Take the vegetable kingdom. Every living plant has life-producing seed, or some method of reproducing itself. The thistle: who can count the number of plants that one thistle can produce in a year? One hundred strawberry plants can be made in ten years to produce more than a thousand million other strawberry plants!

"Take the animal kingdom. Here each living creature has this reproductive power. They say that a pair of sparrows would in ten years, if all their progeny could be preserved, produce as many birds as there are people on the earth—that is, 1,500,000,000. 'Ye are of more value than many sparrows.'

"Just so, this Spiritual Life is intended to spread itself through the world.

"It is to this end it is given to you. God's command to Adam was, 'Be fruitful, and multiply, and replenish the earth.' How much more does this command apply to you and to me! You are to be progenitors of a world of men and women possessed of Spiritual Life; the parents of a race of angels. How this is to be done is another question. About that I shall have something to say as we go along. For the moment, I am simply occupied with the fact that you have to call this world of holy beings into existence by spreading this life.

"Every Officer here is located in a world of death. Sometimes we style it a dying world, and so it is on its human side, but on its spiritual side it is past dying; it is dead. By that I do not mean that the spiritual nature, that is the soul, ever ceases to be in any man. That will never come to pass. Perhaps nothing once created will ever cease to be. Anyway, man is immortal. The soul can never die. Neither do I mean that there is no Spiritual Life.

"By spiritual death we mean that the soul is—Separated from God; no union with Him. In a blind man the organ may be perfect, but not connected.

"Inactive. No love for the things God loves. No hatred for the things He hates. Dead to His interests, His kingdom; dead to Him.

"Corrupt, bad, devilish, etc. What a valley of dry bones the world appears to the man whose eyes have been opened to see the truth of things. Verily, verily, it is one great cemetery crowded with men, women, and children dead in trespasses and sin. Look for a moment at this graveyard, in which the men around you may be said to lie with their hearts all dead and cold to Christ, and all that concerns their Salvation. Look at it. The men and women and children in your town are buried there. The men and women in your city, in your street. Nay, the very people who come to your Hall to hear you talk on a Sunday night are there. There they lie. Let us read the inscriptions on some of their tombs:—

"***Here lies Tom Jones***

"He had a beautiful nature, and a young, virtuous wife, and some beautiful children. All starved and wretched through their father's selfish ways. He can't help himself. He says so. He has proved it. He is dead in drunkenness.

"***Here lies Harry Please-Yourself***

"Mad on footballing, theatres, music-halls, dances, and the like. Nothing else morning, noon, or night seems to interest him. There he is, dead in pleasure.

"***Here lies James Haughtiness***

"Full of high notions about his abilities, or his knowledge, or his family, or his house, or his fortune, or his business, or his dogs, or something. There he is, dead in pride.

"***Here lies Jane Featherhead***

"Absorbed in her hats, and gowns, and ribbons, and companions, and attainments. There she is, dead in vanity.

"*Here lies Miser Graspall*

"Taken up with his money—sovereigns, dollars, francs, kroner, much or little. 'Let me have more and more' is his dream, and his cry, and his aim, by night and day. There he is, dead in covetousness.

"*Here lies Sceptical Doubtall*

"Hunting through the world of nature, and revolution, and providence, and specially through the dirty world of his own dark little heart, for arguments against God and Christ and Heaven. There he is, dead in infidelity.

"*Here lies Jeremiah Make-Believe*

"With his Bible Class and Singing Choir, and Sunday religion, and heartless indifference to the Salvation or damnation of the perishing crowds at his door. There he is, dead in formality.

"*Here lies Surly Badblood*

"Packed full of suspicions and utter disregards for the happiness and feelings of his wife, family, neighbours, or friends. There he is, dead in bad tempers.

"*Here lies Dives Enjoy-Yourself*

"Look at his marble tomb, and golden coffin, and embroidered shroud, and ermine robes. This is a man whose every earthly want is supplied—Carriages, music, friends. There he is, dead in luxury.

"*Here lies Dick Never-Fear*

"His mouth is filled with laughter, and his heart with contempt when you speak to him about his soul. He has no anxiety, not he. He'll come off all right, never fear. Is not God merciful? And did not Christ die? And did not his mother pray? Don't be alarmed, God won't hurt him. There he is, dead in presumption,

"*Here lies Judas Renegade*

"His grave has a desolate look. The thorns and thistles grow over it. The occupant has money and worldly friends, and many other things, but altogether he gets no satisfaction out of them; he is uneasy all the time. There he is, dead in apostacy.

"There are any number of other graves. It is interesting, although painful, to wander amongst them. All, or nearly all, their occupants are held down by a heavy weight of ignorance, a sense of utter helplessness. And all are bound hand and foot with chains of lust, or passion, or procrastination, of their own forging. In the midst of these graves you live, and move, and have your being.

"What is your duty here? Oh, that you realised your true business in this region of death! Having eyes, Oh! that you could see. Having ears, Oh! that you could hear. Having hearts, Oh! that you could feel. What are you going to do with this graveyard? Walk about it in heartless unconcern, or with no higher feeling than gratitude for having been made alive yourselves? Or will you content yourselves with strolling through it, taxing its poor occupants for your living while leaving them quietly in their tombs as hopeless as you found them? Heaven forbid! Well, then, what do you propose? What will you do?

"Look after their bodies, and feed and nourish them, making the graveyard as comfortable a resting-place as you can? That is good, so far as it goes, but that is not very far. Will that content you? Decorate their graves with flowers and evergreens, and wreaths of pleasant things? Will that content you? Amuse them with your music, or the singing of your songs, or the letting off of your oratorical fireworks among their rotting corpses? Will that content you? Instruct them in doctrines, and rescues, and Salvations in which they have no share? Will that content you? No! No! No! A thousand times no! You won't be content with all that. God has sent you into this dark valley for nothing less than to raise these doom-struck creatures from the dead. That is your mission. To stop short of this will be a disastrous and everlasting calamity.

"What do you say? It cannot be done? That is false. God would never have set you an impossible task. You cannot do it? That is false again, for you have done it before again and again. There is not an Officer here who has not called some souls from the dead. Not one. How many thousands—how many tens of thousands, in the aggregate, have the Officers present at this Congress raised from the graves of iniquity? Who can tell?

"Go, and do it again. Go, and look at them. Go, and compassionate them. Go, and represent Jesus Christ to them. Go, and prophesy to them. Go, and believe for them. And then shall bone come to bone, and there shall be a great noise, and a great Army shall stand up to live, and fight, and die for the living God.

"THE SPIRIT OF PURITY

"And now we come to the consideration of the message of the second Spirit. Let us recall his words: 'O Officers, Officers, the Great Father has sent me to tell you that if you would be successful in your campaign against wickedness, selfishness, and fiends, you must yourselves be holy.'

"I come now to the task of showing, as far as I am able, what the plan of life is which God has formed for a Salvation Army Officer.

"What must an Officer be and do who wants satisfactorily to fill up the plan God has formed for him? Of course, there will in some respects be certain striking differences in that plan. But in the main there will be remarkable resemblances.

"The first thing that God asks is, that the Officer shall possess the character He approves.

"You might say the character that He admires. The very essence of that character is expressed in one word—***Holiness***.

"In the list of qualifications for effective leadership in this warfare, The Salvation Army has ever placed Holiness in the first rank. The Army has said, and says to-day, that no other qualities or abilities can take its place. No learning, or knowledge, or talking, or singing, or scheming, or any other gift will make up for the absence of this. You must be good if you are to be a successful Officer in The Salvation Army.

"Let us suppose that a comrade were to present himself before us this morning, and say, 'I am a Salvationist. I want to be an Officer amongst you, and I want to be an Officer after God's own Heart; but I am ignorant of the qualifications needed.' If I were to ask you what I should say to this brother, I know what your answer would be. You would say, with one voice, 'Tell him that, before all else, he must be a holy man.'

"Suppose, further, that I appeared before you myself for the first time at this Congress, and were to say to you: 'My comrades, I have come to be your Leader. What is the first, the foundation quality I require for your leadership?' I know the answer you would give me. You would say, 'O General, you must be a holy man.'

"If there were gathered before me, in some mighty building, the choicest spirits now fighting in The Salvation Army the world over—Commissioners and Staff Officers, Field Officers and Local Officers, together with Soldiers of every grade and class; and suppose, further, that standing out before that crowd, I was to propose the question: 'In what position in our qualifications shall I place the blessing of Holiness?' you know what the answer would be. With a voice that would be heard among the multitudes in Heaven the crowd would answer: 'Holiness must be in the first rank.'

"If this morning I had the privilege of ascending to the Celestial City, and asking the assembled angels in that mighty temple where, day and night, they worship the Great Jehovah: 'What position ought Holiness to occupy in the qualifications needed by Salvation Army Officers in their fight on earth?' you know that angels and archangels, cherubim and seraphim, would join with the Seven Spirits that are before the Throne with one united shout, loud enough to make the ears of Gabriel tingle, and would answer, 'Place it first.'

"If I could have the still greater privilege of kneeling before the intercessory Throne of my dear, my precious, my glorified Saviour, and of asking Him what position this truth should hold in the hearts and efforts of Salvation Army Officers, you know that He would answer: 'Blessed are the pure in heart.' Holiness comes first.

"If, further still, borne on a burning seraph's wings I could rise to the Heaven of Heavens, and, like its holy inhabitants, be allowed to enter the Holy of Holies, where Jehovah especially manifests His glory; and if, prostrate before that Throne, with all reverence I should ask the question: 'What is the first and most important qualification a Salvation Army Officer must possess in order to do Your Blessed Will?' you have His answer already. You know that He would reply: 'Be ye holy, for I am holy.'

"What, then, is that Holiness which constitutes the first qualification of an Officer, and which is asked for by that Blessed Spirit of Purity coming from the Throne of God?

"In replying to this question I cannot hope to do more than put you in remembrance of what you must already know.

"I will, however, to begin with, take the broad ground that Holiness, in the sense in which The Salvation Army uses the word, means entire deliverance from sin. I shall explain myself as I go along. But I begin with the assertion that holy souls are saved from sin.

"You all know what sin is. And it is important that you should, and that you should be able to define it at a moment's notice to whomsoever may inquire. John says: 'All unrighteousness is sin,' That is, everything that a man sees to be actually wrong, that to him is sin. Whether the wrong be an outward act, or an inward thought, or a secret purpose does not affect its character. If the act, or thought, or purpose is wrong to that particular soul it is sin. Whether the wrong be done in public and blazoned abroad before the world as such, or whether it be committed in darkness and secrecy, where no human eye can follow it, matters not; it is sin.

"To be holy, I say, is to be delivered from the commission of sin. Is not that blessed?

"To be holy is to be delivered from the penalty of sin. 'The wages of sin is death.' Holy men are fully and freely forgiven. One of the evidences of the possession of Holiness is the full assurance of that deliverance. Salvation from doubt as to this. Is not that blessed?

"Holiness includes deliverance from the guilt of sin.

"Sin has a retributive power. At the moment of commission it implants a sting in the conscience which, in the impenitent man, lights a flame, which, without the application of the Precious Blood, is never extinguished. In Holiness the sting is extracted, and the fire is quenched. Is not that blessed?

"Holiness supposes deliverance from the defilement of sin.

"Sin pollutes the imagination, defiles the memory, and is a filth-creating leaven, which, unless purged away, ultimately corrupts and rots the whole being.

"In Holiness all the filth is cleansed away. The soul is washed in the Blood of the Lamb. This is the reason for so much being said in the Bible, and in the experience of entirely sanctified people, about purity of heart. Is not that blessed?

"Holiness means complete deliverance from the bondage of sin.

"Every time a sin is committed, the inclination to do the same again is encouraged, and those habits which belong to the evil nature are strengthened until they assume the mastery of the soul, and the soul comes more and more under the tyranny of evil.

"In conversion the chains that bind men to sin are broken, but the tendency to evil still lingers behind. In Holiness the bondage is not only entirely destroyed, and the soul completely delivered from these evil tendencies, but is free to do the will of God, so far as it is known, as really as it is done in Heaven. Is not that blessed?

"Holiness supposes the deliverance of the soul from the rule and reign of selfishness.

"The essence of sin is selfishness; that is, the unreasoning, improper love of self. The essence of Holiness is benevolence. Holy souls are mastered by love, filled with love. Is not that blessed?

"It will be seen, then, that the Officer who enjoys this experience of Holiness will have received power from God to live a life consciously separated from sin.

"A man cannot be living in a God-pleasing state if he is knowingly living in sin, or consenting to it, which amounts to the same thing. Let us look a little more closely at this.

"Holiness will mean a present separation from all that is openly or secretly untrue.

"Any one pretending to be doing the will of God, while acting untruthfully or deceitfully in his dealings with those around him, is not only guilty of falsehood, but of hypocrisy.

"To be holy is to be sincere.

"Holiness means separation from all open and secret dishonesty. This applies to everything like defrauding another of that which is his just and lawful due.

"Holiness also means separation from all that is unjust.

"Doing unto others as you would that they should do to you, may be truly described as one of the lovely flowers and fruits of Purity.

"Holiness means Salvation from all neglect of duty to God and man.

"All pretensions to Holiness are vain while the soul is living in the conscious neglect of duty. A holy Officer will do his duty to his Maker. He will love God with all his heart—such a heart as he has, big or little. He will love and worship Him, and strive to please Him in all that he does. A holy Officer will love his neighbour as himself. The law of love will govern his dealings with his family, comrades, neighbours—body and soul.

"That is a beautiful experience which I am describing, is it not, my comrades? And you cannot be surprised that the Spirit of Purity should bring you the message that it is God's plan of life for you.

"Upon it let me make a few further remarks.

"Holiness is a distinct definite state; a man can be in it or out of it.

"Holiness is enjoyed partially or entirely by all converted people. It can be enjoyed partially. No one would say that every converted man was a holy man, and no one would say that every man who was not perfectly holy was not converted. But I should say, and so would you, that every truly converted man is the master of sin, although he may not be entirely delivered from it.

"Then, again, Holiness is a continued growth in sincere souls. With faith, watchfulness, prayer, and obedience, the power of sin diminishes as the days pass along, and the strength of Holiness increases.

"The line which separates a state of entire from a state of partial Holiness may be approached very gradually, but there is a moment when it is crossed.

"The approach of death is often all but imperceptible, but there is a moment when the last breath is drawn. Just so there is a moment when the body of sin is destroyed, however gradual the process may have been by which that state has been reached. There is a moment when the soul becomes entirely holy—entirely God's.

"By perseverance in the sanctified life spiritual manhood is reached, and the soul is perfected in love; that is maturity.

"Let me illustrate the doctrine of Holiness, in its varied aspects, by comparing its attainment to the ascent of a lofty mountain.

"Come with me. Yonder is the sacred mount, towering far above the clouds and fogs of sin and selfishness. Around its base, stretching into the distance, as far as eye can reach, lies a flat, dismal, swampy country. The district is thickly populated by a people who, while professing the enjoyment of religion, are swallowed up in unreality about everything that appertains to Salvation. They talk, and sing, and pray, and write, and read about it, but they are all more or less in doubt whether they have any individual part or lot in the matter. Sometimes they think they have a hope of Heaven, but more frequently they are afraid that their very hopes are a delusion.

"The land is haunted by troubling spirits continually coming and going, that point to past misdoings and coming penalties. Such venomous creatures as hatreds, revenges, lusts, and other evil passions are rife in every direction; while the demons of doubt and despair seem to come and go of their own free will, leading men and women on the one hand to indifference, worldliness, and infidelity, and on the other to darkness and despair. This wild, dismal territory we will style 'The Land of Uncertainty.'

"In the centre of this unlovable and undesirable country the mountain of which I want to speak lifts its lofty head. Call it 'Mount Pisgah' or 'Mount Beulah,' or, if you will, call it 'Mount Purity'—I like that term the best. But whatever you name it, there it is, rising up above the clouds and fogs of sin and selfishness, and doubt and fear and condemnation that ever overhang the swampy Land of Uncertainty, of which I have given you a glimpse.

"Look at it. There are some monster mountains in the natural world, but they are mere molehills alongside this giant height. Look at it again. Is it not an entrancing sight? Its lofty brow, crowned with a halo of glorious light, reaches far upwards towards the gates of endless day, those living on its summit having glorious glimpses of the towers and palaces of the Celestial City. The atmosphere is eminently promotive of vigorous health and lively spirits. But its chief claim is the purity of heart, the constant faith, the loving nature, and the consecrated, self-sacrificing devotion of those who are privileged to dwell there. It must be a charming place. The multitudes whose feet have ever been permitted to tread its blessed heights think so.

"But while gazing on the entrancing sight, the question spontaneously arises: 'How can I get there?' There is evidently no mountain railway nor elevator on which, while reclining on pillows of ease, and serenaded by music and song, you can be rapidly and smoothly lifted up to the blessed summit. Those who reach that heavenly height must climb what the Bible calls the 'Highway of Holiness.' And they will usually find it a rugged, difficult journey, often having to fight every inch of the way. But, once on the celestial summit, the travellers will feel amply repaid for every atom of trouble and toil involved in the ascent.

"The road to this glorious height passes through various plateaux or stages which run all round the sides of the mountain, each different from the other, and each higher than the one that preceded it. Travellers to the summit have to pass through each of these stages. Let me enumerate some of the chief among them.

"To begin with, there is the awakening stage, where the climbers obtain their first fair view of this holy hill.

"It is here that the desire to make the ascent first breaks out. This longing is often awakened by reading various guide-books or Holiness advertisements, such as ***The War Cry***, or ***Perfect Love***, which set forth the blessedness experienced by those who make the heavenly ascent. Sometimes the desire to ascend the holy hill is awakened by the pure light which every now and then shines from the summit direct into the travellers' hearts. Or, it may be their souls are set on fire with a holy longing to be emptied of sin and filled with love by the burning testimonies of some of the people who live up there, but who come down into the valley every now and then to persuade their comrades to make the ascent. Anyway, it almost always happens when those who read these guide-books and listen to these testimonies begin to search their Bibles and cry to God for guidance, that a spirit of hunger and thirst sets in which gives them no rest until they themselves resolve to take the journey up the side of this wonderful mountain.

"A little higher up, and you reach the starting stage.

"Here those who fully resolve upon seeking holiness of heart first enter their names in the 'Travellers' Book.' On this plateau I observe that there is a great deal of prayer. You can hear the earnest petitions going up to Heaven, whichever way you turn. And, much prayer as there is, you can hear much singing also. One of the favourite songs commences:—

> "O glorious hope of perfect love!
> It lifts me up to things above,
>   It bears on eagles' wings;
> It gives my ravished soul a taste,
> And makes me for some moments feast
>   With Jesus' priests and kings.

"There is another favourite song which begins:--

> "O joyful sound of Gospel grace!
>   Christ shall in me appear;
> I, even I, shall see His face,
>   I shall be holy here.

"But, still ascending, we come to the wrestling stage.

"Here the travellers are met by numerous enemies, who are in dead opposition to their ever reaching the summit.

"I observe that the enemies attack those travellers with doubts as to the possibility of ever reaching the mountain's top, and with scores of questions about apparently conflicting passages of Scripture, and contradictory experiences of Christian people; and, alas! with only too frequent success, for the whole plateau seems to be strewn with the records of broken resolutions relating to the renouncements of evil habits, tempting companions, and deluding indulgences.

"And I observe that lying about are many unfulfilled consecrations relating to friends, and money, and children, and time, and other things; in fact, this stage seems to be a strange mixture of faith and unbelief; so much so that it is difficult to believe that we are on the slopes of Mount Purity at all.

"Here you will find posted on the sides of the rocks in all directions placards bearing the words: 'The things I would do those I do not, and the things I would not do those I do, and there is no spiritual health in me.' And up and down you will also see notice-boards warning would-be travellers not to climb any higher for fear they should fall again.

"But, thank God, while many chicken-hearted souls lie down in despair on this plateau, or retrace their steps to the dreary regions below, others declare that there is no necessity for failure. These push forward in the upward ascent, singing as they go:—

> "Though earth and hell the world gainsay,
>   The word of God can never fail;
> The Lamb shall take my sins away,
>   'Tis certain, though impossible;
> The thing impossible shall be,
> All things are possible to me.

"So, persevering with our journey, higher up, very much higher up, we come to the sin-mastering stage.

"This is a glorious plateau. All who enter it do so by the narrow passage of repentance towards God, and faith in our Lord Jesus Christ; receiving in their souls, as they pass the threshold, the delightful assurance of full and free forgiveness through the Blood of the Lamb.

"Here men and women walk with heads erect in holy confidence, and hearts glad with living faith, and mouths full of joyous song, and eyes steadily fixed on the holy light that streams from the summit of the mount above them. That holy beacon guide is ever calling on them to continue their journey, and ever directing them on the way.

"Those who have reached this stage have already made great and encouraging progress; for God has made them conquerors over their inward foes. The rule and reign of pride and malice, envy and lust, covetousness and sensuality, and every other evil thing have come to an end.

"They triumph on that account, but the conflict is not yet ended. Sometimes the battling is very severe; but with patient, plodding faith they persevere in the ascent, singing as they go:—

> "Faith, mighty faith, the promise sees,
>   And looks to that alone;
> Laughs at impossibilities,
>   And cries, 'It shall be done!'

"And now, close at hand, is the stage of deliverance, where the triumph is begun.

"And now, ten thousand Hallelujahs! let it be known to all the world around, that once on this plateau the separation from sin is entire; the heart is fully cleansed from evil; the promise is proved to be true, 'They that hunger and thirst after righteousness shall be filled.'

"At a great Christian Conference the other day an eminent divine said that The Salvation Army believed in a 'perfect sinner,' but that he believed in a 'perfect Saviour.' This, I contend, was a separation of what God has joined together and which never ought to be put asunder. For, glory be to the Father, glory be to the Son, and glory be to the Holy Ghost, The Salvation Army believes, with its Lord, that a perfect Saviour can make a poor sinner into a perfect saint. That is, He can enable him to fulfil His own command, in which He says: 'Be ye therefore perfect, even as your Father which is in Heaven is perfect.' (*Matthew* v. 48.)

"But there is one plateau higher still which, like a tableland, covers the entire summit of the mountain, and that the maturity stage.

"Here the graces of the Spirit have been perfected experience, and faith, and obedience, and the soul does the will of God as it is done in Heaven, united in the eternal companionship of that lovely being—the Spirit of Purity.

"What do you say to my holy mountain, my comrades?

"Are you living up there? Have you climbed as near to Heaven as that represents? If not, I want to make a declaration which you have often heard before, but which it will do you no harm to hear again, namely, that it is the will of God that you should not only reach the very summit, but that you should abide there.

"Do you ask why God wills that you should reach and abide on this holy mountain?

"I reply it is the will of God that you and I, and every other Officer in this blessed Army, should be holy for His own satisfaction.

"God finds pleasure in holy men and holy women. We know what it is to find pleasure in kindred companions. It is to like to be near them. To want to live with them, or have them to live with us. It is to be willing to travel any distance, or put ourselves to any inconvenience to reach them. According to the Bible, that is just how God feels towards His faithful people. He finds satisfaction in their doings, and praying, and worship, and song. But when there is unfaithfulness or sin of any kind this pleasure is sadly marred, if not altogether destroyed. In such cases the pleasure is turned to pain, the satisfaction to loathing, and the love to hatred.

"Hear what He says of Israel: 'In all their affliction He was afflicted, and the angel of His presence saved them; in His love and in His pity He bare them, and carried them all the days of old.' If for no other reason than the pleasure it will give to God, don't you think every Officer should, with all his might, seek for Holiness of heart and life?

"Another reason why God wants you to live on that blessed mountain is the interest He feels in your welfare.

"He loves you. He has told you so again and again. He has proved His love by His deeds. Love compels the being entertaining the affection to seek the good of its object. He knows that sin is the enemy of your peace, and must mean misery here and hereafter. For this reason among others, He wants to deliver you from it.

"You will remember that by the lips of Peter God told the Jews that He had raised up His Son Jesus, and sent Him to bless them by turning every one of them away from his iniquities. That applies to you, my comrades. You have heard it before; I tell it you again. Holiness is the royal road to peace, contentment, and joy for you. The love God bears you, therefore, makes Him ceaselessly long after your

Holiness of heart and life. Will you not let Him have His way? Will you not do His Will?

"God wants every Officer to be holy, in order that through him He may be able to pour His Holy Spirit upon the people to whom that Officer ministers.

"The men and women around you are in the dark. Oh, how ignorant they are of God and everlasting things! They cannot see the vile nature of the evil, and the foul character of the fiends that tempt and rule them. They do not see the black ruin that lies before them. So on they go, the blind leading the blind, till over the precipice they fall together. God wants their eyes to be opened. The Spirit can do the work, and through you He wants to pour the light.

"The men and women around you are weak. They cannot stand up against their own perverted appetites, the charms of the world, or the devices of the Devil. God wants to pour the Spirit of Power upon this helpless crowd. But He wants holy people through whom He can convey that strength. He works His miracles by clean people. That is His rule.

"There is nothing in the work of the early Apostles more wonderful than the miraculous manner in which they went about breathing the Spirit of Life and Light and Power on the people. But they were fully consecrated, Blood-and-Fire men and women.

"What do you say, my comrades? Will you be holy mediums? Do you not answer, 'Thy will be done'?

"God wants you to be holy, in order that you may reveal Him to the world by your example.

"Men do not believe in God—that is, the real God—the God of the Bible; and they do not believe in Him, because they do not know Him.

"He seeks to reveal Himself to men in various ways. He reveals Himself through the marvels of the natural world; and many say they can see God in the sun, and stars, and seas, and trees. He reveals Himself by speaking to men in their own hearts, and many hear His whisperings there. He reveals Himself in His own Book, and some read and ascertain what is His mind there.

"But, alas! the great multitude are like children. They require to see and hear God revealed before their very eyes in visible and practical form before they will believe. And to reach these crowds, God wants men and women to walk about the world so that those around, believers and unbelievers alike, shall see the form and hear the voice of the living God; people who shall be so like Him in spirit, and life, and character as to make the crowds feel as though the very shadow of God had crossed their path. Will you be a shadow of God?

"God wants you to be holy, in order that you may know what His mind is about the world, and about your work in it.

"He entertains certain opinions and feelings with respect to it. He has His own plan for saving it. He wants to reveal to you what those opinions and feelings are, and to do this so far as it will be good for you and those about you. He wants you to know how you can best fight devils, convict sinners, save souls, and bless the world.

"You can have this wonderful knowledge. Paul had it. He said 'We,' that is, I, 'have the mind of Christ.' God is no respecter of persons. He is as willing to reveal His mind to you, so far as you need it, as He was to reveal it to Paul.

"But to possess this knowledge you must be holy. Sin darkens the understanding, and hinders the perception of truth. A grain of sand in the eye will prevent you seeing the most beautiful landscape in the universe, or the dearest friends you have. It is with the heart that men see divine things, and an atom of sin will darken the brightest vision that can come before you. With a pure heart you can not only see God's truth, but God Himself. Oh, God wants to reveal Himself to you. Will you let Him? But if He is to do so, you must have a clean heart.

"It is God's will that you should be holy, because He wants you to be men and women of courage.

"Courage is the most valuable quality in this War. There are few gifts of greater importance. Only think what it has enabled the Prophets, the Apostles, and the Salvation leaders of modern times to accomplish! How it covered Moses, and Joshua, and David, and Daniel, and Paul, and a crowd of others with glory, and enabled them to conquer men, and devils, and difficulties of all kinds. I shall have something more to say about this before I have done.

"Courage and Holiness are linked closely together. You cannot have one without the other. Sin is the very essence of weakness. A little selfishness, a little insincerity, a little of anything that is evil means condemnation, and loss of courage, which means cowardice and failure.

"'The wicked flee when no man pursueth.' Double-minded people are uncertain, fickle, unreliable in all their ways. 'The righteous are bold as a lion.' Remember Shadrach, Meshach, Abednego.

"God wants you to be holy, in order that He may do mighty works through your instrumentality.

"I verily believe that His arm is held back from working wonders through the agency of many Officers, because He sees that such success would be their ruin. The spirit of Nebuchadnezzar is in them. He cannot build Babylon, or London, or New York, or anything else by their instrumentality, because He sees it would create the spirit of vainglory and boasting, or of ambition; make them dissatisfied with their position; or otherwise curse them and those about them. Look at Saul. What a lesson his history has in it for us all. 'When thou wast little in thine own sight wast thou not made the head of the Tribes of Israel? and the Lord anointed thee king over Israel.'

"Now, I may be asked whether some Officers do not fail to reach the higher ranges of the experience I have here described, and the reasons for this.

"To this question I reply that I am afraid that it is only too true that some Officers are to be found who are willing to dwell in the land of uncertainty and feebleness. They are the slaves of habits they condemn in others. Their example is marred, their powers are weakened for their work, and, instead of going onward and upward to the victory they believe so gloriously possible, they are a disappointment to themselves, to God, and to their leaders.

"If I am asked to name the reasons for their neglect of this glorious privilege, I would say:—

"They have doubts about the possibility of living this life of Holiness.

"They think there is some fatal necessity laid upon them to sin—at least a little, or just now and then. They think that God cannot, or that He will not, or that He has not arranged to save them altogether from their inward evils. They know that the Bible says, over and over again, in a thousand different ways, that the Blood of Jesus Christ cleanses from all sin; and they read God's promise again and again, that He will pour out His Spirit upon them, to save them from all their idols and filthiness; but they doubt whether it is strictly true, or anyway, whether it applies to them. And so, tossed to and fro by doubts about this holy experience, no wonder that they do not seek to realise it in their own hearts.

"Other Officers are kept back from climbing this mountain by the idea that the experience is not possible for them.

"They say, 'Oh, yes, it is good, it is beautiful. I wish I lived up there. How delightful it must be to have peace flow like a river, and righteousness abound as the waves of the sea, and to be filled with the Spirit! But such a life is not for me.' They admit the possibility of Holiness in those about them, and occasionally they push it on their acceptance; but they fancy that there is something about their own case that makes it impossible, or, at least, overwhelmingly difficult, for them to attain it.

"They imagine that there is something in their nature that makes it peculiarly difficult for them to be holy. Some peculiar twist in their minds. Some disagreeable disposition. Some bad, awkward temper. Some unbelieving tendency. Or, they are hindered by something that they suppose to be specially unfavourable in their circumstances—their family. Or, there is something in their history that they think is opposed to their living pure lives—they have failed in their past efforts, etc.

"Anyway, there is, they imagine, some insurmountable obstacle to their walking with Christ in white, and, instead of striking out for the summit of the Holy Mountain in desperate and determined search, relying on God's word that all things are possible to him that believeth, they give up, and settle down to the notion that Holiness of heart and life is not for them.

"Then, other Officers do not reach this experience because they do not seek it; that is, they do not seek it with all their hearts.

"They do not climb.

"They know that their Bible most emphatically asserts that those who seek heavenly blessings shall find them. No passage is more familiar to their minds or much more frequently on their lips, than the one spoken by Jesus Christ: 'Seek, and ye shall find.' And they condemn the poor sinner who lies rotting in the sins which will carry him to Hell, because he won't put forth a little effort to find deliverance. And yet, do not some Officers act very much after the same fashion with respect to this blessing?

"In their efforts they are truly sincere, but they are not much more forward for them. They say 'It is not for me,' and settle down as they were.

"The reason for this is not that the promise is not to them. But it is because they have not been thorough in their surrender; or because they have been wanting in their belief; or because they do not persevere; or because they have been mistaken in some past experience:—

"Another reason why Officers do not find the blessing is the simple fact that they will not pay the price.

"There is something they will not do; or there is something they will do; or there is something they will not part with; there is some doubtful thing that they will not give up. The sacrifice is too great. They think they would not be happy, or some one else would not be happy, or something would not be satisfactory; and so they look and look at the mountain, and long and long, but that is all. They would like to be there, but the price is too great.

"Another reason why Officers fail is neither more nor less than their want of faith.

"This, with sincere souls, is by far the most common hindrance. I have something to say about faith further on.

"And, doubtless, the reason that some Officers fail to reach the upper levels of Mount Purity arises out of their mistaken views as to the nature of this experience.

"You have so often heard me dwell on this view of the subject that I despair of saying anything fresh that will help you. But, knowing that I am on ground where truly sincere souls are often hindered, I will make one or two remarks:—

"I have no doubt that many fail here by confounding temptation with sin.

"They pray—they consecrate—they believe that they receive, and they rejoice. But by and by, when bad thoughts are suggested to their minds, they say to themselves, 'Oh, I can't be saved from sin, or I would not have all those wicked thoughts and suggestions streaming through my soul."

"They confound temptation with sin. Whatever they may say about it, they do not see the difference existing between temptation and sin.

"Some Officers are hindered in the fight for Holiness by supposing that purity will deliver them from serious depression, low spirits, and the like.

"With many sincere souls I have no doubt that one of the most serious hindrances in this strife is the confounding of Holiness with happiness, and thinking that if they are holy they will be happy all the time; whereas the Master Himself was a Man of Sorrows, and lived, more or less, a life of grief.

"Then there comes the last reason I shall notice, and that is the want of perseverance. There are some Officers who have been up the mountain—part of the way, at any rate, if not to the top. But through disobedience, or want of faith, they have no longer the experience they once enjoyed.

"The condition. You say to sinners that they are never to give up. I do, at least. So with those who are seeking Holiness. They must persevere or they will never find it."

Chapter XXVIII
The General as a Writer

None of us have yet any idea how voluminous a writer The General was, because so much of his writing was in the form of contributions to our many publications, or of letters to Officers.

We can only insert here a few, specimens of what he wrote at various dates, and remark that in private letters there was always the very same flow of happy earnest life, the same high ideal as finds expression in the following extracts.

In his ***Orders and Regulations for Field Officers*** he says:—

"It must always be remembered by the Field Officer, and by every one who is desirous of producing any great moral or spiritual changes in men, that the example of the individual attempting this task will be much more powerful than the doctrines they set forth, or any particular methods they adopt for teaching those doctrines, however impressive these may be.

"The correctness of this statement has been proved over and over again in this Salvation War. Everywhere the people measure the truth and importance of what the Field Officer says by their estimate of his character. If he produces the impression in their minds that he is a mere talker or performer, they may listen to his message, and—if he has more than ordinary ability—treat him with a degree of respect; but if this be all, he will be next to powerless in effecting any great change in their hearts and lives. On the other hand, where the life of the Field Officer convinces his Soldiers that he is himself what he wants them to be, truly devoted to God, it will be found that he will possess a marvellous mastery over their hearts and characters. In other words, if he makes his Soldiers feel that he is real and consecrated, he will be able to lead them almost at will; they will follow him to the death.

"The same shot, with the same charge of gunpowder, from a rifled cannon, will produce ten times a greater effect than from one with a smooth bore. The make of the gun gives the extra force to the shot. Just in the same way the truth from the lips of a man whom his hearers believe to be holy and true will strike with a hundredfold more force than the same message will from another who has not so commended himself. The character of the man gives the extra force to the truth.

"The Field Officer, by virtue of his position, stands out before his Soldiers more prominently than any other man. To them he is the Ambassador and Representative of God. He is their Captain, their Brother, and Friend. Their eyes are on him night and day. They regard him as the pattern expressly set for them to copy, the leader who at all times it is their bounden duty to follow.

"How important it is, therefore, that every Officer should be careful to perfect his character to the utmost in order that he may be useful to the fullest extent.

"The Field Officer must lead his Soldiers on to the full realisation of the baptism of the Holy Ghost; he must make them Blood and Fire. The work of the Spirit is to fill the soul with burning zeal for the Salvation of the world. Christ's work must be finished. He has left that task to His people; it can only be continued and carried on to completion by His Spirit working in the hearts and through the lives of His people. The Holy Ghost was promised for this end. This is what His people have, therefore, a right to expect, and without it they are powerless for the War.

"In order that his Soldiers may be effective, the Field Officer must not only act for the purification of his Soldiers, but to have them filled with the Spirit of Christ, in order that they may be competent for the mighty work they have to accomplish.

"This will make them wise. They will understand how to fight, what to say, what to sing, how to pray, and how to talk to the consciences and hearts of men. The Spirit of God will lead them into right methods of action, will show them how to make opportunities, and how to put these opportunities to the best use, when they are made.

"The Holy Spirit will give them perseverance, keeping them going on in the face of difficulty.

"The Holy Spirit will give them power, making them not only willing to endure the Cross, but to glory in it.

"The Holy Spirit will give them the fire of love, the seraphic spirit, the live coal from off the altar, making them both burn and shine. With this they will come to Knee-Drill, to the Open-Air, to face mocking crowds, and to endure the scorn, and hatred, and persecution of men; not merely from a sense of duty, dragging themselves to it, because it is the will of God; or for the good of The Army; or as an example to their comrades; or even for the Salvation of souls; but because they love it, and cannot stay away.

"This baptism will be a fire in their bones, which must have vent. It will be a spirit that must have a voice. It will be a love, a burning love in the heart, which all the waters that earth and Hell can pour upon it, cannot quench a love with which no other love can compare. It will be the Saviour again loving a dying world through His people. It will be Christ indeed come again in the flesh.

"The Soldiers must be baptised with fire. It will give them the Soldier's spirit; and, with that, all a Soldier needs in the way of drill, and duty, and sacrifice will inevitably follow."

In his *Letter to his Officers on his Eightieth Birthday*, he wrote:—

"On the coming 10th of April, in many lands and in many ways, the Officers, Soldiers, and Friends of The Salvation Army will be celebrating my Eightieth Birthday.

"The occasion is one which inspires in me many deep emotions; and, next to the gratitude I feel to Almighty God for the unmeasured blessings He has been pleased to vouchsafe to me, I find the desire to write and tell you, my dear Officers, something of the love and sympathy ever welling up in my heart towards you.

"The times and friends of long ago are sometimes said to have been brighter or better than those of to-day. This may have been the experience of some. It has not been mine. It is true that in the early years of my Salvation Warfare there were battlings and victories of deep interest and value, but no conflicts or triumphs in those far-back times exceeded, or indeed equalled, in value and interest the conflicts and triumphs of my later days.

"It is true that from the beginning I have been associated with many remarkable men and women—men and women whose ability, affection, and devotion to God have been of the greatest service to me. But with, perhaps, one or two exceptions, I have had no co-workers who have excelled, or even equalled, in ability, in affection or devotion, the Comrades who at the present hour are struggling with me all over the world for the highest well-being of their fellows, and for the advancement of the Kingdom of our Lord Jesus Christ.

"Sixty-five years ago I chose the Salvation of men and the extension of the Kingdom of Jesus Christ as the supreme object for which I would live and labour.

"Although that choice was made in my early youth, in much ignorance of the world, and of the religious needs of those about me, still, it was not arrived at without much thought and some information; and that purpose is still, and will be to the end, the object which has shaped and mastered the thoughts, ambitions, and activities of my whole life.

"From the hour of my first Prayer Meetings in one of the cottage homes of my native town, down to the present moment, that object has been the governing principle of my life. The adornments and flowers and music and other pleasant things connected with religious service have all been secondary to efficiency in the search for that object and success in attaining it.

"My hourly usage with regard to every effort I put forth has been to ask myself: What does this action contemplate? What will it achieve? Can it be improved upon? I believe I can say that every conversation and prayer and song and address and Meeting I have had a hand in have been valued in proportion to their ability to promote the realisation of that great purpose.

"No greater mistake can be made with respect to The Salvation Army than to suppose that it is not a school for thought. Perhaps more theories have been produced and more schemes invented by us for gaining the highest ends of the Christian faith (bearing in mind our age and the extent of our work) than by any other religious movement in existence. Indeed, as I have often said in public, when we have so many thousands of hearts inflamed with the love of Christ for sinning, suffering, and dying men, and possessed with a passionate desire for their rescue, you must have the constant evolution of new plans and contrivances for that purpose.

"But, while thus inventive, The Army does not content itself with hopes and theories merely; it seeks to put every fresh idea to the test of practical application, waiting for the issue, before it regards it of permanent value. At least, that has been my own usage, and the practical character of my mind and work has come to be generally allowed.

"While, then, I glory in the fact that our religion is Divine in origin and manifestation, I equally maintain the necessity for human skill, human energy, and human enterprise, in the efforts put forth to establish and extend it; and, accordingly, I have only adopted any efforts so far as they have proved themselves effective in the school of experience.

"So with this confidence in my convictions I proceed once more to push them upon your attention."

In the ***Orders and Regulations for Soldiers***, perhaps the concisest description of earnest living ever written, he says:—

"The Salvation Soldier must have been converted or changed by the power of the Holy Spirit from the old, worldly, selfish, sinful nature, to the new, holy, heavenly, Divine nature; and not only must he thus have received a new heart, but he must have the Holy Spirit living in that heart, possessing it, and working through it, to will and to do the good pleasure of God.

"This is the first and main condition of Soldiership. It is understood that every Soldier has come into the possession of this true Religion by passing through that change which is usually described in The Army as being 'saved.' There is nothing more common throughout our ranks than! the expression, 'I am glad I am saved!'

"As it is impossible for a Salvation Soldier to perform the duties hereafter set forth with satisfaction to himself, and profit to others, unless this change has been experienced, it will be well to describe it rather particularly, so that every Soldier who reads these Regulations will be able to satisfy himself whether he has really undergone this change.

"If on reading this description, any Soldier should have reason to believe that he has not experienced this change, and is still in his sins, or that he has been unfaithful since he did realise it, and is, therefore, a backslider, the first business of such an one will be to go to God and seek Salvation; otherwise it will be impossible for him to be a good Soldier.

"Salvation implies the devotion of the whole life to the accomplishment of the purpose for which Christ lived and suffered and died. It means that the Soldier becomes His disciple.

"Enlisting in His Army, the Soldier receives not only power to walk in His commandments for himself, but to subdue other men to the Lord.

"His new nature now continually cries out, 'What wilt Thou have me to do?'

and carries him forth with the feet of cheerful obedience in the service of his new Master, to weep and suffer, and, if necessary, to die, to bring others into the enjoyment of the Salvation which he himself has found. He lives the same kind of life and is actuated by the same purposes as God Himself."

In ***Religion for Every Day*** he writes:—

"I am always talking to you about what we call religious duties, such as praying and singing, making efforts to save your own soul and the souls of the people about you. In these letters I propose speaking of the things that men call secular, and which many people reckon have nothing to do with Religion. But I want to show you, if I can, that the Salvationist's conduct ought, in every particular, to be religious; every meal he partakes of should be a sacrament; and every thought and deed a service done to God. In doing this you will see that I shall have to deal with many quite commonplace subjects; and, in talking about them, I shall try to be as simple and as practical as I possibly can.

"The first topic to which I shall call your attention is your daily employment, and by that I mean the method by which you earn your livelihood. Or, supposing that, having some independent means of support, you are not compelled to labour for your daily bread, then I shall point out that special form of work, the doing of which Providence has plainly made to be your duty. Because it is difficult to conceive of any Salvationist who has not some regular employment, for which he holds himself responsible to God

"Work is a good thing, my comrades. To be unemployed is generally counted an evil—any way, it is so in the case of a poor man; but it seems to me that the obligation to be engaged in some honourable and useful kind of labour is as truly devolved upon the rich as upon the poor, perhaps more so. Work is necessary to the well-being of men and women of every class, everywhere. To be voluntarily idle, in any rank or condition of life, is to be a curse to others and to be accursed yourself.

"You would utterly condemn me if you thought that I engaged in my work in The Army merely to make a good show, or for some personal profit, and did not care about what God thought of the matter. My comrades, there are not two different standards of work—one for you and one for me. You must, therefore, be under the same obligation to do your work in the house or in the mine or in the warehouse, or wherever the Providence of God has placed you" to please your Heavenly

Master, as I am on the platform, in the council chamber, or wherever my duty may call me.

"But here another question arises. Do you accept Jesus Christ as your Master in the affairs of your daily life? If not, of course, this part of my argument will be thrown away; but if you do, then it will be the most powerful of all.

"At the commencement of His ministry, Jesus Christ announced that He was about to establish the Kingdom of Heaven on the earth. By the Kingdom of Heaven He meant a Kingdom consisting of heavenly government, heavenly laws, heavenly obedience, heavenly power, heavenly love, heavenly joy. These, taken together, constitute the chief characteristics of this Kingdom, and instead of being confined, as it had been hitherto, to a handful of people in Jerusalem and Judea, it was to cover the whole earth.

"Now the subjects of that Kingdom must accept Jesus Christ as their Master and Lord. No one can either come into that Kingdom or remain in it without compliance with this law. You cannot be a son without being a servant.

"But you have written yourselves down as His servants, and said you will 'no longer live unto yourselves,' nor to please the world, but to do the will of Him who has redeemed you; that is, to please Him. Now the Master's province, everybody knows, is, not only to choose the work of His servants, but to get it done, if possible, to His satisfaction.

"He has appointed me my work. He has arranged that I should direct the movements of this great Army, preach Salvation, write Letters for you to read, save as many sinners as I can, and strive to get my Soldiers safely landed on the Celestial Shore. Before all else, I must do this Work, as nearly as I can, to satisfy my Lord—and nothing short of the best work I can produce will accomplish that.

"And as with me so with you. He has chosen your work, if you have put your life into His hands, just as truly as He has chosen mine, although it may be of a different kind. I am writing this letter in the train. I am a poor writer at best. When I was a child my schoolmaster neglected to teach me to hold my pen properly. In this respect he did not do good work, and I have had to suffer for it ever since. Still, I am doing my work as well as I can, in order that it may profit you and please my Lord.

"In settling how much work he will do, a man must have due regard to the claims of his own health. If he rushes at his work without due discretion, and does more than his strength will reasonably allow, he will probably break down, and so prevent his working altogether, or for a season, at least. Whereas, if he exhausts no more energy than he can recover by sleep and food and rest, at the time he can go steadily forward, and by doing so, accomplish a great deal more, in the long run, than he would by temporary extravagant exertion. When speaking on this subject, I sometimes say that I use my body as I should use a horse, if I had one—that is, I should not seek to get the most labour out of him for a week, regardless of the future, but I should feed and manage him with a view to getting the most I could get out of him all the year round. That is, doubtless, the way a man should use his body, and to do this he should take as much time for his food and daily rest as is necessary to replace the energies he has used up by his work.

"In the leisure taken for this purpose, it will be necessary to have specified hours, as otherwise, those who are without principle will take advantage of the weak, and anything like system will be impossible.

"Then, again, when the proper performance of a particular task depends upon the united labour of a number of individuals, who have agreed to work in co-operation, it will be necessary, in the interests of the whole, that each should conform to the regulations laid down, always supposing that such rules are in harmony with truth and righteousness.

"The wishes and interests of employers have also to be taken into consideration. But, in every case, the principle is equally obligatory upon all.

"These duties will demand, and must have devoted to them, a measure of the time at our control. What that amount of time shall be, must be determined by the relative importance of those duties. For instance:—

"There is the work a man can do for his earthly employers, over and above the amount that is considered to be a strict and just return for his wages. Here, again, he must be guided by Jesus Christ's rule, and to do unto his master as he would that his master should do unto him.

"There is the work that he ought to do for his family, apart and beyond the bare earnings of their daily bread. This is work which no one else can do so well, and which, if it be neglected by him, will probably not be done at all.

"There is the effort that every workman should put forth for his own personal improvement. For instance, a youth of seventeen works, we will say, ten hours a day for his employer, who would very much like him to put in another hour at the same task, and would be willing to pay him extra for doing so. This, we will suppose, the youth could do without any injurious effect to his health. But then, by reading his Bible, or cultivating his mind, he might qualify himself to become an Officer, or to fill some other important position, in either case fitting himself for a field of greater usefulness, in the future, than the one he already occupies. Under such circumstances, it must be the duty of that youth to take that hour for his own improvement, rather than to use it to enrich his master or increase his earnings.

"Then, every Soldier of Jesus Christ must duly consider and obey the claims of the Salvation War. That is, he must strive to take his fair share in that conflict. Whether he is his own master, having the direct control of his time, or whether he works for an employer, who only allows him many hours for leisure, he must conscientiously devote much of that time as he can to saving his fellow-men, settling this question, he must use his common sense, and claim the promised direction of the Holy Spirit. God will guide him.

"What I protest against here is the notion, born of indolence and selfishness, which affirms that we should do little, rather than as much, work as is consistent with the maintenance of health, and with the claims arising out of the relations in which we stand to those about us.

"However, circumstances will transpire, during the earthly career of every one of us, calling for self-sacrificing work that must be performed, regardless of consequences to health or any other interest.

"Supposing, by way of illustration, a ship has sprung a leak, through which the water is rushing rapidly in, endangering the lives of both the passengers and crew. Under such conditions, would not every man on board be justified in working night and day to prevent the threatened calamity? Nay, further, would not the laws of humanity call upon every one concerned to do so at the risk of crippling themselves, or even sacrificing life itself, in order to gain the greater good of saving the vessel from destruction, and rescuing a number of their fellows from a watery grave?

Soldiers. God and a sinning suffering world call you to rise up and meet your great opportunity. Do it and do it with your might.

For the present I must say farewell; but always think of me as

Your affectionate General
Williams Booth

CAPE TOWN,
October 12, 1908

AN AUTOGRAPH MESSAGE FROM THE GENERAL

Soldiers. God and a sinning suffering world
cal you to rise up and meet your great opportunity.
Do it and do it with your might.
For the present I must say farewell; but always think of ****
Your affectionate General Williams S. Booth
Cape Town, October 12, 1908

"My contention then, is, that whether in the shop or on the ship, in the parlour or in the kitchen, in the factory or in the field, on the Salvation platform or in the coal mine, whether Officers or Soldiers, we are all alike, as servants of God, under the obligation to do all we possibly can in the service of men; and to do it with the holy motive of pleasing our Heavenly Master.

"Here let me review my warrant for requiring from you the kind of loving labour that I advocate.

"The Bible enjoins it. We have already quoted Paul's words to the Ephesians, in which he says that our work is to be done, 'Not with eye-service as men-pleasers, but as the servants of Christ, doing the will of God from the heart; with goodwill doing service, as to the Lord, and not to men.' That is all I ask for.

"It is enjoined by the doctrine of brotherly love. I cannot understand how any one can suppose, for a moment, that he is living a life acceptable to God unless he is striving, with all his might, to fulfil the Divine command, 'Thou shalt love thy neighbour as thyself.' Your master, or whoever has a claim upon your service, must be included in the term 'neighbour'; and to comply with the command of the Saviour, you must work for that master, or mistress, as the case may be, from the voluntary principle of love rather than the earthly and selfish principle of gain.

"Is not the disinterested method I am urging upon you in keeping with the loftiest ideals the world possesses with respect to work? About whom does it write its poetry? Whom does it laud to the heavens in the pulpit, on the platform, and in the Press? Whose names does it describe the highest in its Temples of Fame, or hand down to posterity as examples for rich and poor, old and young alike, to follow? Is it the man who makes his own ease and enrichment his only aim in life, and who toils and spins for nothing higher than his own gratification? Nothing of the kind. It is the generous, self-sacrificing, disinterested being who uses himself up for the benefit of his fellows.

"Nay, at whom does that same world ceaselessly sneer, and whom does it most pitilessly despise? Is it not the mean and narrow spirit whose conduct is governed by selfish greed and sensual indulgences? Whatever may be its practice, in this respect, the sentiment of the world is in the right direction. It asks for benevolence evidenced by unselfish labour, and admires it when it finds it.

"A paragraph went the round of the newspaper world, a little time back, describing how an American millionaire had decided to spend the rest of his days on a Leper Island in the Pacific Ocean, in order to labour for the amelioration of the miseries of its unfortunate inhabitants. Wonder and admiration everywhere greeted the announcement.

"Shall we go back on all this spirit of self-sacrifice? Shall this kind of thing die out, or only have an existence in poetry books, platform quotations, or anecdote collections? Shall we change over to the 'pound-of-flesh' principle, and hire out the work of our hands, the thoughts of our minds, and the burning passions of our souls, for the largest amount of filthy lucre, and the greatest measure of earthly comfort, that we can obtain for them; so justifying the lying libel on humanity, long since spoken, and still often sneeringly quoted, that every man has his price? Or shall we say that love—the love of God and man—is the highest and divinest motive of labour—a motive possible not only to the sons and daughters of genius, but accessible to the plainest, humblest man or woman who suffers and toils on the lowest round of the ladder of life.

"I argue in favour of this doctrine on the ground of its profitableness to the worker. My readers will probably have asked long before this, How far do these propositions harmonise with the interests of the servant? Ought he not to take his own well-being into account? Certainly. He must have just as true a regard for his own welfare and the welfare of those dependent upon him, as he has for that of others. The command, 'Thou shalt love thy neighbour as thyself,' can only be rightly interpreted by another, like unto it, which reads: 'Whatsoever ye would that men should do to you do ye even so to them.' Therefore, he must ask, that others should do unto him as he would do unto them, supposing they occupied changed positions. This must mean that, while righteously concerned for the interests of others, he must be reasonably concerned for his own.

"But here a little difficulty comes into our argument, arising out of the play of the higher motives of affection. What does love care for gain in its calculations of service? The husband who loves his wife as Christ loved the Church, does not stop to consider the claims of duty, or the advantages following its discharge in toiling for her welfare. He will be willing to die for her, as Christ died for the Church.

"He does not say, 'I will toil for my delicate wife, and deny myself pleasant things, in order to obtain for her the necessaries and comforts she requires, because she would do the same for me, if I were in her place and she in mine.' Nothing of the kind! The wife I spoke of, who told me the other day that she had not had her clothes off for seventeen days and nights in nursing her husband did not make it appear that she thought she was doing anything extraordinary, or that she rendered this service to her companion in life because she felt sure that had he been the wife and she the husband, he would have gladly done the same for her.

"Had the newspapers thought that the American millionaire was going to the Leper Island, with his gold, to make something out of it for himself and family, or to make a name in the world, instead of his being greeted with a chorus of admiration, there would have been a universal chorus of execration at his selfishness. It was because they believed that he was going to make the sacrifice of his own gain, if not of his own self, for the benefit of the poor sufferers, that they praised him.

"Supposing, however, that we come down to the low level of self-interest, we insist then, that those who work from the motive of love, rather than the motive of gain, will not necessarily be sufferers in consequence, so far as this world goes. But it may be asked, 'Will not unprincipled masters or mistresses be likely to take advantage of this docile and unselfish spirit?' Perhaps, nay, doubtless, in many cases, they will. The Salvation Army has been taken advantage of all through its past history, and so have all the true saints of God, because they have submitted to wrong, and have not fought the injustice and false representations and persecutions inflicted upon them from the beginning. It will possibly be so to the end, but that does not affect the principle for which I argue, which is, that we *must* do good work, and as much of it as we can, regardless of what the world may give us in return.

"But, I think, I have sufficiently shown, as I have gone along, that this class of service is not without its earthly rewards, and that every interest of human nature—selfish and otherwise alike—testify to the probability of its proving profitable to those who practise it.

"If, however, the reward does not come in the form of money, or houses, or lands, there will be gain in that which is far more valuable than money and houses and lands, and which money and houses and lands cannot buy. There will be the gain in peace, in satisfaction, and in joy in the Holy Ghost in this life, to say nothing of the gain in the world to come. But, on this point, I shall have more to say another time.

"I remember hearing a gentleman relate the following incident in a large meeting: 'Some time back,' he said, 'I was passing through the streets of Liverpool. It was a cold, raw, wintry day. The streets were ankle-deep in an unpleasant mixture of mud and ice, and battling through it all, the came along a little procession of ragged, haggard, hungry looking boys. Splash, splash, on they went, through freezing slush, at every step making the onlookers shudddered as they stood by in their warm, comfortable coats and furs." In the front rank was a little fellow, who was scarcely more than a bag of bones, half-naked, barefooted, his whole frame shivering every time he put his foot down on the melting snow.

"'All at once, a big boy came forward, and, stooping down, bade the lad put his arms round his neck, and, lifting him up on his back, took his perished feet one in each hand and jogged along with his burden.

"'I was moved,' said the speaker, 'at the sight; and going up to the boy, commended him for his kindness. In his Lancashire brogue the lad replied, "Aye, aye, sir; two feet in the cold slush are not so bad as four." After a while,' said the speaker, 'I offered to carry the little chap myself' but the honest fellow shook his head, and said, "Nay, nay,' Mister; I winna part with him. I can carry him; and he's a-warming o' my back.'"

"And so, if seeking the good of others may not bring as much worldly gain as a selfish course of action, it does ensure that joyful warmth of heart which all loving service brings, and which is among the most valuable of all the treasures of earth or Heaven. Every man who acts on this principle is adding to the general sum of human happiness. What is the sum of celestial happiness, the happiness of God, the happiness of the angels, the happiness of the Blood-washed spirits who are safely landed there? In what does this happiness chiefly consist?

"I reply, Not in the golden streets, the unfading flowers, the marvellous music, nor all the other wonders of the Celestial Land put together, but in Love. Love is the essence of the bliss of Heaven, for 'Love is Heaven, and Heaven is Love.' This happiness we can have below. It is not the love others bear to us that makes our felicity, but the love we bear to them; and, thank God, we can as truly love on earth as we can in Heaven.

"And then, as I have been saying all along, acting on this principle constitutes true religion. As labour done from selfish, fleshly motives is of the earth, and as the results which follow it will perish with the earth, even so labour done to bless mankind and to please God is Divine, and the results flowing out of it must be everlasting honour and joy. Where this principle is carried into effect, every part of human conduct becomes religious—nay, a positive act of Divine worship, and an acceptable song of praise."

Important Events Connected With The General's Life And Work

1827. Jan. 17th Catherine Mumford—afterwards Mrs Booth—born at Ashbourne, Derbyshire
 Apr. 10th William Booth born at Nottingham.
1844. Conversion of Catherine Mumford and William Booth.
1852. Apr. 10th William Booth entered the Methodist Ministry.
1855. June 16th Marriage of William Booth and Catherine Mumford.
1856. March 8th Birth of William Bramwell (now General) Booth.
1859. Mrs. Booth's first pamphlet "Female Ministry" published.
1861. Commenced to travel as Revivalist.
1865. July 5th Commenced Mission Work in East of London.
 First Headquarters opened in Whitechapel Road.
1868. Christian Mission commenced work in Scotland.
1870. Publication of "How to reach the Masses" by the Rev. W. Booth.
1875. Publication of the first volume of music.
1878. First Deed Poll, signed legally, constituting The Christian Mission.
 " Xmas. The name of the Christian Mission altered to The Salvation Army, and the Rev. William Booth assume the title of General.
 First Corps flag presented by Mrs. Booth.
 "Practical Christianity" by Mrs. Booth published.
1879. Dec. 29th Publication of the first number of the "War Cry."
 Formation of the first Salvation Army Band at Consett.
1880. Headquarters removed to Queen Victoria Street.
 Opening of the work in the United States and Australia.

Opening of first Training College.
Publication of first "Orders and Regulations."
"Godliness," by Mrs. Booth, published.
1881. Work extended to France.
First number of the "Little Soldier" issued.
1882. Opening of the Congress Hall and International Training College at Clapton.
Marriage of W. Bramwell Booth and Captain Florence Soper.
Work extended to Switzerland, Canada, Sweden and India.
Publication of "Life and Death" by Mrs. Booth.
First Prison-Gate Home opened in London.
1883. Work extended to South Africa and New Zealand.
1884. "The Training of Children," by the General, published.
First Band Journal issued.
First Rescue Home opened.
1885. "All the World" first published.
Criminal Law Amendment Act passed.
Trial and acquittal of W. Bramwell Booth.
1886. Death of The Army's first French Martyr.
The General paid his first visit to France, the United States and Canada.
First International Congress held in London.
Work extended to Germany.
"Musical Salvationist" published.
Self-Denial Week established.
First "Orders and Regulations for Field Officers" published, and first "Orders and Regulations for Staff Officers" published.
1887. Thousand British Corps established.
First Slum Settlement established.
Work extended to Holland, Denmark and Zululand.
First Crystal Palace Anniversary Demonstration.
Auxiliary League founded.
General paid his first visit to Denmark, Sweden and Norway.
"Popular Christianity," by Mrs. Booth, published.

1888. First Food Depot opened at Limehouse.
Work extended to Norway, Argentine, Finland and Belgium.
" June 21st. Mrs. Booth gave her last public address.
1889. The Petition for the Sunday Closing of Public-houses,
with 436,500 signatures, presented to the House of Commons by the General.
Publication of "The Deliverer."
General visited Belgium, Denmark, Sweden and France.
1890. 25th Anniversary of The Army celebrated at the Crystal Palace.
Oct. 4th. Mrs. Booth's Death.
" " 13th. Funeral Service at Olympia—36,000 present.
" " 14th. Funeral at Abney Park.
Publication of "In Darkest England" by the General.
1891. Work extended to Italy and Uruguay.
General first visited South Africa, Australia, New Zealand and India.
L1,000. 0. 0. subscribed for "Darkest England" Scheme.
General signed "Darkest England" Trust Deed.
Opening of Industrial and Land Colony at Hadleigh, Essex.
Publication of "Social Gazette."
1892. General visited Denmark, Germany and Switzerland.
Publication of "Life of Catherine Booth."
1892. Work extended to West Indies.
1893. General visited Denmark, Sweden, Belgium, Holland and Norway.
1894. International Congress, in connection with the General's Jubilee,
held in London.
General visited America and South European Countries.
Work extended to Java.
1895. General visited South Africa, Australia and various European Countries.
Work extended to Japan and British Guiana.
Naval and Military League established.
1896. General visited Germany, Sweden, Switzerland and Denmark.
Preached to 12,000 in Kings Gardens, Copenhagen.
First Salvation Army Exhibition—Agricultural Hall, London.
Work extended to Malta.

1897. General inspected work in European countries.
1898. General visited United States, Canada and European countries.
"Orders and Regulations for Social Officers" published.
1899. Second Salvation Army Exhibition—Agricultural Hall.
Visited Australia, New Zealand, Ceylon and European countries.
Officers sent to the front to work amongst both sides i
n the South African War.
1900. General visited European countries.
1901. General visited European countries.
Opening of first Inebriates' Home at Hadleigh.
1902. General visited United States, Canada and European countries.
Publication of "Religion for Everyday" by the General.
1903. General visited America, Canada and European countries.
Received by President Roosevelt.
1904. June 24th. The General received by His Majesty,
King Edward the Seventh, at Buckingham Palace.
" June 25th. International Congress opened by the General in London.
" July 23rd. General received by Her Majesty, Queen Alexandra,
at Buckingham Palace.
August. Commenced his Motor Campaign.
Work extended to Panama.
General visited various European countries.
1905. General visited Palestine, Australia and various European countries.
First Emigration Ship sails from Liverpool for Canada with 1,000 emigrants.
The General created Honorary D.C.L., Oxford.
General received Freedom Cities of London and Nottingham.
1906 Establishment of Anti-Suicide Bureau.
General conducted lengthy Campaigns Continental countries.
1907. General visited Japan, America, Canada etc.
General received by Kings of Denmark and Norway,
and Queen of Sweden, and Emperor of Japan.
1908. Work extended to Korea.
General visited South Africa.

1909. General visited Russia, Finland and other European countries.
General received by Kings of Norway and Sweden.
General received by Prince and Princess of Wales, now King and Queen of England.
General received by Queen Alexandra and the Dowager Empress of Russia.
80th Birthday Celebration at Albert Hall, London.
Met with accident involving loss of sight of one eye.
1910. General visited various European countries.
1911. General visited Italy and other European countries.
General conducted International Social Council in London attended by Officers from all over the world.
1912. General visited North European Staff Council in Norway.
" May 23rd. Operation on remaining eye, followed by complete loss of sight.
" Aug. 20th. The General laid down his Sword.

THE END

www.bookjungle.com email: sales@bookjungle.com fax: 630-214-0564 mail: Book Jungle PO Box 2226 Champaign, IL 61825

The Codes Of Hammurabi And Moses
W. W. Davies

The discovery of the Hammurabi Code is one of the greatest achievements of archaeology, and is of paramount interest, not only to the student of the Bible, but also to all those interested in ancient history...

Religion   ISBN: *1-59462-338-4*   Pages:132
                                             MSRP *$12.95*   QTY

The Theory of Moral Sentiments
Adam Smith

This work from 1749. contains original theories of conscience amd moral judgment and it is the foundation for systemof morals.

Philosophy   ISBN: *1-59462-777-0*   Pages:536
                                           MSRP *$19.95*   QTY

Jessica's First Prayer
Hesba Stretton

In a screened and secluded corner of one of the many railway-bridges which span the streets of London there could be seen a few years ago, from five o'clock every morning until half past eight, a tidily set-out coffee-stall, consisting of a trestle and board, upon which stood two large tin cans, with a small fire of charcoal burning under each so as to keep the coffee boiling during the early hours of the morning when the work-people were thronging into the city on their way to their daily toil...

Childrens   ISBN: *1-59462-373-2*   Pages:84
                                          MSRP *$9.95*   QTY

My Life and Work
Henry Ford

Henry Ford revolutionized the world with his implementation of mass production for the Model T automobile. Gain valuable business insight into his life and work with his own auto-biography... "We have only started on our development of our country we have not as yet, with all our talk of wonderful progress, done more than scratch the surface. The progress has been wonderful enough but..."

Biographies/   ISBN: *1-59462-198-5*   Pages:300
                                         MSRP *$21.95*   QTY

www.bookjungle.com *email: sales@bookjungle.com fax: 630-214-0564 mail: Book Jungle PO Box 2226 Champaign, IL 61825*

The Art of Cross-Examination
Francis Wellman

I presume it is the experience of every author, after his first book is published upon an important subject, to be almost overwhelmed with a wealth of ideas and illustrations which could readily have been included in his book, and which to his own mind, at least, seem to make a second edition inevitable. Such certainly was the case with me; and when the first edition had reached its sixth impression in five months, I rejoiced to learn that it seemed to my publishers that the book had met with a sufficiently favorable reception to justify a second and considerably enlarged edition. ..

Reference   ISBN: *1-59462-647-2*   Pages:412   MSRP *$19.95*

On the Duty of Civil Disobedience
Henry David Thoreau

Thoreau wrote his famous essay, On the Duty of Civil Disobedience, as a protest against an unjust but popular war and the immoral but popular institution of slave-owning. He did more than write—he declined to pay his taxes, and was hauled off to gaol in consequence. Who can say how much this refusal of his hastened the end of the war and of slavery ?

Law   ISBN: *1-59462-747-9*   Pages:48   MSRP *$7.45*

Dream Psychology Psychoanalysis for Beginners
Sigmund Freud

Sigmund Freud, born Sigismund Schlomo Freud (May 6, 1856 - September 23, 1939), was a Jewish-Austrian neurologist and psychiatrist who co-founded the psychoanalytic school of psychology. Freud is best known for his theories of the unconscious mind, especially involving the mechanism of repression; his redefinition of sexual desire as mobile and directed towards a wide variety of objects; and his therapeutic techniques, especially his understanding of transference in the therapeutic relationship and the presumed value of dreams as sources of insight into unconscious desires.

Psychology   ISBN: *1-59462-905-6*   Pages:196   MSRP *$15.45*

The Miracle of Right Thought
Orison Swett Marden

Believe with all of your heart that you will do what you were made to do. When the mind has once formed the habit of holding cheerful, happy, prosperous pictures, it will not be easy to form the opposite habit. It does not matter how improbable or how far away this realization may see, or how dark the prospects may be, if we visualize them as best we can, as vividly as possible, hold tenaciously to them and vigorously struggle to attain them, they will gradually become actualized, realized in the life. But a desire, a longing without endeavor, a yearning abandoned or held indifferently will vanish without realization.

Self Help   ISBN: *1-59462-644-8*   Pages:360   MSRP *$25.45*

www.bookjungle.com email: sales@bookjungle.com fax: 630-214-0564 mail: Book Jungle PO Box 2226 Champaign, IL 61825

QTY

	Title	ISBN	Price
☐	**The Rosicrucian Cosmo-Conception Mystic Christianity** by *Max Heindel*	ISBN: 1-59462-188-8	$38.95
	The Rosicrucian Cosmo-conception is not dogmatic, neither does it appeal to any other authority than the reason of the student. It is: not controversial, but is: sent forth in the, hope that it may help to clear...	New Age/Religion Pages 646	
☐	**Abandonment To Divine Providence** by *Jean-Pierre de Caussade*	ISBN: 1-59462-228-0	$25.95
	"The Rev. Jean Pierre de Caussade was one of the most remarkable spiritual writers of the Society of Jesus in France in the 18th Century. His death took place at Toulouse in 1751. His works have gone through many editions and have been republished...	Inspirational/Religion Pages 400	
☐	**Mental Chemistry** by *Charles Haanel*	ISBN: 1-59462-192-6	$23.95
	Mental Chemistry allows the change of material conditions by combining and appropriately utilizing the power of the mind. Much like applied chemistry creates something new and unique out of careful combinations of chemicals the mastery of mental chemistry...	New Age Pages 354	
☐	**The Letters of Robert Browning and Elizabeth Barret Barrett 1845-1846 vol II** by *Robert Browning* and *Elizabeth Barrett*	ISBN: 1-59462-193-4	$35.95
		Biographies Pages 596	
☐	**Gleanings In Genesis (volume I)** by *Arthur W. Pink*	ISBN: 1-59462-130-6	$27.45
	Appropriately has Genesis been termed "the seed plot of the Bible" for in it we have, in germ form, almost all of the great doctrines which are afterwards fully developed in the books of Scripture which follow...	Religion/Inspirational Pages 420	
☐	**The Master Key** by *L. W. de Laurence*	ISBN: 1-59462-001-6	$30.95
	In no branch of human knowledge has there been a more lively increase of the spirit of research during the past few years than in the study of Psychology, Concentration and Mental Discipline. The requests for authentic lessons in Thought Control, Mental Discipline and...	New Age/Business Pages 422	
☐	**The Lesser Key Of Solomon Goetia** by *L. W. de Laurence*	ISBN: 1-59462-092-X	$9.95
	This translation of the first book of the "Lernegton" which is now for the first time made accessible to students of Talismanic Magic was done, after careful collation and edition, from numerous Ancient Manuscripts in Hebrew, Latin, and French...	New Age/Occult Pages 92	
☐	**Rubaiyat Of Omar Khayyam** by *Edward Fitzgerald*	ISBN: 1-59462-332-5	$13.95
	Edward Fitzgerald, whom the world has already learned, in spite of his own efforts to remain within the shadow of anonymity, to look upon as one of the rarest poets of the century, was born at Bredfield, in Suffolk, on the 31st of March, 1809. He was the third son of John Purcell...	Music Pages 172	
☐	**Ancient Law** by *Henry Maine*	ISBN: 1-59462-128-4	$29.95
	The chief object of the following pages is to indicate some of the earliest ideas of mankind, as they are reflected in Ancient Law, and to point out the relation of those ideas to modern thought.	Religion/History Pages 452	
☐	**Far-Away Stories** by *William J. Locke*	ISBN: 1-59462-129-2	$19.45
	"Good wine needs no bush, but a collection of mixed vintages does. And this book is just such a collection. Some of the stories I do not want to remain buried for ever in the museum files of dead magazine-numbers an author's not unpardonable vanity..."	Fiction Pages 272	
☐	**Life of David Crockett** by *David Crockett*	ISBN: 1-59462-250-7	$27.45
	"Colonel David Crockett was one of the most remarkable men of the times in which he lived. Born in humble life, but gifted with a strong will, an indomitable courage, and unremitting perseverance...	Biographies/New Age Pages 424	
☐	**Lip-Reading** by *Edward Nitchie*	ISBN: 1-59462-206-X	$25.95
	Edward B. Nitchie, founder of the New York School for the Hard of Hearing, now the Nitchie School of Lip-Reading, Inc, wrote "LIP-READING Principles and Practice". The development and perfecting of this meritorious work on lip-reading was an undertaking...	How-to Pages 400	
☐	**A Handbook of Suggestive Therapeutics, Applied Hypnotism, Psychic Science** by *Henry Munro*	ISBN: 1-59462-214-0	$24.95
		Health/New Age/Health/Self-help Pages 376	
☐	**A Doll's House: and Two Other Plays** by *Henrik Ibsen*	ISBN: 1-59462-112-8	$19.95
	Henrik Ibsen created this classic when in revolutionary 1848 Rome. Introducing some striking concepts in playwriting for the realist genre, this play has been studied the world over.	Fiction/Classics/Plays 308	
☐	**The Light of Asia** by *sir Edwin Arnold*	ISBN: 1-59462-204-3	$13.95
	In this poetic masterpiece, Edwin Arnold describes the life and teachings of Buddha. The man who was to become known as Buddha to the world was born as Prince Gautama of India but he rejected the worldly riches and abandoned the reigns of power when...	Religion/History/Biographies Pages 170	
☐	**The Complete Works of Guy de Maupassant** by *Guy de Maupassant*	ISBN: 1-59462-157-8	$16.95
	"For days and days, nights and nights, I had dreamed of that first kiss which was to consecrate our engagement, and I knew not on what spot I should put my lips..."	Fiction/Classics Pages 240	
☐	**The Art of Cross-Examination** by *Francis L. Wellman*	ISBN: 1-59462-309-0	$26.95
	Written by a renowned trial lawyer, Wellman imparts his experience and uses case studies to explain how to use psychology to extract desired information through questioning.	How-to/Science/Reference Pages 408	
☐	**Answered or Unanswered?** by *Louisa Vaughan* Miracles of Faith in China	ISBN: 1-59462-248-5	$10.95
		Religion Pages 112	
☐	**The Edinburgh Lectures on Mental Science (1909)** by *Thomas*	ISBN: 1-59462-008-3	$11.95
	This book contains the substance of a course of lectures recently given by the writer in the Queen Street Hall, Edinburgh. Its purpose is to indicate the Natural Principles governing the relation between Mental Action and Material Conditions...	New Age/Psychology Pages 148	
☐	**Ayesha** by *H. Rider Haggard*	ISBN: 1-59462-301-5	$24.95
	Verily and indeed it is the unexpected that happens! Probably if there was one person upon the earth from whom the Editor of this, and of a certain previous history, did not expect to hear again...	Classics Pages 380	
☐	**Ayala's Angel** by *Anthony Trollope*	ISBN: 1-59462-352-X	$29.95
	The two girls were both pretty, but Lucy who was twenty-one who supposed to be simple and comparatively unattractive, whereas Ayala was credited, as her Bombwhat romantic name might show, with poetic charm and a taste for romance. Ayala when her father died was nineteen...	Fiction Pages 484	
☐	**The American Commonwealth** by *James Bryce*	ISBN: 1-59462-286-8	$34.45
	An interpretation of American democratic political theory. It examines political mechanics and society from the perspective of Scotsman James Bryce	Politics Pages 572	
☐	**Stories of the Pilgrims** by *Margaret P. Pumphrey*	ISBN: 1-59462-116-0	$17.95
	This book explores pilgrims religious oppression in England as well as their escape to Holland and eventual crossing to America on the Mayflower, and their early days in New England...	History Pages 268	

www.bookjungle.com *email*: sales@bookjungle.com *fax*: 630-214-0564 *mail*: Book Jungle PO Box 2226 Champaign, IL 61825

QTY

The Fasting Cure by *Sinclair Upton* ISBN: *1-59462-222-1* $13.95
In the Cosmopolitan Magazine for May, 1910, and in the Contemporary Review (London) for April, 1910, I published an article dealing with my experiences in fasting. I have written a great many magazine articles, but never one which attracted so much attention... *New Age/Self Help/Health Pages 164*

Hebrew Astrology by *Sepharial* ISBN: *1-59462-308-2* $13.45
In these days of advanced thinking it is a matter of common observation that we have left many of the old landmarks behind and that we are now pressing forward to greater heights and to a wider horizon than that which represented the mind-content of our progenitors... *Astrology Pages 144*

Thought Vibration or The Law of Attraction in the Thought World ISBN: *1-59462-127-6* $12.95
by *William Walker Atkinson* *Psychology/Religion Pages 144*

Optimism by *Helen Keller* ISBN: *1-59462-108-X* $15.95
Helen Keller was blind, deaf, and mute since 19 months old, yet famously learned how to overcome these handicaps, communicate with the world, and spread her lectures promoting optimism. An inspiring read for everyone... *Biographies/Inspirational Pages 84*

Sara Crewe by *Frances Burnett* ISBN: *1-59462-360-0* $9.45
In the first place, Miss Minchin lived in London. Her home was a large, dull, tall one, in a large, dull square, where all the houses were alike, and all the sparrows were alike, and where all the door-knockers made the same heavy sound... *Childrens/Classic Pages 88*

The Autobiography of Benjamin Franklin by *Benjamin Franklin* ISBN: *1-59462-135-7* $24.95
The Autobiography of Benjamin Franklin has probably been more extensively read than any other American historical work, and no other book of its kind has had such ups and downs of fortune. Franklin lived for many years in England, where he was agent... *Biographies/History Pages 332*

Name	
Email	
Telephone	
Address	
City, State ZIP	

☐ **Credit Card**   ☐ **Check / Money Order**

Credit Card Number	
Expiration Date	
Signature	

Please Mail to: Book Jungle
                    PO Box 2226
                    Champaign, IL 61825
or Fax to: 630-214-0564

ORDERING INFORMATION

web: *www.bookjungle.com*
email: *sales@bookjungle.com*
fax: *630-214-0564*
mail: *Book Jungle PO Box 2226 Champaign, IL 61825*
or PayPal *to sales@bookjungle.com*

Please contact us for bulk discounts

DIRECT-ORDER TERMS

20% Discount if You Order Two or More Books
Free Domestic Shipping!
Accepted: Master Card, Visa, Discover, American Express

www.ingramcontent.com/pod-product-compliance
Lightning Source LLC
Chambersburg PA
CBHW080446170426
43196CB00016B/2709